I HAVE ALWAYS been delighted at the prospect
of a new day, a fresh try, one more start,
with perhaps a bit of magic waiting
somewhere behind the morning.

J. B. Priestley

about the
AUTHOR

ELLEN DUGAN, also known as the Garden Witch, is a psychic-clairvoyant who lives in Missouri with her husband and three children. A practicing Witch for over twenty-four years, Ellen also has many years of nursery and garden center experience, including landscape and garden design. She received her Master Gardener status through the University of Missouri and her local county extension office. Look for other articles by Ellen in Llewellyn's annual *Magical Almanac*, *Wicca Almanac*, and *Herbal Almanac*. Visit her website at:

WWW.ELLENDUGAN.COM

From the author of *Garden Witchery*

BOOK OF WITCHERY

Spells, Charms & Correspondences
for Every Day of the Week

Ellen Dugan

Llewellyn Publications
woodbury, minnesota

FIRST EDITION
First Printing, 2009

Portions of this book originally appeared in *7 Days of Magic* (Llewellyn, 2004)

Book design and editing by Rebecca Zins
Chapter opener artwork from *Old-Fashioned Floral Designs* (© 1990, 1999 Dover Publications, Inc.)
Cover design by Ellen Dahl
Cover image © PhotoDisc
Tarot cards from *Universal Tarot* by Roberto De Angelis are reprinted by permission from Lo Scarabeo

Llewellyn is a registered trademark of Llewellyn Worldwide, Ltd.

Library of Congress Cataloging-in-Publication Data

Dugan, Ellen, 1963-
 Book of witchery : spells, charms & correspondences for every day of the week / Ellen Dugan.
    p.   cm.
 "Portions of this book originally appeared in *7 Days of Magic* (Llewellyn, 2004)."
 Includes bibliographical references and index.
 ISBN 978-0-7387-1584-1
 1. Witchcraft. 2. Magic. I. Title.
 BF1566.D85 2009
 133.4'4—dc22

                                                                        2009024018

Llewellyn Publications
A Division of Llewellyn Worldwide, Ltd.
2143 Wooddale Drive, Dept. 978-0-7387-1584-1
Woodbury, MN 55125-2989
www.llewellyn.com

Printed in the United States of America

other books by
ELLEN DUGAN

Garden Witchery: Magick from the Ground Up
(Llewellyn, 2003)

Elements of Witchcraft: Natural Magick for Teens
(Llewellyn, 2003)

Cottage Witchery: Natural Magick for Hearth and Home
(Llewellyn, 2005)

Autumn Equinox: The Enchantment of Mabon
(Llewellyn, 2005)

The Enchanted Cat: Feline Fascinations, Spells & Magick
(Llewellyn, 2006)

Herb Magic for Beginners: Down-to-Earth Enchantments
(Llewellyn, 2006; also available in Spanish as *Magia con las hierbas*)

Natural Witchery: Intuitive, Personal & Practical Magick
(Llewellyn, 2007)

How to Enchant a Man: Spells to Bewitch, Bedazzle & Beguile
(Llewellyn, 2008)

Garden Witch's Herbal: Green Magick, Herbalism & Spirituality
(Llewellyn, 2009)

Acknowledgments

A special word of thanks to my husband, Ken, and our three children, Kraig, Kyle, and Erin. When this deadline got moved up, you all encouraged me in your own ways, and you kept the snarky comments to a bare minimum on my absentmindedness and crankiness while writing under a wicked deadline.

To John Absey, reprint editor, who enthusiastically jumped at the idea of me expanding the original manuscript. Without his enthusiasm, this project would not exist. For Elysia Gallo, who makes me work harder and smarter and who keeps me on my toes with deadlines. To Becky Zins, who I love working with and for being the best editor anyone could ask for.

A special thank-you goes to Heather. When I complained to her one day about not being able to figure out a name that clicked for this particular book, Heather thought about it a moment and instantly conjured up a great new title.

For my friends and covenmates, for all their love and continued support—especially Mickie, for the arts and crafts information; Sandy, for the illuminating data on the Norse gods and goddesses; and Ember, my fellow witchy writer who cheerfully supplied on-the-spot information on crystals and gemstones. Also a special thanks to Mary Butler, for the additional information on tiger's-eye, the talks on puppy training, and for being a friend. For Jenn M., for being a sister Witch. "Love ya—mean it!"

Finally, to Jen: thanks, dahling, for letting me bounce ideas off of you, for riding shotgun on the 2008 trip to Salem, and for listening when I need to vent. Thanks for helping me look at full moon magick from a different perspective and for being my first witchy belly-dancing buddy.

contents

MONDAY

37

TUESDAY

❧

73

WEDNESDAY

❧
107

THURSDAY

145

FRIDAY

185

Saturday

227

Full Moon Witchery

271

Introduction
A Book of Shadows

THE LOVE OF learning, the sequestered
nooks, and all the sweet serenity of books.

Henry Wadsworth Longfellow

Why a Book of Shadows, you may wonder? Over the years, I have had more requests for this type of book than anything else. When I began teaching public classes on witchery, practical magick, and the Craft, I based every single class I taught from the correspondences in the original version of this book, *7 Days of Magic*. But I have always wanted to take a shot at expanding and intensifying that original little manuscript. However small the size of that manuscript may have been, the original book was packed full of daily correspondences, spells, and lessons on how to incorporate witchery into each and every day of the week. In essence, it *was* a Book of Shadows—it was *my* Book of Shadows, containing a collection of spells, charms, and correspondences, all of it witchery that worked well and that I had created, written down, and successfully practiced and then went on to teach to the public.

So here we are. You hold in your hands not an old book with a new cover. No, indeed. This book is bigger, better, and more in-depth; the information has more than doubled in size. The fundamentals that you have come to expect from me are still here, but now there is even more magick to try your hand at. For example, you will find enchanting and new daily meditations, potion and philter recipes, Witch crafts, full moon magick, and rituals that are more intense and much more involved, in addition to the classic crystal, color, herb, tarot card, and deity magick.

This Book of Shadows is meant to kick-start your own brand of creativity, and it will give you many fresh ideas on how to build your own personal brand of witchery and magick. I promise that this book will keep you happily conjuring seven days a week—because, as I always say, magick is where you find it, and creativity is the key.

WITCHERY FOR THE WEEK

> WRITE IT ON your heart that every
> day is the best day in the year.
>
> *Ralph Waldo Emerson*

Magick is all around us at all times. Enchantment can be found in each moment of every day of our lives. In this frantic and crazy world that we live in, it is more important now than ever to stop and take a few moments for yourself and your witchery. Each day, set aside some private time just for you. Then use this personal time to connect to the wonder, divinity, and magickal energies of that specific day. If you've got only ten minutes to spare for magick, then incorporate your intuition and your knowledge of the Craft to use every bit of that time wisely.

Magick doesn't have to be complicated. You are not any less of a Witch if you choose to keep things straightforward and basic. Who says you have to spend an hour setting up and then performing your spells? Certainly not me. If you keep things uncomplicated and practical, you'll enjoy it more—and you'll be working magick more often. Witchery isn't limited only to the sabbats and to the occasional full moon; magick happens twenty-four hours a day, seven days a week.

Every day is a bewitching day, Sunday through Saturday. Each day holds its own planetary correspondences, deity associations, magickal energies, and applications. A clue to how these magickal traditions started is to consider how the days of the week got their names in the first place. To the ancients, there were seven known planets, or celestial bodies, in the heavens. These were the sun, moon, Mercury, Mars, Venus, Jupiter, and Saturn. Back in the day, folks believed that the seven planets all revolved around the earth—that whole "the earth is the center of the universe" thing. They also believed that the movements of the planets signified the will of the gods and their direct power over human affairs.

Sunday is obviously named after our closest star, the sun. Monday was named after the moon. All of the other names for the days of the week are actually inspired by a combination of the old Roman and Norse deities and mythologies. Each day of the week has its own energies and specialties, and the day itself may affect people in different ways. For example, do Mondays make you cringe? Why? They are not always the start of the work week. For those of us who work weekends, Monday is just another day. It is, however, the moon's special day of the week. What kind of magickal work could you possibly perform on a Monday?

Well, on that sacred day of the moon, you could work for increased psychic abilities or you could connect with a lunar god or goddess. If a full moon happened to fall on a Monday, this could infuse extra magickal power into any lunar spell. Sounds like a double whammy to me. How could you use this information in your own brand of witchery and magick?

Techniques for Newer Witches

Over the years, I have met many newer Witches who are often confused and overwhelmed by daily magickal correspondences. They rub their foreheads and give me a pained expression as they ask, "Tuesdays are for what?" Goddess knows I've fielded this question many times with my students, magickal friends, and my covenmates. Some magickal practitioners break a sweat after taking one look at those massive correspondence charts and planetary hours. I can totally sympathize.

While serious astrological charts and the accompanying information make my eyes cross (I think it reminds me too much of math), you can and should still learn more about the individual magickal associations of all the days of the week. Daily planetary information and magickal associations will help you figure out the hows, whys, and whens of magick working the way that it does. Once you learn how to apply the daily correspondences, you turn up the power and the volume of your Craft. In essence, this gives you more unique magickal tools in your repertoire, and this will then allow you to creatively experience more options.

Inspiration for Experienced Witches

For those Witches who wonder what the point is of relearning what they perceive to be very basic material, try looking at daily correspondences in a whole new way. It really doesn't matter how old you are. Whether you are in your late teens or in your seventies, many experienced Witches have trouble working successfully with the daily magickal correspondences, so they face boredom and burnout. Whatever scenario you are dealing with, either is frustrating.

The topics covered in this Book of Shadows—the daily correspondences, meditations, theme spells, tarot card associations, Witch craft projects, potion recipes, and other natural accessories—are like building blocks. You can successfully add this magickal information to the Witchcraft that you already practice. Before you know it, you've increased your knowledge of the Craft, expanded your understanding of magickal correspondences, tried your hand at creating some of your own spells, and stepped up in the ranks.

EXPANDING YOUR MAGICKAL TOOLBOX

> FOR ALL A rhetorician's rules
> Teach nothing but to name his tools.
>
> *Samuel Butler*

Mastering the daily magickal correspondences actually expands the size of your magickal toolbox. You know that fun little "mental toolbox" that you cart around inside your head? Think of all the ways you will be able to personalize and advance your witchery! Instead of wasting time wondering which item, color, herb, or other magickal prop best harmonizes with what theme, you'll already know, leaving you free to focus on the task at hand. When you free up your mind and focus on your magick instead of worrying if you have all the correct items, you allow so much more room for the spells and witchery to manifest—and without a bunch of expectations or worries slapped all over them. Remember that the most advanced magick springs from the hidden lessons that you began with. There are layers in magick and worlds within worlds. Are you willing to take the time to carefully investigate them?

Whenever I teach public classes, I always ask how many students know their daily correspondences by heart. The response ranges from horrified to confused. At a recent class I taught while on tour, there were over thirty-five people in attendance, and not a single one of them knew their basic daily magickal correspondences from memory. These students also included a few third-degree practitioners from another established tradition. I will admit that it took me a moment to recover from my surprise. How can someone say they are a third-degree high priestess and not know their daily correspondences? And most importantly, why were they not taught this essential and foundational information? I say "foundational" because you will use this daily magickal information as a foundation on which to build your own witchery and magick every single day.

My theory for this common lack of knowledge is that the daily correspondences are a magickal topic that is simply not focused on. However, it certainly should be. The surprising truth is that many practitioners do not know their daily correspondences by heart—such as what specific planet or which crystals, colors, herbs, plants, or flowers correspond with a particular day, or even which deity lent its name to any particular day of the week. And that always shocks the hell out of me.

I once had a student get so hostile about that topic that she threw a tantrum in class. Why, she had studied for years, she sputtered at me. Did I understand just how many books she owned on the Craft? However, during all of her "how dare yous," she missed the whole point.

What finally stopped her tangent was when I cheerfully asked her how often she actually cast spells. She had no answer for that one. She really turned red when I gently asked her if, when the mood struck her and she began to create her own personal magick, did she waste a lot of time looking everything up? Or instead, by her knowing the basic correspondences, was she able to use her knowledge of what items work harmoniously together, thereby leaving her free to apply her intuition to create her own personalized spells?

The tantrum-throwing student's mouth hit the floor. And I saw several people in class have an *aha!* moment when the information hit home. And this, my friends, is the entire point: if you want to have the freedom to create your own personal brand of witchery, then you need to have a solid foundation on which to build. Learning and studying the daily correspondences and the magickal theme of the day allows you to open up amazing possibilities for awesome witchery for each and every day. It is, quite simply, all up to you. How much do you want to learn, and how far do you wish to advance your own witchery?

HOW TO USE THIS BOOK OF SHADOWS

> BOOKS ARE THE quietest and most
> constant of friends; they are the most
> accessible and wisest of counselors,
> and the most patient of teachers.
>
> *Charles W. Eliot*

This book has separate chapters for each day of the week and an additional chapter on full moon magick. This way, you can apply the knowledge you gain on the individual days of the week and apply it to your full moon magick. For example, if the full moon falls on a Friday, what daily energies are already in play? How could you add those successfully into your witchery? Within these chapters, you will find a listing of the specific magickal correspondences for the individual day. Each chapter is also broken down into several enchanting sections. These sections are:

AT-A-GLANCE CORRESPONDENCES: A quick reference list for you to check out, this is an at-a-glance listing of the bewitching accessories and natural items that correspond with that particular day of the week.

DAILY MAGICKAL APPLICATIONS: The specific captivating attributes for the featured magickal day. A smidgen of history and lore about the highlighted day and how it got its name.

DEITIES: Information on an eclectic mix of the coordinating deities of the day.

MEDITATIONS: A guided meditation for the day that focuses on that day's magickal theme—a lesson to be learned and a journey to take. Where will your meditations take you?

MAGICKAL PLANTS & FLOWERS: Flowers, herbs, and plants that share the same astrological significance of the featured day. Doses of daily garden witchery and herbal spells, including flower fascinations and natural magick.

COLORS, CANDLES, METALS & CRYSTALS: What colors you can wear to help unify the day's energies. Spell candles to burn and magickal candle aromatherapy. Harmonizing metals and crystals to wear, carry in your pocket, or group around a candle. A complementary color and crystal spell or two. (Please note: If you are wondering where to find all of the various scented and colorful candles that are mentioned throughout this book, try taking a look at the little votive candle. Votives come in an impressive array of colors and scents. They are inexpensive and have a very high oil content, which means their wonderful and magickal scents are released immediately as they are burned. If you have ever burned a votive candle, you will have noticed that they turn to liquid wax right away—which is why you should always burn votives inside of a votive cup, otherwise you'll get a big puddle of wax all over your work area. Check them out for yourself. Votives are a great, affordable candle to use in your own custom-made magick.)

POTIONS, PHILTERS & OILS: Recipes for personalized magickal philters and potions for each day's magickal theme. Each daily recipe will have directions, a supply list, and its own spell to enchant your homemade philter. Also, you will discover a handy listing of the classic essential oils that coordinate with each bewitching day.

TAROT CARD ASSOCIATIONS: Got a tarot deck and want to use it for more than the occasional reading? Try using certain coordinating cards as props to focus on while you perform your daily spells and charms. You'll be amazed at how well they work!

DAILY WITCH CRAFTS: Let's put some craft back into your Witchcraft. Each day's chapter features a handmade craft project for you to create, along with a spell to enchant and empower the item.

CUSTOM-MADE DAILY MAGICK: A potpourri of magickal information, a smidgen of foods and bewitching spices—tips and tricks on how to take all of the information that is presented and inspire you to begin creating your own rituals and personalized magick. How to put all of the information together, plus even more theme spells and charms for the day.

RITUAL FOR THE DAY: A more intense and longer magickal working—in other words, a ritual. Each of the day's featured rituals will correspond with that day's specific magickal theme.

WITCHERY FOR EVERY DAY
put your heart into it!

A LOVING HEART is the
beginning of all knowledge.

Thomas Carlyle

These daily spells and rituals should signify something important to you. If you want to see the best results possible, then you have to put your heart into it! To create a positive change, you need to focus on the desire and the will. Creating loving change, or a positive transformation, is the ultimate goal of every Witch.

Yes, spells, charms, and rituals can be used for many purposes: connecting to deity, encouraging love, increasing prosperity. You may also perform magick for protection and healing, or even to boost your own creativity. This magick may take only a few moments, or it may take a bit longer. It's up to you. Now, if you're wondering how all of these daily spells, charms, magickal projects and so on *really* work, I have some thoughts on that. To begin with, performing a spell can help us to focus on the sacred, and it actually slows us down.

As we begin to work magick, our minds shift to a calm and centered place. As we go through the process of setting up for the spell, it forces us to concentrate on the task at hand. This helps to bring us into a calmer, more focused attitude. That quiet focus is heightened when you add a little personal power and connect with deity. Then the magick that we perform is helping us concentrate on the present while at the same time allowing us to deal with any past problems. And, finally, it encourages us to be creative and to visualize our future in a more positive, life-affirming way. Most magick users will agree that there are several elements to the good performance of a ritual or a meaningful spell. Check out this list below—you'll get the idea.

THE ELEMENTS OF SPELLWORK AND RITUAL

CERTAIN THINGS ARE everlasting.

Magic is one of them.

Laurie Cabot

PURPOSE: This is the purpose of the ritual. Are you focused? Did you take a moment to ground and center and to put aside all negativity? Is your intention pure? Are you sincere?

SEQUENCE: Every ritual has a clear beginning and end. Write up a quick outline. You may find it helpful to refer to page 301, where a daily spell worksheet has been provided for you. This will help you sort things out, set things up, and get ready to go.

SACRED SPACE: Spells and rituals cause a change in consciousness, as they take place outside of ordinary life. Toss a pretty scarf or piece of fabric over a card table or the kitchen table, or be bohemian and sit on the floor. You may care to work your daily magick in a special spot, such as your altar or household shrine. Perhaps you'll want to set up in the garden or on the patio. Wherever you choose to work your witchery, make it a sacred space. By this I mean a clean, happy, and pleasant environment.

SUPPLIES: Most rituals employ complementary colored candles, oils, herbs, crystals, and other props. You will find lots of information in this Book of Shadows—such as daily meditations, Witch craft projects, recipes for personalized potions, and complementary tarot cards—in each of the daily chapters that will harmonize with that day's specific magickal energy. All of these correspondences and featured magickal components will work in tune with each other, as they have the same sort of energy, or vibration.

Why Daily Correspondences Are Important

When you add complementary natural items such as coordinating crystals, candles, herbs, flowers, and colors to your daily spells and charms, you can increase the effectiveness of your witchery. How, you may ask? Well, these items will help link your Witchcraft together with that day's magickal energies. A good example of this is the power of color.

Every day of the week has its own specific magickal colors. This practical type of magick should never be underestimated, even by the more experienced Witch. If you select a color that harmonizes with your personal energies or goals for the day, then you will flourish.

As you begin to focus on daily magickal correspondences, you will realize that the simple use of crystals, oils, flowers, and colors can not only positively influence your personality but your thoughts and life as well. These daily correspondences and coordinating natural items can actually strengthen the punch of a charm. They will allow you more creative ways to personalize your Witchcraft, and they will help to unify your spellwork.

A Word on the Daily Deities

As to the deity listings in this book, these will be an eclectic mix of gods and goddesses from all over the world and from many magickal cultures. Now, I am aware that this idea will cause some traditionalists to clutch their chests in horror . . . hence the term *eclectic*. So what if you're calling on a Greek sun god and a Celtic goddess of light? If they are both solar deities, then they wouldn't really be incompatible. They are merely different representations of the same type of solar energy from separate magickal cultures.

Come on, folks . . . relax. The best way to learn something new is to experiment and have a little fun. The planet will not stop revolving just because you mixed pantheons. Follow your instincts; see who speaks to you. Build a relationship with a deity, and see what they can teach you about yourself and magick. You will never know what possibilities are out there unless you try. The world is wide, and the sky's the limit when it comes to finding a friendly deity. The gods and goddesses are many; mix and match as you like.

ADVANCING YOUR MAGICKAL SKILLS

> MAGIC IS MADE in the mind. It is
> first and foremost an act of will.
>
> *Marina Medici*

The trick to advancing your magickal expertise is to create your own personal style of witchery. Many experienced practitioners loudly complain about a lack of advanced techniques or materials, which always makes me wonder if they have ever considered studying, experimenting, and creating their own advanced magick. So let's consider this for a moment. What is your specialty? What type of magick do you feel you excel in? Maybe your specialty is creating oils and potions or making handmade magickal items and tools. Possibly your gift is working with the crystals and the stones, or you really have a knack for herbal spells and charms. Perhaps you're an adept at the tarot, or you're skilled at working the candles; well, now is the time to find out where your talents lie!

Listen to your instincts. Use your imagination, and follow your heart. No one knows your tastes and preferences better than you do. So take a look at the magickal information and correspondences presented here, and use them as a starting point. Open up that magickal toolbox in your brain, and develop the magick of your mind. Learn something new; stretch the boundaries of your knowledge and experience in the Craft. Add some new information to your current repertoire, and begin exploring all the possibilities for advancing your witchery.

Are You Psyched? Great, Let's Go!

So now that you are intrigued and enthusiastic, wouldn't it be handy to have a Book of Shadows that you could just flip open on any day of the week? A book where you will find all sorts of enchanting things—meditations, inspiring ideas, witchy arts and crafts, potion and philter recipes, herbal information, magickal correspondences, deity information, quick practical charms, natural magick, and rituals and spells that would coordinate for that specific day of the week?

Well, my friend, look no further. Let's start working and learning about all of the days of witchery. The seven days of the bewitching week are filled with all kinds of earthy enchantments, practical magick, and witchy wisdom. Let's get your creative juices flowing! The motivation you need to craft your own more advanced and personalized magick might be only a page or two away. So pick a day, any day, and let's get started!

Seven are the days of the magickal week,

Look inside this book for the secrets they keep.

Success, prosperity, love, and strength they hold,

To uncover their meanings, one must be bold.

Craft new magickal objects, potions, and embrace herbal lore,

Incorporate this wisdom into what you knew from before.

Let us embark on this journey one day at a time,

May your witchery be strong and true, come rain or shine.

Sunday

A CHEERFUL FRIEND is like a
sunny day, spreading bliss all around.

John Lubcock

At-a-Glance Correspondences

PLANETARY INFLUENCE	Sun
PLANETARY SYMBOL	☉
DEITIES	Helios, Sunna, Brigid
FLOWERS & PLANTS	Carnation, chrysanthemum, marigold, St. John's wort, sunflower
METAL	Gold
COLORS	Gold, yellow, yellow-orange, neon shades of orange and yellow, hot pink
CRYSTALS & STONES	Carnelian, diamond, amber, tiger's-eye, quartz crystal
ESSENTIAL OILS	Bergamot, calendula, carnation, cedar, cinnamon, frankincense, orange, rosemary
TAROT CARDS	The Sun, Ace of Wands, the Chariot
FOODS, HERBS & SPICES	Orange, cinnamon

DAILY MAGICKAL APPLICATIONS

The Latin term for Sunday, our first day of the week, is *Dies Solis* ("sun's day"). In ancient Greek, it was called *Hemera Heliou*. In the Old English language, it was known as *Sunnandaeg*; in Middle English, *Sonenday*. All of these titles mean the same thing: the day of the sun.

What do you think of when you feel the sun shine down on you? What sorts of enchantments and energies do you think would be complementary to a day named after our closest star? Sunday brings those bright solar energies into your life and has the magickal correspondences of success, promotion, leadership, pride, light, generosity, warmth, fitness, and personal growth. Astrologically, the sun symbolizes the conscious self and rules the zodiac sign of Leo.

The charms and spells that would complement this magickal day of the sun are ones for personal achievements of any kind—such as if you are seeking fame and wealth, working for that much-deserved promotion at work, or being acknowledged for a job well done. Health issues, increasing personal power, or simply sticking to your diet and being proud of what you have accomplished all fall under the sun's golden influence.

DEITIES

Getting to know more about the various pantheons and assorted deities helps you figure out who to call on and when. Learning more about the assorted deities helps you specialize your magick. In other words, you go to specific gods for particular needs. Why is specializing so important? Well, you wouldn't call a plumber if you needed your fuse box repaired, would you? Here is a bit of information on some of the deities associated with light, success, and the sun.

There are many mythological connections between the sun and a male deity. These gods of light and fire sometimes seem to be direct contrasts to the more feminine powers of the night, water, and the moon. However, there are goddesses of light, fire, and the hearth flame as well. In truth, if you take a good look at various mythologies, you can typically find something for everyone.

Oh—and yes, there are also female solar deities as well. Take a look at Sekhmet, the Egyptian lion-headed goddess of war. There is a Japanese goddess of the sun called Amaterasu, and probably the most well-known feminine solar deity is Sunna, the Norse goddess of the sun. Sunday got its name by being "Sunna's day."

Sunna

Sunna (pronounced SOO-*nah*) drives her horse-drawn chariot across the daytime sky. According to Norse mythology, the horses' names are Allsvinn and Arvak, which mean "very fast" and "early rising." Sunna is the divine representation of the sun, and she was much loved by the Norse people as a giver of life. Here is a deity with some pretty potent agricultural ties. And this makes sense, as without Sunna's light and magick, crops did not flourish. Sunna is chased across the daytime sky by the wolf Skoll. From time to time, Skoll catches up with Sunna and takes a bite out of the sun, which appears to us here on earth as a solar eclipse. Sunna is characterized in modern art as a beautiful woman with golden hair. Traditionally, she was simply viewed as the sun in the sky. Symbols for this Norse goddess include a sunburst, a flaming sun, horses, and Sunna's golden chariot.

Helios

Do you feel that you need the extra drive, ambition, and power of the god of the sun, who sees all and watches over us as he blazes through the sky? Try picturing a buff, chariot-driving, golden-haired centurion—that would be Helios, the Greek god of the sun.

Helios was thought of as the physical representation of sun. He was portrayed as sometimes wearing a golden helmet or having a golden halo. He was often characterized in art as a handsome man draped in a white, sparkling tunic and cloak. Helios drove his blazing sun-chariot across the sky from east to west, every day. The golden chariot was pulled by his four white horses, named Pyrois, Eos, Aethon, and Phiegon. Symbols for this sun god include the chariot, the rooster, the globe, and his four white horses.

Brigid

The Celtic goddess of the hearth and flame, Brigid is a triple goddess of light, inspiration, and healing. She is often associated with smithcraft, well-being, and poetry. There are many variations on the name Brigid, including Breed, Brigit, Brighid, and Brigitania. The goddess Brigid was also known as the "Bright One" or the "Bright Arrow." Often depicted as a woman with long, braided, red-gold hair, this beloved goddess of the Celts once had a sacred fire that was tended in Kildare, Ireland. In medieval times, abbey nuns tended the perpetual flame. In ancient times, it was Brigid's priestesses. Recently, Brigid's flame was relit. This goddess of Erin (Ireland) will always bring illumination to those who seek her out.

Brigid keeps the home fires burning. She is the guardian of the hearth and the goddess of flame, light, and the sun. If you have a fireplace in your home, Brigid is the deity to guard, or ward, it. On my mantle, there is a framed picture of the triple Brigid. She watches over the home and wards our wood-burning stove and the surrounding hearth. No fireplace? Well, then, the kitchen stove is the next logical choice. Try setting out a little arrangement of three white pillar candles. Keep them lit when you are home, and watch them set an enchanting mood. You could devote them to Brigid by carving a triskele (⚬) on the sides of the candles. Those burning candles bring to mind the sacred perpetual flame at Kildare.

Another magickal symbol for Brigid is a cauldron, as Brigid was thought to have been the keeper of the cauldron of inspiration. A lesser-known symbol for Brigid is the shamrock, which could be another symbol for those candles if you have trouble carving a neat triskele. The shamrock, or three-leaf clover, was thought to represent the triple aspect of this goddess in olden times.

SUNDAY'S WITCHERY

Today's guided meditation was inspired by my morning workout. I am an early riser, and I enjoy getting up and going for a walk first thing in the morning and watching the sun come up. In my way of thinking, this leaves the rest of the day free to write, answer emails, run errands, and catch up on housework without me trying to figure out and then plan when I am going to find time to do my workout for the day. Since I work at home, my schedule is pretty flexible, but being a hopeless Virgo, I am happier when I have some type of routine.

As I write this, it is an early Sunday morning in mid-October. Currently, here in Missouri, we are having what the locals call an "Indian summer"—meaning it has been very warm and sunny despite the autumn season, and the temperatures are around eighty degrees Fahrenheit during the days and in the lower sixties at night. Just a week ago, the temperatures were much more seasonal and cooler. But I think Mother Nature enjoys messing with us just a bit. Maybe we will have fall-like temperatures . . . and maybe we won't. However, the leaves are really starting to turn colors now, and my chrysanthemums are in all their glory in the front gardens, putting on a show in the solar colors of bright yellow, red, and orange.

Meditation

> I SAW TWO clouds at morning,
> Tinged with the rising sun,
> And in the dawn they floated on,
> And mingled into one.
>
> *John Gardiner Calkins Brainard*

Visualize that you are comfortably standing or sitting outdoors in your favorite spot in nature. Perhaps you are standing on a sandy beach or are overlooking the edge of a mighty river. You may find yourself sitting in the grass in a pretty meadow, tucked under a mossy tree at the edge of the forest, or perched on a flat boulder on top of a mountain or on a desert floor. See where your mind takes you.

Take a moment to savor the peace and quiet of this time. There are no demands on you, and you are blissfully alone. Look above you and see the deep blue sky that only comes in the brief moment before sunrise. Turn your head and notice that to the east, the color of blue is different and that a few clouds appear to be illuminated even though it is still dark. Now look to the west and see the stars still bright in the sky. As you turn your head gently back and forth, you become aware of how quickly the color of the nighttime sky is changing. Slowly you notice that the entire sky is becoming brighter.

The birds begin to increase the volume of their early morning song, as if to welcome the new day. The stars above you, one by one, begin to wink out. And the eastern sky is brightening with an orange-pink glow. This rosy color begins to reflect in the clouds that are floating toward the eastern horizon, and you smile as you watch the amazing show of colors that you are witnessing. You feel hopeful as you see the glimmer of the sun begin to ease its way over the horizon; for a second, you close your eyes and visualize Helios or Sunna beginning their journey across the daytime sky. The clouds to the east turn gold against a sky the color of a robin's egg, and as the sun rises even higher, you get caught up in the beauty of the moment and watch as the sky loses all traces of the night. Day has truly begun.

Today is the day of the week that is devoted to the sun and all solar magick. What better way to honor it than to watch the sunrise and witness a new day being born? Take a deep breath and center yourself. Know that all things are possible. The day spreads out before you, full of possibilities and magick. While you are in this meditative state, make a promise to yourself to go outside and do something active today. Take a walk, ride your bike, go for a jog, or play outside with your kids or your pets. Walk in the rain, play in the snow, kick around in the autumn leaves, work in the yard, or plant some flowers. Just get out into nature and be thankful for your life, your health, and the body that you have. Success, sunshine, and happiness are all around you. All you have to do is grab hold of it with both hands and explore all the enchanting possibilities that are in your world.

Now take another deep breath and ground and center. Look around one last time and see the sun shining brightly down upon you. Take some of that solar energy and magick with you today as you work and play through your day. Open your eyes and return to awareness. Stretch out gently, and now go enjoy your successful and sunshiny day. Blessed be.

Magickal Plants & Flowers

Chrysanthemum

The chrysanthemum, or mum, is a classic fall flower. Botanically, they are called *Dendranthema* hybrids. The planetary correspondence of the mum is the sun, and the elemental association is fire. In the language of flowers, the mum says "cheer." And the various colors of this flower have different magickal applications. Classically, the mum will bloom in the spring or the autumn. However, the chrysanthemum always blooms when the daylight and nighttime hours are fairly equal. In fact, nurseries across the United States trick mums into blooming in the fall through a process called vernalization. How do I know? I used to do this every year when I worked at local nurseries. Every June, nurseries start out with a tiny sprig of a mum hybrid and plant it in a large pot. They allow the plant to grow, and then pinch it back every few weeks, removing flower buds and encouraging the plant to branch out and to grow fuller. Eventually, in late August or sooner, depending on the climate and local growing season, they leave the now much larger and bushier plant alone, and the flower blossoms begin to set. Then, as the nighttime temperatures get cooler and the daylight and nighttime hours begin to become more balanced, the plant knows it's time to bloom. This is why, come September, you see dozens of varieties of chrysanthemum parading their brilliant fall colors at roadside stands and nursery displays across the country. According to flower folklore, the chrysanthemum will repel ghosts and roaming spirits. It is generally a cheery, happy, and protective flower. As you would expect, mums do best in rich soil and in sunny gardens.

Marigold

The common garden marigold (*Tagetes*) is a powerful little magickal flower. While its scent is strong and maybe unpleasant to some folks, don't turn up your nose at it! This flower's astrological correspondence is the sun. According to folklore, it was thought that if you gathered marigolds at noon, it would double their solar energy. The marigold is used to encourage wealth and riches. It also helps keep wandering spirits away. By the way, the pot marigold (*Calendula officinalis*) is edible, and its flower petals may be added to salads or used as garnish.

St. John's Wort

The herb St. John's wort (*Hypericum perforatum*) is a perennial herb, blooming typically once a year right around midsummer. St. John's wort is a classic summer solstice herb and is often incorporated into sabbat rituals. This flowering herb is also associated with the sun, and its magickal properties include health, happiness, and protection from faerie magick or trickery. Try gathering the blossoms for a good luck charm, or work with the green foliage and tuck it into a vase with other magickal flowers for its protective qualities.

Carnation

The carnation (*Dianthus caryophyllus*) is one of my favorite solar flowers. As cut flowers, they are inexpensive to purchase, and you can even grow a fragrant and tiny variety of them in the garden quite easily from seed. (Look for the popular perennial dianthus at your local nursery or garden center.) These dainty pink perennials for the garden are also called clove pinks (or simply "pinks") and are also known as Sweet William or the gillyflower. Whether you work with the multicolored large or miniature varieties of the carnation from the florist or grow your own little perennial dianthus, the carnation's spicy aroma is uplifting and healing. Here is an extra little flower/color magick tip for you: try working with yellow- and orange-colored carnations to give your Sunday flower fascinations an extra boost! A flower fascination is a simple floral type of magick that usually only employs a flower or two. The term *fascination* is defined as "to bewitch or to hold spellbound by an irresistible power." Therefore, a flower fascination is simply the act of working spells with magickal flowers.

Sunflower

The sunflower (*Helianthus annuus*), while very easy to grow in the home garden, may only bloom for a few months out of the year—typically late June throughout September. However, these days it is available to us year-round, and it is a very popular flower in the florist's trade. So, if you don't have any blooming in the garden at the moment, pop into your local florist and pick up an inexpensive stem or two for Sunday spells. In the language of flowers, the sunflower symbolizes "high hopes and adoration." If you've ever grown sunflowers in the garden, then you have noticed how they turn their faces toward the sun throughout the day. These sun-worshipping flowers are perfect for you if you are looking to stand out in a crowd or are seeking fame and riches.

Garden Witch Tip

HERE IS A practical tip for working with fresh flowers. If you'd like your flowers to stay fresher in the vase for a longer period of time, then give the bottom of the stems a fresh diagonal cut with a knife or scissors just before you plunk them into a water-filled vase. Also, strip off any lower leaves from the stems that may be below the water line. (The only thing you want in the water is the stems.) Change your water every other day so the flowers will stay fresher longer. Adding a bit of white soda, such as 7-Up, to the water is rumored to keep flowers fresher longer, too.

A *Sunflower Spell*

If possible, work this flower fascination outside. Set a sunflower or two into a vase full of clean water. (If you work with flowers from the garden, you may have to arrange those thick stems in something more substantial, like a decorative metal bucket or heavy vase, so the weight of the stems won't tip over the vase.) At the third line of the spell (below), turn to face the sun. Close your eyes and tip your face up to its light. Remember, while working your way to the recognition, promotion, or raise that you so richly deserve, to be fair and not to step on anyone else as you climb that ladder of success. Repeat the following spell three times:

I will stand head and shoulders above the crowd

I call for wealth and fame; I'll shout it out loud

Like a sunflower, I turn to face the bright sun

Grant me power and triumph, and let it harm none.

Close the spell by saying:

For the good of all, with harm to none

By blossom and leaf, this spell is done.

Put the sunflowers in a spot where you can see them every day to remind you of the flower fascination. Enjoy them until they begin to fade. When it's time to dispose of them, do it neatly. Recycle them by adding them to a compost pile.

COLORS, CANDLES, METALS & CRYSTALS

Colors

Colors for the day include all shades of yellow, yellow-orange, and metallic gold. Actually, the associated metal for Sunday is gold. If you have any gold jewelry, such as a ring, a pair of earrings, a necklace—or even a fun and funky piece of costume jewelry shaped like a sun, such as a pin or pendant—today is the day to wear it and to enchant it. Hold up the jewelry to the sunlight and ask for the energies of the day to imbue it with wealth, purpose, and achievement. Try asking Helios to bless it with drive and ambition. Request that Sunna consecrate you with her radiance, or ask Brigid to strengthen it with her light and divine inspiration. Then you can wear the sun-charmed jewelry any time that you feel the need for a little extra sunshine, warmth, and success.

If you care to coordinate your outfit with the bright energies of the sun, then try a shirt, blouse, scarf, or accessory in any of these warm colors. If you're feeling really adventurous, try the bright colors of hot pink, neon orange, and neon yellow.

A *Colorful Sunny Day Spell*

Try working this spell on a gloomy, rainy Sunday, or any day. It will lift your spirits, no matter what the weather.

Slip on your sunny outfit or wear your sun-themed jewelry, and then take a moment to imagine yourself either on a sun-drenched beach or in the middle of a bright meadow with the sun streaming down on you. Now picture that a little of the sun's warmth is soaking into the bright colors or jewelry that you are wearing. Do you feel a bit warmer? While you are visualizing this for a moment or two, repeat the following spell three times:

> *Even though the skies may be cloudy and gray*
> *I will wear the colors of the sun today*
> *For the colors of yellow, gold, and orange, you see*
> *Work their own sunny magick; so mote it be!*

Close the spell by saying:

> *For the good of all, with harm to none*
> *By color and light, this spell is done!*

Then take a deep breath, blow it out, and go dazzle 'em today!

Candles

Candle colors for today include yellow and gold. In magick, the color yellow is used to aid communication, knowledge, and creativity. The color gold represents royalty, the God, riches, wealth, and fame. For centuries, candles have been lit to welcome deity and to symbolize a connection to the magickal realms. In actuality, a burning candle is a physical symbol of your spell. Watch for gold metallic tapers and pillar candles around the winter holidays; you can usually pick them up on sale. Yellow may be harder to find, so keep your eyes peeled. For my candle magick, I like to work with scented votives. They come in all colors and lots of yummy fragrances. Try looking for citrus scents to bring health, and cinnamon scents for success and prosperity. These bewitching scents will help link your solar magick with a little magickal aromatherapy.

Metals & Crystals

As stated earlier, the bewitching metal for today is gold. Gold is intimately linked to the sun's energies. It is associated with sun gods and goddesses and a majestic or regal type of energy. Gold has the powers of health, wisdom, prosperity, and success. Gold is also thought to guarantee a long life. Wearing gold jewelry will increase your personal power and give a boost to your self-confidence. Gold, whether white or yellow, has a projective and masculine energy. Also, it's good to know that wearing gold jewelry mixed in with your silver jewelry will help to bring balance into your life and magick.

CARNELIAN: The carnelian has the elemental associations of fire. This stone ranges in colors from pink to orange and red. It encourages protection, courage, healing, and sexuality. The carnelian can help you focus on your true path in life, and it will help you make smart decisions and become more organized, plus it can help influence the making of successful choices. Carnelian is thought to bolster a nervous public speaker and will aid in removing doubts and negativity. This is a stone loaded with positive energy, and it keeps you moving forward. Carnelian stones are a good choice for any type of magickal work that affects your job and career. In ancient Egypt, rings of carnelian were worn to calm anger and remove jealousy and hatred.

TIGER'S-EYE: The tiger's-eye is a fun tumbled stone to keep around. A very popular stone for magickal use, it too is associated with the element of fire and encourages protection, bravery, and good luck. Tiger's-eye also promotes prosperity and personal protection. On an interesting note, the tiger's-eye stone will also aid in psychic protection, especially if it includes a cat's-eye marking (by this I mean that the markings or stripes in the stone will have the shape of a feline pupil). As my Witch friend Mary says, "The cat's-eye mark allows you to see past any crap that might get in the way of your protection," thus enabling you to see what's coming before it happens.

QUARTZ CRYSTAL: The quartz crystal is a powerful stone. It has both projective and receptive, or masculine and feminine, energies. The quartz crystal is associated with the elements of fire and water. Quartz crystals are often used to top wands, and there is good reason for that. Basically, a clear quartz crystal point is an amplifier. It intensifies, or multiplies, the powers of any other stones that it is in contact with. The crystal points will also amplify your personal power. If you carry it in your pocket or wear a quartz crystal point in your jewelry, it will increase your psychic abilities and your chances of success. A quartz crystal point may be used in healing and health spells as well. The crystal point is rubbed over the affected area to draw out the illness or the pain. Try holding a quartz crystal at the base of your skull or placing the stone on your forehead to help draw out a headache.

AMBER: Amber is associated with the goddess Freya (this Norse goddess of love and sexuality will be featured in Friday's chapter). Amber is associated with the sun and the element of fire, and it possesses all of the qualities that you would come to expect: healing, strength, fame, power, and success. Unlike many gems, amber is thought to be warm to the touch, because amber came from a living tree. This makes it a gemstone of vegetative origin as opposed to mineral origin like most gemstones. The ancient Greeks called amber *elektron*, which means "of the sun," owing to the fact that if amber is rubbed against natural fibers, such as silk or wool, it will build up static electricity, holding an electrical charge. Perhaps it is for this reason that amber jewelry is traditionally worn by both high priestesses and priests.

Amber is a gorgeous and popular magickal "stone" (it's actually a fossilized resin). Baltic amber comes in a milky and golden tones, and is readily available in the natural shades of honey gold and orange. It may have bubbles, tiny bits of ancient bark, or even an insect within it. Amber may also come in the hues of white, red, brown, blue, and green. You should be aware, though, that much of the commercial green amber is heated to enhance its color and to make it appear sparkly and deep toned. Truly unenhanced green amber is very rare and expensive. Today, amber beads and amber jewelry, no matter what their color, are worn for healing purposes as well as to boost the power of any spells that you cast. Amber radiates a positive and sunny energy, making it perfect to incorporate into any Sunday spells. Also, this gemstone has the reputation of making the wearer irresistible.

DIAMOND: Beyond being a girl's best friend, the diamond promotes spirituality and self-confidence. The diamond has the elemental correspondence of fire, and it has a projective energy. Due to the way that the stone flashes and reflects when direct light hits it, it is also considered a defensive stone. If you own any diamond jewelry, no matter what the size, it falls under the category of an associated stone of the sun. Diamonds are the birthstone for April. A diamond is also rumored to promote fertility and to keep your sexuality on track, as it is thought to cleanse and remove any blocks to the root chakra.

Empowering Your Magickal Stones

A GREAT WAY to empower any type of crystal or stone is to have the sun give them a little zap of energy. Similar to empowering your golden jewelry, hold the crystals or tumbled stones in the palms of your hands. Then lift up your hands toward the sun for a moment or two, quietly giving them a little shot of the sun's might and magick. (Try the sunny beach or meadow visualization if it will help.) Slip the tumbled stones in your pocket or place them around a spell candle, and you're ready to go!

Sunday Crystal Spell for Success

If you enjoy working with crystals, try this natural magick spell for ambition and success. Carefully look over the spell before performing it. Either set up this spell outside or facing a sunny window. Opportune times of the day to work this sunny spell are sunrise and noon.

Gather one each of the following: a small piece of amber, a tiger's-eye tumbled stone, and a quartz crystal point. With a safe, flat surface on which to set up the spell, place a yellow candle and a candle holder in the center, and arrange the stones in a ring around the candle. Have a lighter or matches handy to light the candle.

Speak the following spell three times:

Around a yellow candle I create a ring

Choose tiger's-eye, amber, and quartz, it's just the thing

I call the god Helios for drive and success

Today's ambitions and career goals he will bless.

Close the spell by saying:

For the good of all, with harm to none

By the sun and stones, this spell is done.

Allow the candle to burn out on its own. Please remember to not leave your burning candle unattended. Pocket the sun-kissed stones and keep them with you, in your pocket or purse, for a week.

Potions, Philters & Oils

I thought it would be interesting and fun to add another dimension to this Book of Shadows by including essential oils that coordinate with the day's magickal energies as well as a recipe or two for potions. Now, technically, it is generally thought that a magickal potion is to be brewed or steeped over heat, while a philter is mixed together like a potion but the ingredients are not brewed. Another definition of a philter is simply "a magickal liquid" (which says classic potion to me). Potion and philter recipes both typically contain the following: water or a base oil, various essential oils, and other magickal ingredients such as herbs, flower petals, shed animal fur, or even tiny chips of crystals.

The magickal philters featured in this Book of Shadows are not meant to be taken internally. These philters, or potions, if you prefer that term, may simply be used to anoint and to bless objects—for example, for consecrating a spell candle. Use a cotton ball or swab to apply the philter to the object or candle. Though the homemade philter and potion recipes in this book smell wonderful, they are not intended to be perfumes either, so be smart and safe. Because of the possibilities of allergies or other medical problems, I would not recommend applying these mixtures to bare skin. Also be sure to wash your hands thoroughly after applying the philters to an object, and avoid contact with your eyes and mouth. These recipes are for charms and spells only, and are not to be ingested. If you wish to carry the scent with you, then I recommend applying the philter to a cotton ball and tucking it inside of a sachet bag.

When you look for bottles for your potions or philters, check the arts and crafts stores for small decorative bottles and jars. Make sure they will seal up and that the neck of the bottle will be large enough for you to pour the mixture into easily. You will probably want to invest in a few small funnels to make it easier. But when you are perusing the decorative glass bottles at the local stores, keep in mind that you want something that is affordable, small, sturdy, sealable, and easy to use. If you can find colors associated with the day's magick, that's even better. Look around and see what you can come across.

The charms that are suggested in all of the daily philter and potion recipes can be easily found in a jewelry-making section of the arts and crafts store. Look for a small package of celestial-themed charms in silver and gold tones.

Also keep in mind that the herbs, crystals, colors, and oils featured in this chapter give you even more information to experiment with. All of the featured items in this chapter are linked to the sun and solar magick. So take a good look at the recipes and other spells that are featured here to see how you can personalize them and make them uniquely your own.

Philter Recipe for
Health, Wealth & Success

- A small decorative glass bottle with a lid or a stopper
- A clean dropper to easily add the essential oil
- A tiny golden sun charm
- 6 inches gold ribbon
- A label and a pen (to list the ingredients and to decorate and mark the bottle)
- ⅛ cup base oil like sunflower oil
- 9 fresh or dried sunflower petals
- Small chips or a tiny piece of carnelian
- 13 drops essential carnation oil

Pour your base oil into the bottle until the bottle is three quarters of the way full. Then add the tiny carnelian chip, the sunflower petals, and finally the essential carnation oil. Add the lid, hold your fingers over the top to avoid any spills, and then carefully shake up the mixture.

Hold up the mixture to the sunlight and allow the sun's beams to illuminate the mixture within. Wipe off the outside of the bottle and use the label to list the ingredients and the use of the potion. Finally, decorate the bottle by attaching the label and tying the gold ribbon around the neck of the bottle. Add the golden sun charm to the streamers of the ribbon so it is visible from the front of the bottle. Knot the charm into place. As you finish tying the bow, hold the bottle in your hands and repeat the charm below:

This philter carries the power of the sun

For health, wealth, and success, the charm is begun

The stone adds power and the element of fire

The sunflower brings fame and will grant my desire

Carnation oil to bring good health and to bind it fast

Now blend all together and make my witchery last

By the power and might of this day of the sun

This philter is magickally blessed, with harm to none.

Store the philter bottle in a safe, dry place that will be out of direct sunlight (try an upper cabinet). Make sure to keep all philters and potions well out of the reach of children and pets.

Essential Oils

All of the following essential oils are associated with the sun. I have specifically chosen oils that are easy to find in either health food, scent, arts and crafts, or local metaphysical/magickal supply stores.

- Bergamot
- Calendula
- Carnation
- Cedar
- Cinnamon
- Frankincense
- Orange
- Rosemary

TAROT CARD ASSOCIATIONS

The tarot cards that are linked to the fiery energy of the sun's day are the Ace of Wands (or Rods) for power and clout; the Major Arcana card the Sun, which symbolizes both joy and attainment; and another Major Arcana card, the Chariot, which signifies ambition, the drive to succeed, and the willpower to overcome any obstacles in your path.

Ace of Wands

The suit of Wands is classically associated with the element of fire. The Ace of Wands is a nice visual boost to job and career spells. In fact, the suit of Wands, or Rods, typically represents both your career and business life. This tarot card in particular corresponds to a successful career and business savvy; it can symbolize success, accomplishments, and moving to a new home or receiving a promotion. Basically, it symbolizes that you are moving up in the world. Work with this tarot symbol for help in obtaining your career goals and personal ambitions.

The Sun

The Sun symbolizes joy and personal achievement. This is the card to work with on a Sunday; its imagery is perfect for all of the magick that is associated with a Sunday. It can be used to help you focus on high ideals and may help encourage you to be strong as you pursue your ambitions. This card traditionally portrays a young blond child riding a white horse while the sun shines down upon him. The white horse is a traditional symbol of the sun, just like

Helios's four white steeds. Work with this card to bring joy, enthusiasm, motivation, and movement into your life.

The Chariot

The Chariot is a wonderful card to work with when personal goals of any kind are the concern. This card often portrays a chariot driver who controls the direction of his path without the use of reins; in other words, he is guiding his course by the strength of his willpower alone. The Chariot card often appears in a tarot reading when a challenge of some kind must be faced. It is a powerful symbol of strength and determination. This card symbolizes a person who will succeed no matter what obstacles they face or how many unexpected curves they may encounter on life's road. Try adding this card to healthy weight loss spells. It will help you stay motivated and to keep on working toward your fitness goals.

An Evaluation/Promotion Tarot Spell

Got an evaluation coming up at work? There is nothing worse than having to go over a review form. You know you deserve a good raise, but how much will your manager or the company be willing to dole out? Or are you trying for a promotion? Sounds like it's time to hedge your bets, so to speak. Try your hand at this tarot spell.

Gather the following:

- A carnelian tumbled stone for success and to boost your career or a quartz crystal point for extra power
- 1 yellow or gold candle (white will do in a pinch—it's an all-purpose color)
- Our three featured tarot cards: the Ace of Wands, the Sun, and the Chariot
- An item in sympathy with the spell that you are casting

You can also add the health, wealth, and success philter to this spell if you wish. Just anoint the spell candle with the solar-powered oil you have created.

What exactly is an item of sympathy? It is any item that is sympathetic to what you are working for. Since this is a job-related spell, an item in sympathy could be your recent paycheck stub, ID badge, or your business card. So, with that thought in mind, adding this sympathetic item to your other correspondences only helps to unify the magick. It does this by uniting the energies and giving you something very specific to focus on.

Arrange your items in front of the candle. If you wish, anoint the spell candle with the philter. Now, light the spell candle and focus on the cards and your item of sympathy, and then repeat the spell below three times. Check out the last line of the spell and adjust this as necessary.

Just like the golden child who rides under the sun
I call for recognition of a job well done
This spell candle illuminates my way
Bringing success and wealth to all my days
Goddess, bless my ambitions, they are fair and true
While this higher career goal/promotion I do now pursue.

Close the spell by saying:

> *For the good of all, with harm to none*
> *By the sun and stars, this spell is done.*

Let the candle burn until it goes out on its own. Keep the carnelian in your pocket or purse, and the cards and your item of sympathy together and on your person for one week, until the following Sunday.

DAILY WITCH CRAFT
solar pocket talisman

Here is a Witch craft that ensures that you carry a pocket full of sunshine at all times. Use this talisman to remind yourself that the sun's power and energy is always with you. This will encourage your outlook on life to be sunny, and it can help keep any of your solar-themed spells going strong and yourself magickally motivated.

- Yellow- or orange-colored oven-bake clay such as Sculpey or Fimo
- A pinch of ground cinnamon
- A nail to inscribe the clay with
- A baking sheet
- Your oven

To begin, knead the orange or yellow clay to make it more flexible. As you do, add a pinch of the cinnamon (a solar herb) to the clay, and work it into the material. Next, flatten and shape out a small circle. Go for the size of a large coin-sized disc, about ¼ of an inch or 6 mm thick. Now take the nail and gently inscribe a sun on one side of the talisman. Flip over to the back and inscribe the names of Helios and Sunna on the other side.

You can make this talisman depiction of the sun as simple or as elaborate as your artistic ability allows. Place the disc on the baking sheet, and bake the clay following the manufacturer's directions—typically at 130 degrees; the length of time is approximately fifteen minutes, though it depends on how big your disc is. This is an estimate only, so read the directions on the oven-bake clay for further guidance.

When the talisman is done baking, allow it to cool. Then consecrate the talisman, and you'll be ready to go! Here is a charm that will bless your new solar talisman. You can certainly add a solar-colored spell candle or crystals to this spell if you wish. Take a look at the at-a-glance correspondences at the beginning of the chapter and see what you would like to add to the spell to make it more personal. Once the talisman is finished, hold it up to the sunlight and repeat the consecration charm:

> In Helios and Sunna's name, this talisman I do bless
> This pocket magick brings to me wealth, happiness, and success
> I invoke the powers of the sun into this spell of mine
> With harm to no one, this charm is done and sealed up with a rhyme.

Now clean up your craft supplies, tuck that talisman into your pocket, and enjoy the rest of your day.

Custom-Made Daily Magick
a recipe for success

Here is where you take everything that you have learned in this chapter and tie all of the Sunday correspondences together. If you are still confused, think of the daily correspondences this way: choosing complementary correspondences is not unlike selecting the ingredients for a batch of homemade chocolate-chip cookies. If you add a little chopped nuts to the cookie batter or an extra splash of vanilla, you get a more deluxe version of an otherwise basic cookie. Now, if you were to throw something like carrots into the recipe for chocolate-chip cookie dough, that wouldn't even complement the other ingredients, would it? Nope. It would just be uncomplementary, weird, and make for a very unappetizing final product.

The reason for this cookie-spell analogy? Well, spells and charms are not unlike recipes. With a spell, you gather your ingredients, mix them together, and work the complementary ingredients for the desired outcome. So, learning how to correctly work with daily magickal correspondences is a clever way to jazz up an otherwise basic, or elementary, spell.

With that thought in mind, here are a few more Sunday spells for you to consider.

Sunday Sunrise Spell for Illumination

Here is a spell that invokes the aid of the triple goddess Brigid. This spell is meant to warm you up from the inside out. This will cause you to have a magickal sparkle and for your lovely personality to shine right through. If you don't feel particularly lovely at the moment, then maybe it's time for a change. This should help you to improve your outlook and cheer you up. Brigid is probably one of the more popular goddesses that modern Witches work with. I think it is because she is so welcoming, strong, and feminine, all at once.

For this spell, try working outside at sunrise. You can also beef this up by adding some natural correspondences, such as stones or flowers, to the spoken verse to help tie the energy together. You could include tiger's-eye, amber, and carnelian. Set these stones around your candles. Slip a few stems of a sun-associated flower into a vase. Try draping the workspace with a gold-colored cloth—celestial fabrics that feature bright yellow suns would be a smart choice. Or just set up in view of a sunny window and let the sunshine illuminate the workspace naturally.

Repeat the spell below three times:

> *Sunday starts off the week with its bright golden glow*
> *This day brings fame, wealth, and causes friendships to grow*
> *Light a gold and yellow candle to ensure success*
> *I call on the goddess Brigid, my spell she will bless*
> *Her light glows inside me, from within my soul will shine*
> *Leadership, health, and growth will all appear in good time.*

Close the spell by saying:

> *With all the power of three times three*
> *As I will it, then so shall it be.*

You can work this spell whenever you feel the need for a little extra personal power. As before, you may keep the stones in your pocket for a few days, or tuck the flowers from the spell into your hair or pin them onto your jacket like a tiny corsage. This will ensure that you carry a bit of Brigid's magick throughout your day.

RITUAL FOR SUNDAY
fitness and health spell

There is more to life than just climbing the ladder of success. How about personal goals, like going on a diet or beginning an exercise program or promising to live a healthier lifestyle? How about promising to exercise on a regular basis? If you want to lose weight, then eat healthier: add more veggies and fruits, drink lots of water, and avoid sweets. Also, take a walk.

Sidewalks are free, baby! Lace up your tennis shoes and hit the pavement. You don't need to join a gym to start losing weight. I should know. I have lost over sixty pounds in the past fifteen months on my own—no crazy diets, no food programs, no gym membership. So, how did I do it? I started out by walking for a half-hour every single day. And I'll be honest: at first I thought I was going to die. Just a stroll around the neighborhood at first made my feet and knees ache so badly. But I refused to give up; I was in it for the long haul. After all, I didn't get to a size 22 overnight; I knew I wouldn't get back to a size 14 overnight, either.

Yes, I had bad days . . . at first, all those skinny little chicks in my neighborhood bouncing along at the local high-school track in their fancy, matching, expensive workout outfits were very discouraging. There I was, trucking along in old, faded shorts and various huge Pagan festival T-shirts, sweating and trying to breathe, while they jogged around the track, making it look effortless. There were days I would plot hideous demises for them as they easily bopped by me. And I kept myself going by laughing at myself—and of course at my various fantasies of catching up with them and then breaking them in half with one arm (I think exercise makes me a bit blood-thirsty). However, it did help me to stay motivated and to keep walking.

Eventually I began to walk for longer distances, then I started doing hikes along the river with my husband. I took belly-dancing classes, broke out my sons' old weight set and started lifting weights in my office at home, and eventually I even started to jog, which surprised the hell out of me.

It started with me challenging myself by asking myself if I could jog one lap and not pass out. Yes, I could. Then after a while, I wondered, could I jog two laps? And on it went, slowly over about six months, until today, believe it or not, I can actually jog a mile. How's that for magick? Honestly—as a kid, I could not run the 200-yard dash. So if I could start jogging when I turned forty-five, I know that you can handle walking.

Did you know that for every pound that you lose, it takes four pounds of pressure off your knees? Yes, that's very true. Losing weight—and keeping it off—also lowers your risks for heart disease, cancer, and diabetes. This is your body and your future we are talking about. Why shouldn't you be as happy and as healthy as possible? I'm sick of hearing about how Pagans are typically "big" people. Baloney. I think that's just wrong. Now, just so we are clear, I'm not talking about getting down to a size double 0. No, indeed; I'm talking about losing some pounds, becoming more active, and getting in shape for health reasons. Set a realistic weight-loss goal, and go for it. My goal was to get back to a size 14, not a size 4. It's a healthy weight-loss goal for me, and I am so glad I stuck with it.

Becoming more fit—making your heart stronger and your body healthier—is a magickal goal that falls under the associations of the sun. So if you want to try it for yourself, get out there and just do it!

Sunday Fitness Ritual

- 1 plain, white seven-day jar candle
- Essential orange oil
- A small, thin screwdriver
- An item of sympathy
- An orange
- A knife to cut the orange into sections
- A small plate or saucer
- The Chariot tarot card

For this fitness spell, you will once again need an item in sympathy with your goal. If that is weight loss, then add a photo of yourself or a tiny lock of your hair. Maybe you have an item of clothing that you want to lose weight to be able to wear. Then cut

out a picture of the item and post it up where you can see it. Since part of your goal includes eating more healthily, as in more fruits and veggies and avoiding sweets, we will add an orange, which is another natural symbol for the sun, to this ritual.

To begin, set up a white seven-day jar candle. Take the screwdriver and carefully push it straight down inside the top of the candle wax. Now lift the screwdriver back out, thereby making a deep hole in the wax. Do this three times, so you have some channels to put the oil into. Set the screwdriver aside. Next, use a clean dropper and squirt the essential orange oil down into the openings you've made inside the jar candle. This way, you have a scented and consecrated jar candle without a big pool of oil on top of the wax, which would make the flame go out.

Place your item of sympathy next to the jar candle. Add the Chariot tarot card to help you keep up your willpower to stick to your healthier lifestyle and exercise routine. If you want to get really fancy, do an Internet search for an image of the Chariot tarot card, print it out, and paste it to the jar candle. Next, quarter the orange and arrange it on a small plate. Arrange the candle and sympathy item to the left of the plate, with the orange in the center and the tarot card to the right.

Now, light the seven-day jar candle. Hold your hands over the orange and focus on your lifestyle-change goals. Don't make excuses about how you don't have time or how you think you might fail. Don't go there. Neutralize those negative thoughts. Stay positive, and don't think about anything but how you will succeed. Believe in yourself. Finally, repeat the following spell three times, and when you are finished with the spell, eat the enchanted orange for a healthy snack.

> On this magickal day of the bright golden sun,
> Now grant me the willpower to get this job done.
> The Chariot will help me stay committed to my goals.
> I will lose weight in a healthy way while taking a stroll.
> As this jar candle burns, so my magick has begun.
> I will meet my goals with a little boost from the sun.
> I am healthier, leaner, and stronger, this much is true,
> Lord and Lady, protect and guide me in all that I do.

Close the spell by saying:

In no way will this spell reverse or place upon me any curse.[*]

For the next seven days, you will repeat this spell with your hands on either side of the jar candle. (Eating the orange is optional on the following days.) Repeat the spell verse just before you go for your daily walk.

Now get out there and walk. Make that a nice brisk walk, and go for some hills: it's better for you than walking on a flat surface all the time, plus it keeps things challenging for your body. Start with thirty minutes per day. Yes, you can walk the dog or put the baby in the stroller and push the little urchin along for the ride. Just move! Don't be afraid to change your routine of where you walk. Go to the park, go to the local high-school track and do laps, change things up so you don't get bored. Also, if the weather is bad outside, then go to the mall and "mall walk." Where I live, those mall walkers are intense—Goddess help you if you get in their way or on their route. Other options include doing an exercise DVD or belly-dancing video at home. Keep active, and be conscious of everything you eat. Choose smarter foods and eat smaller portions. Another tip is to keep a food journal. Write down everything you eat. It really does help.

Bottom line: keep at it and do not give up. If I can do it, you can do it. Make it fun, and realize that the change will come gradually. Don't give up after a week. Keep going; it takes time to make a lasting lifestyle change. Magick is, after all, about personal transformation. What better way to transform than by starting with your own body

---

[*] This closing line was written by a famous British Witch named Sybil Leek. This is a great little all-purpose rider to close out any spell.

and your own health? You can do anything that you set your mind to if you are willing to work hard. I foresee a lot of svelte, sexy, and stronger Witches out there!

Now, take all of the information that you have absorbed from this chapter and add it to spells that you perform on a Sunday. When you decide to sit down and work out how to write and then cast your own spells, refer to the information that was presented in this chapter and create your own personalized magick. Refer to the various spells and charms and adapt them to suit your needs. Check out the worksheet on page 301. Make a few copies of it, and get to work!

Those ambitious, successful spells and charms will be heightened by working on the day of the week that has the planetary influence of the sun. So light those sunny candles, wear some luminous colors, and break out the gold jewelry! Bake up some cinnamon rolls or low-fat cinnamon muffins for an enchanting family breakfast. Take an orange with you to eat at lunch today. Try using a little magickal aromatherapy and burn some cinnamon-scented incense to encourage success and wealth today. Make the talisman to keep your solar magick with you. Sprinkle some dried marigold petals around your house—or across the threshold—to pull triumph and protection toward you and your family.

Get outside and tip up your face to the sun. Take a walk outside, and soak up some sunshine! Acknowledge the power of Sunna or Helios as they blaze across the sky and bring courage and motivation into your life. Sit outside at sunrise on a Sunday morning and bask in its warm, rosy-golden glow. Acknowledge Brigid as the inner, creative spark of imagination and inspiration. She can help these gifts burn brightly within your own soul. Use your imagination and create your own brand of witchery and magick. Here comes the sun, and it's your turn to shine!

Monday

THE MOON SHINES bright
in a night such as this…

Shakespeare

At-a-Glance Correspondences

PLANETARY INFLUENCE	Moon
PLANETARY SYMBOL	☽
DEITIES	Mani, Meness, Thoth, Selene
FLOWERS & PLANTS	Bluebell, jasmine, gardenia, white rose, white poppy, moonflower
METAL	Silver
COLORS	White, silver, pale blue
CRYSTALS & STONES	Moonstone, pearl, quartz crystal, sapphire
ESSENTIAL OILS	Gardenia, jasmine, lemon, lemon balm, lily, myrrh, sandalwood, Stephanotis
TAROT CARDS	The Moon, the High Priestess
FOODS, HERBS & SPICES	Melons, chamomile, wintergreen

DAILY MAGICKAL APPLICATIONS

Monday is named after the moon. The Latin term for Monday is *Dies Lunae* ("moon's day"); in the Old English language, this day was *Monandaeg*; in Greek, it was *Hermera Selenes*. All of these different names and languages translate to the same thing: the "day of the moon."

Working with the different phases of the moon is an important skill that takes a bit of time for Witches to learn. So why not cut to the chase and experiment with the day of the week that is dedicated to the moon in all of its magickal energies and aspects?

Magickally, Monday encourages the lunar energies of inspiration, illusion, prophetic dreams, emotions, psychic abilities, travel, women's mysteries, and fertility.

DEITIES

Typically, when folks talk about deities associated with the moon, the Goddess in her three aspects of Maiden, Mother, and Crone comes to mind. The Triple Moon Goddess is a basic principle of Wiccan belief. Understanding and working with this trinity of goddesses is often a starting point for folks who are new to the Craft. These three different aspects of the Goddess correspond to the various lunar phases: the Maiden for the new to waxing moon, the Mother for the full moon phase, and the Crone for the waning to the dark of the moon. One of the better-known trinity of goddesses is the classic Greek trio of Artemis the Maiden, Selene the Mother, and Hecate the Crone.

However, there are a few male gods of the moon as well. And why not, I ask you? What's wrong with a little equal time for the God? Let's not forget that the balance of male-female energies, or partnership of the God and Goddess, is an important part of our belief system.

While researching this moon god topic, I came across some information about a horse-riding Japanese god of the moon named Tsuki-Yomi and a little-known Baltic god named Meness. Wow, these were new ones for me. Also, the Norse have a god who is linked to the moon. The most well-known moon god, though, is probably the Egyptian god Thoth. He was worshiped throughout the Early Dynastic period and then into Roman times.

Meness

Meness is a Latvian fertility moon god depicted as a young man wearing a star-covered silver cloak. He is crowned with stars and journeys in a chariot that is drawn across the heavens by a gray horse. I like the idea of him silently swooping across the night sky, keeping an eye on us. Meness was known as a protector of travelers and a patron of soldiers. You will find a spell or two working with Meness later in this chapter.

Mani

Mani is the Norse god of the moon. He is described as the personification of the physical moon, and he is Sunna's brother. He is also referred to as the "shining god." Mani's lunar magick holds a softer, shadowy likeness to his sister Sunna's bright solar power, for the moonlight illuminates, yet it also conceals. In Norse mythology, Mani guides the course of the moon and determines its waxing and its waning. Mani is also a chariot-riding deity, and he is followed through the sky by his two children: his son, Hjuki, and his daughter, Bil.

Thoth

Thoth (pronounced *Tote*) is the ibis-headed god from Egypt who wore on his head both a crescent and a lunar disk. Thoth was believed to have regulated the seasons and to have helped keep the lunar phases on track. He was regarded as a magus, the greatest of all magicians. Thoth was a fair and benevolent god of wisdom, astronomy, and practical skills, and he presided over education and books. He was a patron deity of the scribes, and his protection included written medical and mathematical knowledge. Thoth had a wife named Sheshat, and her title was Mistress of the House of Books. Sheshat was a goddess of writing, stars, books, history, and invention. She was depicted as a woman with a star on her brow who wore an inverted, or horns-down, crescent moon on her forehead. Thoth is a powerhouse of magickal power and wisdom. Try calling on him on a Monday night and see what he has to teach you.

Selene

Selene is a Greek goddess of the full moon. She is often portrayed within the face of the full moon as a beautiful winged woman wearing a golden crown. There are Homeric hymns dedicated to Selene, as she was a very influential goddess of her time. One of the lines gives a romantic description of the goddess: "From her golden crown the dim air is made to glitter as her rays turn night to noon." The final section of the hymn reads, "Her great orbit is full, and as she waxes a most brilliant light appears in the sky. Thus to mortals she is a sign and a token."

Selene is a favorite goddess of modern Witches. Why? Well, her specialties include helping you find practical, commonsense answers to your problems. Solutions appear quickly within a day or so. When you call on Selene, you basically get broom-side assistance. Now, before someone starts imagining a dramatic *flash-boom!* accompanied by a swirl of fairy dust, hang on for a second . . .

Selene sends her practical solutions quietly and in unexpected ways. Plus, best of all, spells and prayers dedicated to Selene get results almost every time. However, if you don't pay attention, you may miss the magick. Selene is subtle. Watch closely, and see how she sends in her magickal assistance in a practical, no-nonsense fashion. Symbols for Selene include white flowers, the bluebell, and, of course, the moon.

Monday's Witchery

Today's guided meditation focuses on the lunar deities featured in this chapter. There is something alluring about staying in tune with the moon as it waxes and wanes through its cycles. I think one of the most profound exercises any Witch can do is to watch the moon every day, weather and clear skies permitting, and to learn where the moon rises, sets, and is to be found in the sky. Yes, during certain phases, you will be able to see the moon in the daylight skies. To me, that is always a powerful time to do any type of magick. Since both the sun and moon are present in the sky, you'll have quite a bit of magickal punch to tap into.

Meditation

MEET ME BY moonlight alone,
And then I will tell you a tale...

J. Augustus Wade

Visualize that you are walking quietly outside in a moonlit garden. As you let yourself into the garden, you follow your instincts and walk along the path. The scent of night jasmine wafts through the garden; enchanted, you wander about, enjoying the sights, sounds, and scents of the garden. A small fountain gurgles nearby, and an almost full moon illuminates your trail. You walk over to see the fountain and choose to sit in a spot under a draping tree, close to where a flowering vine is twining its way up an arbor.

Sit down on the soft green grass and relax. Take a few breaths in and out, and let all your worries fade away. Movement catches your peripheral vision, and you turn your head to notice that the moonflower blossoms are shuddering and quivering and then suddenly, before your very eyes, they begin unfurl their bright white petals. Enchanted, you lean back with your spine resting upon a trunk of a tree. You look up through the branches of the tree and realize that you are sitting beneath a willow. You smile to yourself and think that the gods and goddesses have guided you to this spot, for the willow is a tree that belongs to the moon and all her magick.

As you sit and relax in the moonlit garden, you notice hawk moths have gathered around the moonflowers and are sampling the nectar within. There is peace, serenity, and contentment here in this place, and as you contemplate the night sky, you see a large shadow pass silently by. A moment later, an owl begins to call softly through the night. As you relax in this moonlit garden, you think you hear footsteps on the garden path. Curious, you lean forward and see two figures walking arm in arm before you.

One of the figures is a woman, hauntingly beautiful, with silvery-blond hair and a shining coronet upon her brow. She is draped in a luminescent white gown and she smiles at her companion as they move along the garden path. Her companion is a handsome young man with dark hair. He wears a dark silver-colored cloak scattered with twinkling stars. As you watch, somewhat hidden under the draping willow branches, you have to smile, as it appears the two of them are old friends. As they laugh and talk softly back and forth, you have a moment to wonder what the two of them are plotting.

They begin to move past where you are sitting, and the man stops his companion and gestures to the willow tree. He bends over, pulls a few draping branches aside, and smiles at you.

"Hello, child," he says kindly. He holds out his hand. You accept the hand and rise to your feet to stand before the two of them.

Now that you can see them clearly, you realize that these two are not just regular people wandering the garden. Their ages are impossible to determine, and your eyes water as you have a difficult time focusing on them directly. There is magick afoot in this garden, and your mind scrambles to identify them. Then you begin to realize that this is Selene and Meness, both deities of the moon. Part of your brain wonders what a Greco-Roman goddess and Latvian god are doing hanging out together. Selene answers your unspoken question quietly with a question of her own.

"Do you not have many different kinds of friends yourself?" Her question makes you smile, and you nod your head. As you stand before them, they regard you with gently smiling faces and begin to speak to you. Take a moment to listen to what they have to say. Use your heart and listen carefully, for things are not always as they seem under the light of the moon.

As they finish communicating with you, you bow your head in thanks for the wisdom they have shared with you. Meness touches a fingertip to the center of your forehead and then takes your hand and presses something there. "Watch for our sign in the night sky," he tells you and then pats your head as if you were a small child. And you realize that, to him, you *are* a child, for the deities of the moon are ageless and timeless.

He steps back and holds out his other hand for the goddess. She brushes a hand over your cheek as she leaves and smiles as she whispers farewell. Selene accepts Meness's arm, and together they move farther into the dark of the garden. A cloud passes over the moon and then, as the light peeps through again, they are gone.

You look down at the palm of your hand and discover a small moonstone. Laughing, you run your hands across your face in wonder and realize there is a moonflower tucked behind your ear. You smile and thank Selene and Meness. Deciding it's time to return home, you begin to make your way out of the garden. As you reach the garden gate, you look up to regard the moon and see that there is a rainbow effect around it in multicolored rings. Well, they did tell you to watch for a sign . . . You blow a kiss to the moon and, smiling, you begin the journey home.

MAGICKAL PLANTS & FLOWERS

Bluebell

Bluebells are linked to the moon because of the tale of Selene and her handsome lover Endymion. The botanical name for the bluebell is *Endymion nonscriptus*. Selene could not bear the thought of losing Endymion to old age and death, so she cast a spell on her lover, thereby keeping him eternally handsome and youthful. Her lover sleeps away eternity with a smile, while Selene visits him in his dreams. As she visits Endymion, the moon wanes to dark. When Selene returns to her duties once again, the moon waxes to full. Mythology states that Selene bore Endymion fifty beautiful but sleepy daughters. Is it any wonder that he is always smiling? On an interesting final note, in the language of flowers, the bluebell means "constancy." Adding bluebells to a love or romance spell will gain special attention from Selene.

Jasmine

Jasmine (*Jasmine officinale*) is a flowering vine that has an extraordinary scent. In magickal herbalism, the delicate jasmine bloom is associated with the moon. Night blooming jasmine is a natural for lunar enchantments and charms. The jasmine flowers were thought to promote prophetic dreams and to help encourage a spiritual love. In aromatherapy, jasmine is used to lift your spirits and help you relax.

Gardenia

Another scented lunar flower, the gardenia (*Gardenia jasminoides*) is a blooming shrub bearing incredibly scented flowers. The essential oil from gardenias is often used in perfumes. Gardenias are popular as a bridal flowers due to their creamy white color and romantic, old-fashioned scent. In the language of flowers, the gardenia symbolizes feminine charm and a secret love. Magickally, the gardenia encourages love and mysticism.

White Rose

The white rose (*Rosa* spp.) traditionally symbolized purity and love, which explains its popularity in the bridal flower trade. The white rose is a sacred symbol to many goddesses. A full-blown, or opened, white rose is a symbol of Selene, the full moon goddess. The different phases of a rose blossom may also be used to symbolize the different phases of the moon: a tight bud to represent the new moon, a partially opened bud for the waxing moon, a fully opened rose for the full moon, a rose just beginning to fade but still lovely for the waning moon, and rose hips for the dark of the moon.

White Poppy

The white poppy (*Papaver* spp.), another of Selene's sacred plants, is also an enchanting flower. The poppy comes in many colors: red, orange, purple, and white. The nectar of the poppy flower makes the bees in the garden giddy. There are many varieties of poppies available today; consider adding some of them to your garden at home. On an amusing note, in the language of flowers, it symbolizes "drifting in a peaceful sleep." (No wonder Selene claimed it!)

Moonflower

The moonflower (*Ipomoea*), which is mildly toxic, is an annual flowering vine that blooms in late summer–early fall. Part of the morning glory and the sweet potato family, moonflowers have an intoxicating scent. And, just as you would imagine, they only bloom at night. On cloudy, cool morning in the early fall, the trumpet-shaped flowers may stay open for a while. Moonflowers are a natural when it comes to working a little Monday night moon magick. Try gathering a bloom and floating it in a bowl of water. I often float a bloom in my small garden fountain in the backyard. Or leave the blooms on the vine and work your moon magick spell while you sit nearby and enjoy the fragrance.

A Moonflower Dream Spell

Traditionally the moonflower carries the message of "I am sustained by your affections," just like Endymion was sustained by Selene's love. Try this moonflower-inspired spell and send your lover a sweet dream of you.

Gather from the garden a white rose, a single moonflower blossom, or any of the lunar-associated flowers that were mentioned above. Float the bloom in a fountain or a birdbath, or use a clear glass bowl. If you use a bowl, hold the bowl in your hands and concentrate on the lunar symbolism both of the round, moon-shaped, circular bowl and the white flower floating within. If you use a fountain, then adapt this accordingly. Close your eyes and gently concentrate on your partner. Picture in your mind a happy time or future event that you are both looking forward to. Open your eyes and repeat the following spell three times:

> My love, while you sleep I will send you a sweet dream
>
> By the light of the moon, things are not as they seem
>
> I cast upon the water petals from a white flower
>
> May Selene now bless my spell in this enchanted hour.

Close the spell by saying:

> For the good of all, with harm to none
>
> By moonlight and dreams, this spell is done.

Note: Be sure to leave the theme of the dream up to the dreamer. You are suggesting only, not manipulating the outcome or coercing their private thoughts. This spell also works well when your partner is having trouble sleeping and you want to encourage a restful night's sleep. Brew up a cup of chamomile tea and set it next to the candles. When you are finished with the spell, give the tea to your partner and wish them a good night. It should work like a charm.

COLORS, CANDLES, METALS & CRYSTALS

Colors

Colors for this lunar day may include white, silver, and pale blue or gray. If you want to feel a little more witchy on Mondays, then try adding a little color magick to your outfit by adding these lunar colors. Any soft, shimmery fabrics in delicate lunar colors would work out nicely as well. Add a silver pin shaped like a moon, and you're all set and ready to go!

Lunar Illusion Color Magick Spell

Feel the need to blend in or to go about your business quietly, without drawing attention to yourself? There are times when we all need to be, well, a little subtle. Now, before you get in a huff at what I am suggesting, think about it for a moment. Sometimes even those of us who are naturally outgoing need to tone things down a bit—like when you have had an argument with your mother or are approaching your boss about an issue at work or are taking on one of your kid's teachers at school. There are times when it is simply inappropriate to swagger into situations with your six guns a-blazing.

For those times when discretion, tact, and a little magickal strategy is called for, this lunar illusion spell will help to keep you centered and calm. If you need to work magick discreetly, or for those times when being subtly witchy is the way to go, this sort of quietly clever magickal control goes a long way in situations when tempers are frayed and emotions are high. This glamoury-type of enchantment is particularly useful when you want to win people over to your side or for when you are quietly working magick to smooth over sticky situations.

Choose your outfit with care. Think of quiet, lunar types of colors with silver jewelry. No matter what your personal style is, whether you slip on a gray business suit, tug on a white sweater, or pull on a comfortable denim shirt in a soft blue, this lunar illusion will work. Take a moment and imagine yourself standing on the quiet moonlit shores of a lake. Feel yourself becoming serene and filled with the power and magick of the moon. Now, wrap a little of the moon's light and glamour around you. Do you feel more centered and focused? Good. Now believe that you can calmly and quietly handle this situation. Repeat the spell below three times:

> *The lunar shades of magick are white, silver, and blue*
> *Charm, mystique, and illusion they grant softly to you*
> *Peace and serenity are the order of the day*
> *May this spell smooth all obstacles that are in my way.*

Close the spell by saying:

> *For the good of all, with harm to none*
> *With color and light, this spell is done!*

Take a deep breath, and let it out slowly. Now, coolly go and deal with the crisis.

Note: Remember, this spell works to smooth situations over, not to eliminate them. In other words, you can glide in, fix the situation, and then quietly ease back out. It also makes people see you in a different light, so be ethical and make sure you use this spell fairly.

Candles

Candle colors for today include white, silver, and pale blue. Keep your eyes open for celestial-themed candles with moons and stars on them. Try your hand at a little candle-magick aromatherapy. Look for the following scented votive candles to coordinate with your lunar enchantments: gardenia-scented candles promote spirituality and love; jasmine-scented candles encourage peace, sleep, and psychic dreams; sandalwood, a highly spiritual scent, may be used to support meditation and helps to set an excellent magickal mood. All of these enchanting fragrances correspond to Monday and the moon's gentle magick.

Metals & Crystals

The associated metal for Monday is silver. Silver is a receptive metal and is identified with the lunar energies of the Goddess. Silver is the metal of emotions, magick, psychic abilities, and peace. Charging or empowering silver jewelry works along the same lines as the directions that were given in Sunday's chapter for enchanting gold jewelry, the main difference being that you want to work in the moonlight as opposed to the sunlight. This time, hold the jewelry up to the light of the moon and ask either Selene to enchant it or Thoth to imbue it with wisdom and knowledge.

The crystals and stones that are linked to Monday and to the moon are the quartz crystal, moonstone, pearl, and sapphire. Moonstones and quartz crystals can easily be purchased at nature-theme stores or at most magick or metaphysical shops. These two tumbled stones are typically inexpensive, so pick up a couple of your favorites and keep them on hand for crystal magick and spells. If you own jewelry with pearls or sapphires in them, consider working with them for other lunar spells.

QUARTZ CRYSTAL: The all-purpose quartz crystal makes yet another appearance in this book. Why? Because the quartz crystal is linked to both the moon and the sun. It also has associations to the fifth element in magick, that of Spirit. This crystal has both feminine and masculine—receptive and projective—properties. Quartz crystals set in silver evoke lunar and feminine energies, thanks to the silver. This jewelry combination is very popular with magick users and Witches today. Quartz crystal points may be used to tip wands, and the stones are also excellent for clearing the chakras, the energy centers of the body. Use your quartz crystal points for extra power for any ritual, spell, or charm.

PEARL: Pearl has the elemental association of water and is the birthstone for the month of June. Pearls are created when a piece of grit such as sand gets inside the shell of certain species of a living clam, mussel, or oyster. The animal, in an effort to minimize the irritation, coats the grit with a material called nacre. Layers of this coating are deposited on the irritant until, after a few years, a pearl is formed. There is a debate on whether or not pearls are ethical to work with. Some magickal folks do not care to work with pearls, as the oyster has to be killed to retrieve the pearl. However, if you already own any pearls, this is an excellent opportunity to perform moon magick with them.

Natural pearls come in a range of colors, such as white, yellow, pink, and black. They are considered to be receptive and are a classic moon symbol. They are often worked into goddess magick, women's magick, and good fortune and fertility spells.

SAPPHIRE: The element associated with the blue sapphire is water, and it is the birthstone for the month of September. The sapphire is from a group of gems known as corundum. While blue is the main color of the sapphire, it does come in other colors as well. Technically, different-colored sapphires are called "fancies." Sapphires may be pink, yellow, orange, purple, and green. Interestingly, there are no red sapphires, because a red sapphire is actually considered to be a ruby. (Rubies are also from the corundum group.) Actually, rubies and sapphires are often found together, with one of the colors more prevalent than the other.

This fabulous precious stone is incorporated into rituals and magick for protection, sorcery, and healing. Wearing sapphire jewelry will also increase your psychic abilities. Blue sapphires are also considered to be a love stone, which makes them a more romantic choice for wedding jewelry than a diamond. Sapphires also will increase your spirituality, and if worn while meditating, they can increase divine knowledge.

You may care to enchant these lunar stones by placing them on a windowsill that receives the moonlight or by setting them in a dish and leaving them in the garden on the night of a full moon, letting them soak up some lunar energy. If you own any pearl or sapphire jewelry, then let it stay indoors on a moonlit windowsill. (I wouldn't recommend leaving your good jewelry outdoors overnight.)

MOONSTONE: The moonstone is linked to the sea and to the moon. The elemental association for the moonstone is water, and it is a receptive stone. It is employed in all types of moon magick. Tumbled moonstones are enchantingly affordable and come in a range of colors—white, beige, pearly gray—and these stones are gorgeous and shimmery. As jewelry, white moonstones are typically set in silver. Wearing moonstone earrings, rings, pendants, or bracelets can increase your sensitivity to psychic impressions, though, so if you are already sensitive enough, limit your exposure to moonstones.

Personally, I adore moonstones; however, I do not wear them as often as I'd like. I never wear my moonstone earrings or my moonstone pendant when I do psychic readings. Why? Because when I do, I typically get overloaded with information—rather delicate, personal information that the client may not have wished for me to know. Also, moonstones tend to turn up my mediumship abilities to full blast. So I do not wear my moonstone jewelry during psychic work unless I want to spend my day talking to all the client's dead relatives, who can be very demanding—once they have someone to talk to, they typically do not shut up—and yeah, they do follow me home, which is very disruptive.

This is not the case for everyone, but if you do counseling, assist in physical therapy, perform healing work such as Reiki, or give tarot readings to the public, you are already sensitive. Moonstone jewelry may really help you "up your game," so to speak, and become incredibly empathic to others, or it may cause you some psychic overload and emotional distress. In other words, you may feel so overwhelmed and so emotionally worn out by other people that you need a break. It's like having a psychic hangover; it feels like all the symptoms of drinking too much without the actual drinking. And believe me, psychic hangovers suck big time. So you'll have to experiment to see how moonstones set in silver affect you.

Truthfully, they may not bother you at all. I know plenty of folks who work beautifully with the moonstone for psychic work and tarot readings. Just remember, when moonstones are set in silver, it only increases their receptive powers. There is no reason to be alarmed; just use this moonstone information to your advantage in the future.

Try carrying a piece of tumbled, polished moonstone in your pocket to celebrate your connection to the moon and all its energies. Or keep the opalescent stone with your divinatory tools. I like to surround spell candles with a ring of tumbled moonstones to give my candle spells a boost of lunar magick. The moonstone is wonderful for use in the following types of spells: safe travel, increasing psychic powers, boosting your empathy, gardening, and self-awareness. It is a classic Goddess stone. Since the moonstone is often used as a talisman to promote a safe journey, I think it's time to conjure up a moonstone travel spell with one of the featured deities for Monday.

Moonstone Travel Spell

This spell will call on Meness, the patron moon god of travelers. We met Meness earlier, in the meditation for Monday. I suggest setting up this spell in the evening. Find a spot that faces east or that is illuminated by moonlight. Or try setting this up under the moon, in the garden, or on the porch or your outside deck. Get some atmosphere going! Try using a scented candle, such as jasmine or gardenia, to coordinate the fragrance with the moon's energies.

Gather the following items:

- A photo of your destination, your travel itinerary, or your airline tickets
- 4 small tumbled moonstones
- A scented white votive candle and holder
- A lighter or matches

Set up this spell on a safe, flat surface. Light the candle and place it in the holder. Place your paperwork/tickets or itinerary to one side of the candle. Arrange the four stones in a circle around the holder. Place your hands on the travel paperwork, and ground and center. Then repeat the following spell three times:

Meness, patron of travelers, watch over me

Whether I travel in the air, on land, or sea

Like a talisman in my pocket a stone will I tuck

Moonstones do encourage a safe journey and bring good luck.

Take one of the stones and keep it in your pocket while you travel. You may close the spell by saying:

For the good of all, with harm to none

By the moon and stars, this spell is done.

Gather up your papers and tuck them away for your trip. Allow the candle to burn out on its own. If you performed this outside, then move your candle and the remaining stones indoors to let the candle safely finish burning. Never leave your candles unattended.

POTIONS, PHILTERS & OILS

Today is the time to create philters and potions that work in harmony with your lunar magick. Since the moon is directly linked to psychic abilities, today is the day—no matter what phase the moon happens to currently be in—to create a psychic power philter (or potion, if you prefer). There are many variations to lunar magick. After the philter recipe, you will find more information about the lunar phases and their effect on psychic abilities.

Philter Recipe for Psychic Power
- One clear or blue glass bottle with a stopper or lid
- A clean dropper
- 6 inches silver ribbon
- A small moon-shaped charm
- A label and a pen (to list the ingredients and
  to decorate and mark the bottle)
- ⅛ cup almond base oil (almond is associated with the moon)
- 13 drops sandalwood oil (a lunar oil that is both spiritual and protective)
- 3 white rose petals
- 3 willow leaves or a pinch of dried willow bark
- A tiny moonstone chip

Pour the base oil into the bottle until the bottle is three quarters of the way full. Then add the moonstone chip, the rose petals, willow, and finally the essential sandalwood oil. Close up the bottle with the lid, place your fingers over the lid, and carefully shake up the mixture.

Hold up the mixture to the moonlight and allow the moonbeams to illuminate the philter within. On the label, list the ingredients and the use for this potion. Decorate the label by drawing moons or whatever else you think would add to the moon magick. Attach the label to the glass bottle (wipe off the outside of the bottle first). Finish up by threading the moon charm onto the ribbon and then tying the silver ribbon around the neck of the bottle. As you finish tying on the bow, hold the bottle in your hands and repeat the charm below. (Notice there is a place for you to insert which phase of the moon you happen to be currently in. This way, you can customize the philter for specific psychic abilities.)

> *This philter holds the powers of the moon*
>
> *May it increase my psychic power soon*
>
> *The stone adds lunar power and empathy*
>
> *The herbs and oil increase the power times three*
>
> *During this ___ quarter's enchanting moon phase*
>
> *I'll work easily with my powers through the day*
>
> *This potion is enhanced by the moon's magick so bright*
>
> *My psychic talents will now blossom and come to light.*

Store the philter bottle in a safe, dry place out of direct sunlight. Make sure that you keep all potion and philter bottles well out of reach of children. Now, if you want to get really creative, you can adapt the charm for the philter to work in any of these following lunar energies (which means you could literally create four different lunar philters, one for each phase and psychic influence of the moon).

Phases of the Moon and Their Psychic Associations

The different phases of the moon do have an effect on your psychic talents. Here is the information, along with tips for working with your divinatory tools, such as runes or the tarot. Consider how this lunar phase/psychic information will affect the spells that you cast on a Monday. It will all depend on what phase the moon is in when you cast, which means you have lots to learn and plenty to experiment with. There are many layers to witchery and magick. The best way to up your game and to increase your skills is to practice, experiment, and see how the magick works for you.

FIRST QUARTER: (new moon to the waxing half moon) Now is the time
when your psychic power is starting to build; you may feel more "tuned
in" and more compassionate and sensitive to other people's emotions. Your
dreams and their divinatory meanings become clearer. You may notice
that your animal allies, or totem animals, show up more in your life, so pay
attention to their messages. Work your divinatory tools now to get a clear
picture of what is beginning to unfold in your life at the present time.

SECOND QUARTER: (waxing half moon to the full moon) During this lunar
phase, your emotions and senses get turned up to "high." (Think of it as
riding a psychic wave of sorts: it builds as the full moon gets closer, peaks,
and then you start to ride downward.) Precognitive dreaming is more
likely to happen during this particular lunar phase. At the full moon phase
itself, you will probably notice everything in a more detailed and magickal
way, so work with it when it hits. Intuition and clairvoyance abilities will
peak as the moon waxes to full. Employ your favorite divinatory tools now
to see the past, present, and future.

THIRD QUARTER: (day after the full moon until the waning half moon) As
the moon wanes, the focus begins to turn within. Pay attention to your
inner voice—your instincts and gut hunches. This is not the time to
ignore that inner monologue. You may find that you are "hearing between
the lines," meaning you are hearing or sensing what is unspoken, so think
before you speak. Ride the back of this wave of lunar energy and realize
that the energies around you can be used to your benefit. Tune in to your

own spirit and meditate. Work with divinatory tools now to see what is hidden from you.

FOURTH QUARTER: (waning half moon until the new moon) At this point of the moon phase, some folks may find that their psychic talents go on holiday, or you may notice that they come howling in with an all-out assault on your senses. The reason for this is, I believe, that during this last waning lunar phase, all psychic work turns within. This often forces a person to contemplation, and it nudges them into turning their psychic abilities and all that focus within. Then they gain the opportunity for self-discovery. Work with your divinatory tools now to gain an appreciation for what events and people have led you to this point of your life. By looking to the past, we can acquire a good overview on what has brought us to the point we are standing at now. Then we may gain understanding, wisdom, and insight.

Essential Oils

These essential oils are all linked to the moon. Again, I have chosen scents that should be easy for you to get your witchy hands on. Essential oils that correspond with the moon and Monday's magick are:

- Gardenia
- Jasmine
- Lemon
- Lemon balm

- Lily
- Myrrh
- Sandalwood
- Stephanotis

These scents would be fabulous to add to spell candles—you can always add a drop or two to a plain white tealight candle or work these essential oils into potions and philters of your own design. So take a whiff of their bewitching fragrances, and see which ones you prefer for your own lunar enchantments.

TAROT CARD ASSOCIATIONS

The tarot cards that are associated with the moon's day are the Major Arcana cards the Moon, which symbolizes illusion, and the High Priestess (or Popess), which means intuition, dreams, and magickal powers. Adding these cards as props to any moon magick spell will give you something to focus on, and the classic tarot card symbols are ancient and powerful.

The Moon

The Moon is an intriguing tarot card. Often this card is interpreted as a time of disillusionment or despair, but not always. This card is a symbol for the Crone Goddess, and it also signifies illusion and development of psychic powers. This is the card to work with and meditate on when you feel that there are hidden forces at work or when you may not be seeing things as they really are—you know, the new boyfriend who seems

too good to be true? The boss who seems to have a hidden agenda? You get the idea. In the classic illustration of this card, it shows both a dog and a wolf howling at the full moon. These may be symbols of the tamed and untamed personality, or the conscious and unconscious mind.

The High Priestess

The High Priestess symbolizes wisdom, mystery, feminine power, and magick. This card typically represents the Goddess in her aspect as the Maiden. This card is the one to work with when you want to increase and call on your inner natural magickal powers. The High Priestess is strong, tough, wise, and unyielding. This is a woman of power. In the classic illustration of this card, the priestess holds a scroll and a quill, which represents wisdom and knowledge. And believe me, working with this card or having it turn up in a reading reinforces that you are strong enough to wield your magickal power wisely. We all have our own magick; dig deep and see if you can call it out. If you want to learn how to be more empathic and tune in to your natural psychic abilities (and everybody has those, too, by the way), this is the card to meditate on and to focus on in your spellwork, as it brings strength, insight, and understanding.

Increasing Psychic Powers Tarot Spell

Feel like working for a little increased intuition or psychic ability? Here is a Monday night tarot spell that will help you increase your psychic talents and focus on your own powers. This spell will incorporate many of the bewitching accessories that were mentioned earlier in this chapter, such as candles, aromatherapy, and crystals. You can always add a few drops of your new lunar philter to an unscented white candle. Try carving a moon on the side of that plain candle, and *ta-da!* Instant lunar candle of your very own creation. If you choose to add essential oils to the white candle instead, I would probably go with jasmine or sandalwood, as both are equated with the moon, and they are spiritual scents that help encourage intuition and empathy.

- 1 plain white candle, taper or votive
- 1 coordinating candle holder
- Lighter or matches
- A few tumbled moonstones or a quartz crystal point (to increase psychic abilities)
- Lunar philter or essential oils associated with the moon
- The High Priestess and the Moon tarot cards
- A pinch of silver glitter or star-shaped confetti

Place the Moon and the High Priestess cards on either side of the candle. Arrange the crystals on the work surface around the tarot cards. Also have that silver star confetti or glitter close at hand.

Make the work area pretty and magickal. Try adding a silvery or shimmery piece of cloth to drape over the area. Prop up the cards so you can focus on them during the spell. Arrange the other accessories in a way that pleases you, and take a moment to center yourself. Repeat the spell below three times. On the last line, sprinkle a bit of glitter or confetti on the floor in a circle going clockwise around you.

> *I call upon the Lady to open my heart*
> *In olden times, prophecy was the Witch's art*
> *Clear sight, empathy, and intuition now bring*
> *In all seasons, fall to winter, summer to spring*
> *By the powers of water, fire, earth, and wind*
> *With stardust and moonlight, may my visions begin.*

Now, sit inside of the circle that you just cast on the floor with the confetti and allow your mind to drift and your intuition take over. Lay out a quick tarot spread and see what the cards have to tell you about the current situation. A very simple card spread to use is to deal out three cards: one for the past, one for the present, and the final card to represent the future. Meditate on the cards for a moment or two. Close the spell by saying:

> *As I close this spell, I bring harm to none*
> *By moonlight and magick, my spell is done*
> *In no way will this spell reverse or place upon me any curse.*

You may either let the candle burn until it goes out on its own or pinch it out and save it to use when you do a tarot card reading at a later time. If you start to experience vivid dreams, then start a dream journal and keep track of them. Pay attention to your "gut hunches," and start listening to your inner voice. Everyone has psychic abilities of some sort. Don't deny any psychic experiences that you have, no matter how small they may seem. Instead, write down your experiences and validate them. You receive more psychic impressions and become more comfortable with your own intuition when you begin to acknowledge the experiences instead of brushing them off.

DAILY WITCH CRAFT
dream catcher

A dream catcher is created to be a net in which to catch bad dreams and negativity. It is typically hung up and over a sleeping area and in a place where the morning sunlight can illuminate the webbing and "burn off" the unpleasant dreams. Here is a new, witchy spin on the traditional dream catcher.

- One 12-inch thin grapevine wreath
- 3 yards pale blue ribbon
- 3 yards silver ribbon
- 3 yards white ribbon
- White, gray, or blue feathers (you may use fallen feathers too)
- A low-temperature glue gun
- Black pipe cleaner
- A silvery moon-shaped charm (check the jewelry-making aisle)
- Assorted glass and metal beads in lunar colors of white, silver, and blue

Create this dream catcher on a Monday, the day associated with the moon and all its magick. If you are working in a waxing moon, then enchant the dream catcher to increase your protection and to promote a good night's sleep. If you are making this craft in a waning moon phase, then enchant it to ward off and keep away negativity and bad dreams.

To begin, take one of the colors of the ribbon and weave a five-pointed star inside of the wreath. If you want to get fancy, you can thread a few of the beads onto this ribbon as you go; it's up to you. You may need to add a drop of glue to the ribbon to keep the pentagram from sliding around. Weave the star into the wreath and keep the points even. When finished, tie off the ribbon, and then turn the wreath so the pentagram has one point up.

Take the second color of ribbon and create a bow. Use the pipe cleaner to wire the bow onto the wreath. You may thread some of the beads and the moon-shaped charm onto the dangling streamers of the bow. Tie a few attractive feathers at the end of the streamers as well. Remember to take your time and enjoy the process.

Next, arrange some of the feathers along the side of the wreath in a pretty arrangement, and glue them on. Use the remaining ribbon as a hanger and loop it at the top of the wreath so it can dangle from the ceiling or a curtain rod. Adjust the length as necessary. (Any leftover ribbon may be used to wrap around the wreath or for future crafty projects.)

Please note: you can make this project smaller if you wish. Use a miniature grapevine wreath about six inches across and then scale the ribbon down to one yard per color. Go with whatever size dream catcher, large or small, that you like the best.

Once the dream catcher is decorated to your liking, hold it in both hands, and ground and center. Then repeat the following charm over it:

With Monday's witchery, I create a dream catcher

To keep away bad dreams and to create peace and laughter

By color magick of white, silver, and blue

This wreath is enchanted, and its purpose is true

Feathers are traditional, and they sweep evil away

I am blessed with lovely and sweet dreams for all of my days

By all the power of the day of the moon

Lunar gods, bless this spell and grant me a boon.

Now hang up your dream catcher, and enjoy the magick you have created and enchanted with your own two hands.

CUSTOM-MADE DAILY MAGICK

Here are a few more moon-associated spells for you to try your hand at. The first spell calls on Thoth, the Egyptian god of wisdom and magick. If you wish to try and "beef up" your magickal prowess, so to speak, then working with Thoth is the way to go. As Thoth was considered the greatest of all magicians and a benevolent god to boot, he should be able to help you cleverly increase your powers and help you to gain a little magickal wisdom while you are at it.

The Spell of the Magus

Try working this spell on a Monday while both the moon and the sun are in the sky at the same time. During certain phases of the waning moon, the moon can be seen in the morning sky (or in the new to waxing moon phase, in the evening sky just before the sun sets). This time—when both the sun and the moon are visible in the sky—is believed to be a time of incredible magickal power.

Choose a small pillar style of white candle. Inscribe the candle with a lunar symbol. Anoint the candle with sandalwood oil to increase your spirituality. Next, light the white candle and place it in a candle holder on a safe, flat surface. Gather a few almonds in a dish off to the side of the candle holder. Almonds are sacred to Thoth and are thought to grant wisdom. *Note:* If you are allergic to nuts, then substitute a white wintergreen-flavored mint. Wintergreen is also associated with the moon.

Repeat the spell below three times:

> Thoth, Egyptian god of wisdom and of the moon so white
>
> Hear my call: grant me might and power on this special night
>
> Honor and integrity creates its own power
>
> Grant me wisdom and strength in this magickal hour.

At the final repetition of the spell, eat the almonds/mint, then close the spell by saying:

> As I consume these nuts/this mint, I take into myself
>
> the wisdom and benevolence of Thoth
>
> For the good of all, with harm to none
>
> By the moon and stars, this spell is done.

Keep an eye on the candle; let it burn until it goes out on its own. Meditate on the old saying that with great power comes great responsibility. Be sure you are fair and wise in all of your magickal actions. If you are unsure of your motives, then contemplate Thoth, use your imagination, and see what he has to tell you.

Ritual for Monday
selene's ritual

This ritual calls on Selene, our featured lunar goddess of practical magick and commonsense solutions. Look over the ritual before you begin, as you will need a few supplies. This spell is also a good one to work on the night of a full moon, no matter what day of the week it is. Simply adjust the opening line—try saying instead, "On the night of Selene's enchanted full moon"—and you're good to go. Happy casting!

- 1 white taper candle
- 1 silver taper candle
- 2 candle holders
- A white rose in a vase
- Matches or a lighter
- Sandalwood incense and an incense holder

Set up this ritual on a safe, flat surface. Arrange your work area so that you can see the moon, no matter what phase she is in. When you are ready to begin, light the candles and the incense. Center yourself, and repeat the spell below three times:

Monday is the magickal day of the moon
In this enchanted time, hear this Witch's tune
See the white and silver candles burning so bright
I call the goddess Selene for her help this night
Practical solutions are her shining gifts, you see
Lady, show me the way; as I will, so mote it be.

Lift up your face to the moon and take nice deep, even breaths. Concentrate on the moon, and let your mind drift. Allow your eyes to blink naturally as you meditate on Selene, Lady of the Moon, and what messages she may have for you. If it helps, close your eyes; just keep your face tipped so the light of the moon shines down on you. If you like, read the guided meditation in this chapter and see if that jump-starts anything for you. After you are finished meditating, close the spell by saying:

Selene, I thank you for your time and care

I close this spell now by the powers of earth, water, fire, and air.

Snuff out your illuminator candles. You may save these candles to use on the full moon or anytime you call on Selene. Enjoy the rose until it starts to fade, then carefully gather the petals and spread them out to dry in a single layer. After they have dried, store them in an airtight, nonporous container (old glass canning jars are ideal for this purpose). Then use those enchanted petals in lunar philter and potion recipes or in any spell where you need to speed things up. Keep your eyes open, and see how Selene's power and your moon magick go to work in your life.

Think for a moment on all of the witchery, magick, and enchantments that you discovered in this moon-themed chapter. Don't be afraid to adjust these spells to suit your own specific needs. Any of the gentle, illusory, and dreamy charms and spells from this chapter can be enhanced when you work on the day of the week that is dedicated to the moon. Also, there is that handy-dandy spell worksheet on page 301 for you to copy and work with. Mondays are a fantastic day to boost your psychic abilities and to tune in to your intuition and empathy. It also gives you the opportunity to work with a different lunar phase each and every Monday, which means in one month you could work four different types of moon magick on Mondays. How's that for adding to your repertoire? You are going to have mad skills in no time at all.

So light up those lunar scented candles and add a little mystique to your outfit by wearing an enchanting lunar color. Wear your sparkling silver jewelry and maybe add a pair of dangling silver earrings or a pendant shaped like a crescent moon. Create lunar potions and philters; make a dream catcher and give it as a gift to someone you love. Burn some sandalwood or jasmine-scented incense today to inspire the glamour and magick of the moon. Slice up a favorite variety of melon for a snack or share it with your love and enjoy his or her lunar and romantic qualities. Brew up a cup of chamomile tea, enchant it with a little moon magick, and relax and get a good night's sleep.

Most importantly, get outside tonight and watch the moon for a while. What phase is she in? What color was the moon as she rose? Why not start a journal and write down at what location the moon rises and sets for a few seasons? This is a great way to teach you to tune in and to become more aware of the moon and the influence that she pulls into our lives. Try calling on Selene for her magickal assistance, and call Thoth for wisdom and strength. Get to know the Norse Mani and the Latvian Meness. These gods of the moon have plenty to teach, and if you allow their influence to cycle through your life, you'll receive many blessings. Be imaginative, and create your own personal lunar magick and witchery. Go on . . . the moonlight becomes you.

Tuesday

At-a-Glance Correspondences

PLANETARY INFLUENCE	Mars
PLANETARY SYMBOL	
DEITIES	Mars, Tyr/Tiw, Lilith
FLOWERS & PLANTS	Holly, snapdragon, thistle
METAL	Iron
COLORS	Red, black, scarlet, orange
CRYSTALS & STONES	Bloodstone, garnet, ruby, red jasper
ESSENTIAL OILS	Basil, ginger, pennyroyal, pine
TAROT CARDS	Five of Wands, Six of Wands, Strength
FOODS, HERBS & SPICES	Allspice, peppers, carrots, garlic, ginger

DAILY MAGICKAL APPLICATIONS

Tuesday is the day associated with the planet Mars. In mythology, Mars was the Roman god of war. If you're wondering how this day came to be named, it's because to the Norse, Anglo-Saxon, and Germanic people, this day was Tiw's day (Tuesday). Tuesday actually got its name from the Norse deity Tyr, Tiw, or Tiu, who was also a god of battles and courage. This deity was very similar to the Roman Mars, and the names of the days of the week became switched and substituted as the Germanic peoples replaced the older deities with their own gods. So the name was changed from the Latin *Dies Martis* ("Mars' day") to the Old English *Tiwesdaeg.*

The Norse god Tiw, or Tyr, was known for his sense of justice, discipline, and integrity. This day's planetary influence brings with it the aggression, bravery, and honor of soldiers, as well as the passion and strength of those of us who must fight for what we believe in.

DEITIES

Mars

Mars may have been originally a god of vegetation, but as time went on he became more closely linked to Ares, the Greek god of war. Mars was one of the major deities of the Roman pantheon. He was a patron god of soldiers and was often portrayed as wearing a cape, a suit of armor, and a plumed helmet. Mars' symbols include a shield and a spear. It is believed that the month of March got its name from the Roman god Mars, in part due to the violent swings in the weather, not unlike Mars' temperament.

Tyr/Tiw

Tyr, or Tiw, is the Norse god who lends his name to Tuesday. He was best known for the binding of the Fenris, a big, bad, and ravenous wolf. Tyr managed to bind Fenris but lost his sword hand in the process. Tyr is known for his courage in defense of his clan. He was the deity of warriors, and his devotees were said to have marked Tyr's rune onto their swords for protection and to ensure that they would win their battles. (The rune is tiewaz—it looks like an arrow that points to the sky.) There is more to Tyr than just fighting, however; he is also a god of justice and law. In addition to the rune tiewaz, Tyr's symbol is the sword. This Norse god brings a fair resolution to any conflict, as he is a god of courage, strength, wisdom, meditation, and (of course) fighting skills.

Lilith

Lilith is the divine lady owl and the original bad-ass chick. She is often portrayed as a dark, winged, beguiling sorceress. Our most familiar image of Lilith comes from a terra-cotta relief from Sumer, dating back to about 2000 BCE. She is shown as an attractive winged woman with clawed feet. In modern times, she is popularly imagined as the beautiful vampire and the ultimate femme fatale. It is easy to envision Lilith as a raven-haired seductress draped in flowing black, her ebony wings swirling around her. She is thought to be ethereally beautiful, with pale skin, dark red lips, and perhaps a small flash of elongated teeth. Seductive, aggressive, and dangerous—Lilith is all of these things.

According to the Zohar, a Kabalistic work from the thirteenth century, Lilith is described as a seductive redhead draped in crimson, wearing many "ornaments." Oh, and there are also some passages about her having white skin, rosy cheeks, and a seductive mouth, which seems to me like they are describing makeup and jewelry. While this makes us roll our eyes and giggle today, that was very scandalous—downright provocative and, dare we say, titillating—back in the thirteenth century. This version of Lilith illustrates her as a woman standing at the crossroads, waiting for some hapless male to wander into her trap so she can then pounce on him. (Gee, sounds like somebody in the old days was absolutely terrified of a woman's sexuality and power, doesn't it?)

To modern practitioners, Lilith is a patroness of Witches and a goddess of sexuality, wisdom, female equality, power, and independence. While Lilith is not traditionally linked to a Tuesday, I don't see why we couldn't work with her on this day. Perhaps it's time to make some new traditions. Sometimes you gotta go with your gut—personalize your witchery and magick! Go with what you think will work best for you. After all, Lilith's feisty and fiery qualities are perfect for a Tuesday. Today is the ideal day for a big dose of in-your-face female empowerment! These aggressive and strong characteristics are just what is called for.

TUESDAY'S WITCHERY

Today's guided meditation takes you on a journey to meet the god of war. This guided meditation challenges you to draw your own conclusions and to decide for yourself what you consider to be the ultimate soldier. Keep your mind open about what you think he will be like; I imagine you are in for a surprise. Also, it is a quest of sorts to go and gather your spiritual weapons, and it is a test to see if you will wield these weapons wisely. Have a good journey.

Meditation

COURAGE IS NOT the absence of fear,
but rather the judgment that something
else is more important than fear.

Ambrose Redmoon

Imagine that you are walking along an old dirt road in the middle of a summer afternoon. The temperatures are warm but not uncomfortable, and as you walk along the road, you work up a light sweat and enjoy the sensation of stretching your legs and soaking up the sunshine. To one side of the road, a woodland is green and luxurious. On the other side, a field is planted with crops that appear to be thriving. You come to a crossroads and wonder which way to turn. Do you go straight ahead or turn left or right? You decide to go straight ahead, and you follow the curve of the road as the woods come closer to the path you are traveling along. You are so busy admiring the trees in the woods that you don't see the stranger approaching until he is fairly close to you. Your heart gives an unpleasant thump as you realize that you did not hear this person or get any inkling that you were no longer alone on your walk until the last possible second.

You look over to check out the other traveler and notice that he appears to be wearing a long red jacket, which you realize is a bit warm to be wearing on a day like today. Curious, you walk closer and realize that the man has stopped in the center of the road and is regarding you just as curiously. He stands as if ready for action, and you wonder what in the world he expects to have to be ready for.

As you walk closer to the person, you realize that the jacket is not a jacket at all, it is in fact a cloak. Oh, boy. The other traveler appears to be fairly brawny and he looks to be in excellent shape. You shift to the far side of the road to politely pass him, and the man shifts to block you. There is nothing threatening about him, he just seems to be making it clear that you are not going past him.

You smile politely, and then stop and back up a few paces. "I'm sorry," you begin in a friendly tone, "is this a private road?" As an answer, he just glowers at you. *Well, then,* you think to yourself and begin to turn around and go the other way. No point in having your walk interrupted by this guy. Confidently, you turn around and go back to the crossroads and start back for home. A short time later, the same man is once again standing in the middle of the road in front of you, with a neutral expression. Apparently, he is waiting for you.

This time, you realize there was no way he could have appeared in front of you that quickly without you seeing him travel around. Now that you are aware that something is afoot, you stop and plant your hands on your hips. You take a careful look at this man and think to yourself that he is much more than he appears.

Is that a jacket or is it, in fact, a cloak? Is it merely decorative, or is it well worn and battle stained? Are those boots or sandals on his feet? What is that tucked under his arm—a fur-covered, horned helmet or a bronze battle helm? Now that you think about it, you are having a hard time focusing on his overall appearance. Every time you think you make out what he has on, it subtly shifts. Blinking your eyes, you see that now he is wearing a tartan and has flowing, long hair and a blue-painted body like a Pict warrior of old. Then that image shifts as well, kaleidoscoping from one image to the next. Look at him carefully, and let him show you what he wishes you to see.

What is your idea of the perfect warrior? Does he appear as a samurai, graceful, disciplined and silent, or does he seem to embody a Native American warrior, one who is resourceful, instinctual, and in tune with the land? Is this deity appearing to you in modern battle gear, the fatigues of a twenty-first-century soldier in a flak jacket and camouflage, or is it an old-style Norse leather tunic with a fur vest and pants? Is he appearing to you as a Spartan soldier with a plumed bronze helmet, or do you see more of a medieval knight in well-used chain mail and metal armor? What do you envision? What does this god have to teach you?

His hair appears light, then dark; short and martial, then long and untamed. He is both clean shaven and bearded, and his features and coloring shift constantly from ebony to bronze complexions, to golden and then to pale skin tones. His eyes are round and blue, then almond shaped and black, next a warm brown, then a striking hazel. Those eyes change to stormcloud gray and then a brilliant green. He appears elegant, tall, and lean one moment, and the next he is rough, stocky, and brawny. He is all of these images of a male warrior in his prime, and dozens more. Your mind races to keep up with the various types of soldiers in different cultures and times that he presents to you. Feeling a little overwhelmed, you shake your head to clear it. Then you take a deep breath, lift your chin, and in a challenge, you meet his gaze square-on.

"Who are you?" you ask.

Wow. He does not seem to care for that question; he sputters and swears in an exotic language and stalks around the road. He levels you with a furious look and begins waving his arms in a fine temper at your audacity for having asked for his name. Well, good grief. Leave it to you to go on a meditation and to confront a god with an attitude. You let him wind down and wait him out. You stand silently and put a respectful expression on your face and consider him for a moment. Hmmm . . . it really should come as no surprise that a god of battles would be hot tempered, after all.

Suddenly, he stops and takes a deep breath. He appears to be struggling to hold back his impatience and his temper, and he turns quickly and marches up, into your face. "I am many, I am one." He thumps a fist on his chest and announces, "I am the spirit of battle and the soul of the warrior. I have countless names." He glowers down at you for a moment, and then you nod your head in acknowledgement, and he appears to settle down a bit.

He regards you intensely for a moment longer, and then he smiles slightly. "Take this," he demands, and then he hands you a weapon. Look carefully at this gift. It may be a sword, a spear, an axe, or another type of weapon. Respectfully, you take the weapon and close your hand firmly around it. It vibrates in your hand, and you feel the energy run up your arm, across your chest, and rush down to your toes. He explains to you that this astral weapon is for you and you alone. He informs you that if you have need, he will answer your call and gift you with courage and strength. All you have to do is to visualize the psychic weapon you now hold in your hands, and then his courage, cunning, valor, and strength will come storming in. He states that it is up to you to know when the time is appropriate to use his gift. He also reminds you that the most successful warriors temper their battles with knowledge and wisdom—the knowledge of comprehending when and where to strike, and the wisdom to know when not to.

You thank him for the gift, and as you watch, the astral weapon fades away. He gruffly tells you that though it may be unseen at the moment, it will always be close at hand should you need it. He tells you to be on your way. Thank the god and then turn to go back home, down the path you began your meditative journey on. You resist the urge to look over your shoulder for a time, but you eventually give in to see if he is behind you and watching. He is gone, but you have the feeling he is hidden and watching somewhere, probably plotting and hatching new battle tactics. You smile to yourself and realize that this warrior god will always be close by and ready to spring into action if needed.

Now, take a deep, cleansing breath and ground and center. Look around one last time at this place, and see the sun shining brightly down upon the fields. Practice conjuring up the feel of that protective astral weapon in your hand, and become familiar with its strengthening presence. Keep the idea of protection, power, and strength with you today as you move through your day as carefully and fully aware as a warrior. Take in a final deep, cleansing breath, and slowly blow it out. Open your eyes and return to awareness.

Magickal Plants & Flowers

A few of the plants associated with the planet Mars and Tuesdays are the thistle, holly, and snapdragon. Now, if you think about it, two of these plants have prickles on them: thistles can have very prickly stems, and the leaves of the holly typically have sharp, pointy ends. The snapdragon, a favorite cottage-style flower of mine, has the elemental association of fire and is also aligned with Mars. All of these magickal plants are utilized for their protective and fiery qualities. This trio of magickal plants is often worked into hex-breaking and defensive magick. Now, just because these plants have the ability to break a hex or to stop evil doesn't mean that you will have to use them for that on a regular basis.

Before you start running around in a panic, worrying about someone trying to zap you with a naughty spell, relax. In actuality, a hex is typically a rare occurrence. Also remember this: people who hex and curse do so from a position of weakness. That's the bottom line. They are actually afraid—of you—so they decide to strike out with magick, which is pretty stupid and self-destructive. And nine times out of ten, it only creates more havoc in their own lives.

Most often what you are sensing when you start to wonder if you are under the gun, so to speak, is emotional exploitation, jealousy, and envy that has been directed at you. Happily, these Mars-associated plants will help to shield you from petty jealousies and your average manipulation, which occurs more often than anything else.

Manipulation is not always a magickal problem; sometimes it's an everyday one—from the coworker who cons you into doing their job for them, or the well-meaning in-laws who think that if they just apply enough pressure, then, perhaps, you will fall in line, to the person or partner who thinks they can just walk all over you because you always give in. As to envy and jealousy, well . . . the grass is always greener, as they say. Don't let other people get you down. Just because someone else has their knickers in a twist doesn't mean you have to sit there and take all that spite. You can fight back ethically with protection work and by tapping into a warrior's energy. So, no worries about the sky falling, okay? These everyday scenarios are typically the types of negative emotions, situations, and problems that you will face.

Mars plants tend to be protective plants, and when you apply a little practical witchery and common sense with their magickal qualities, you get an unbeatable combination.

Thistle

Also known as the bull thistle (*Cirsium vulgare*), this wildflower has the elemental association of fire. According to herbal folklore, when thistles are allowed to grow in the garden, it is thought to protect the home from burglary. Thistles grown in containers by the front or back door are supposed to have the power to ward off evil and negativity. If you feel the need to break up any negative energy or manipulative intentions that you believe may have been sent your way, then thistle is the plant to work with. Thistle is a wildflower and often volunteers in the garden. If you have a sunny spot well out of the way of young children, who need to watch out for the thorny leaves and prickly stems, consider letting it grow wild. In the language of flowers, thistle symbolizes independence and austerity.

Holly

The holly (*Ilex*) comes in many varieties and species. Its elemental association is fire. Not all hollies bear fruit (in other words, berries). The female holly will produce the berries, while the male produces small greenish flowers for pollination and a few berries. One male holly will pollinate many female hollies. Check with your neighbors and see if they have a male variety; if not, you will have to pick one up so they can pollinate, and the female holly will then produce lots of pretty berries for you. The holly has the charming folk name of "bat's wings." If you take a good look at most modern varieties of holly, you can see how those leaves look a bit like the shape of a bat's wing.

When the holly shrub is grown in the garden, it is thought to protect the home from lightning and roguish magicians. Classically, the holly plant is partnered up with the ivy for Yule celebrations. In this scenario, the holly is considered to have masculine qualities, and the ivy, feminine ones. According to the language of flowers, the holly symbolizes good will, foresight, and a happy home.

If you feel that you might have fallen under the crossfire of a less-than-ethical practitioner, a problematic coworker, or (more likely) a meddling relative, then try adding holly leaves to your spellwork.

Snapdragon

Snapdragons (*Antirrhinum*) are also linked to the element of fire, and they are a very protective flower. They have the adorable folk names of "calf's snout" and "dragon's snout," and are a great magickal flower. They grow happily in most gardens and thrive in containers. If you pinch off the flowering tops after they fade, they will keep blooming for you all season long, until bitter cold sets in. As a matter of fact, as I write this, it is November, the local temperatures are in the high thirties, and my red and yellow snaps are happily blooming away in my Witch's garden.

Snapdragons can break any manipulative intentions or bad mojo that might be tossed your way. Try a little flower magick on those problematic relatives or nosy neighbors and give them a small container planted full of red snapdragons. That should help to break the animosity between the two of you. As a cut flower, snapdragons are available at most florists year-round and come in many colors. Try red for protection and yellow for wisdom. Look for orange colors for energy and passion. In the language of flowers, the snapdragon says you are beautiful but dangerous. Well, doesn't that floral definition go along nicely with the theme of this chapter?

If you feel the need for a little reinforced protection at work, then arrange a couple of snapdragon stems in a vase and set them on your desk. Not only will the flowers perk you up, but they will create a sort of no-fly zone around you, where other people's head games and office dramas will pass you right by. If you are not allowed to have flowers at work, try picking up a few packages of snapdragon seeds in the winter or spring. Tuck a package of the seeds in your desk or, if things are really bad, then try discreetly sprinkling just a few seeds across the troublemaker's desk or on their office floor, where they will be sure to walk on them.

The Warrior Spell

Let's combine these magickal protective and fiery plants for a kick-ass flower fascination. Hey, it's a Mars day, after all! Everybody has a bad day or goes through trying times. Life can throw you a curve, and then you find yourself in the middle of a painful situation. Before you know it, your self-confidence is shot, and you feel victimized and wonder how in the world this ever happened. When tough situations come your way, concentrate on Mars' warrior-like and feisty qualities, then take a deep breath and let go of your fear.

As you prepare to work this spell, take a good look at what you are so worried about or afraid of. Give yourself some time, and deal with your emotions. If you find yourself shedding a few tears, it's no big deal. You probably needed the release that only a good cry can bring. (So what if your nose is red? It's a Mars color, after all.) Take a few minutes and concentrate on being braver, stronger, and able to handle anything that life tosses your way. Remember, you are not a victim! Turn that fear into an ally, and channel that energy into protection instead. Take this as an opportunity to be brave and strong and to deal with the problem. Now, blow your nose, wash your face, and take a deep breath. Be a calm and powerful magickal warrior! You can do it, I know you can.

Gather from the garden three stems of snapdragons (red, if possible), a stem or two of blooming thistle, and nine holly leaves. Combining these three plants will invoke protection and encourage passion and bravery. If you cannot locate a live thistle, then consider looking for dried thistle at an herb shop or at the arts and crafts store. As for the snapdragons, you can always go to the florist if they are out of season, or during the spring and summer months, purchase a six-pack of the annual to add to your magickal gardens. Then the snapdragons are readily available for your flower spells and for you and your family to enjoy.

Arrange the flowers in a water-filled bud vase and then position the holly leaves in a circle around that. Add a red ribbon to your flowers to help reinforce both the magick of a Tuesday and Mars' fiery qualities. Take a red ink pen and a piece of paper, and write down the challenge that you are facing. Set this list under the vase and within the circle of the holly leaves. Ground and center yourself. Let go of your anger, and put your game face on. Now, repeat the spell below three times:

> *Mars' fiery energy now encircles me*
> *A Witch is a warrior; I set my fears free*
> *Purple thistle, holly leaves, and snapdragons three*
> *Passion, courage, and bravery now send to me*
> *I release all my worries—they have no more power*
> *This warrior's spell is cast by leaf and by flower.*

Close the spell by saying:

> *For the good of all, with harm to none*
> *By herb and thorn, this spell is now done!*

Let the flowers stay in the vase for a few days until they begin to fade. Then gather up the components from this spell and tuck the holly leaves and flowers into an envelope. Seal it, then tie the red ribbon around the envelope, and take it right out and into the garbage. Drop it in and brush off your hands. Slap the lid on the can and strut away.

So, do you feel more confident? Good. Now put all this garbage behind you. People only have the power to hurt you when you let them. Next time you have to see or deal with them, be confident, be friendly, and give them a cocky smile. That ought to confuse the hell out of them. Rise above and conquer!

COLORS, CANDLES, METALS & CRYSTALS

Colors

Colors for the day include red, black, scarlet, and orange. Black is for boundaries and fighting negativity; it's great for protection spells. Scarlet is a daring, passionate hue that adds *oomph* to candle spells. Remember, our girl Lilith was fond of scarlet; I wonder if that's where the term "scarlet woman" came from? Finally, the color orange is used in spells for energy, courage, vitality, and charisma.

The color red is considered by many Asian cultures to be a lucky and sacred color. Red is believed to promote power, strength, and fame, and is, of course, associated with the element of fire. Red is the color for wedding attire for both the bride and groom in Indian cultures. Plus, in China, it is traditional for a bride's gown to be red; also, a proud father of a newborn son will hand out red eggs. It is also thought that wearing red ribbons will direct and retain positive chi, or energy.

If you care to coordinate your outfit with the warrior energy of the day, then try adding a cherry-red scarf or blouse. Ladies, you may want to wear Lilith-inspired red lipstick or crimson-hued lingerie. Guys might want to go with a red sweater or a fiery-colored tie. If you're a casual sort of person, then try sporting a red T-shirt, sweatshirt, or even bright red socks!

Candles

Candle colors for today include all shades of red, from oranges to scarlet to deep burgundy. Also, try working with black candles to absorb negativity and to break bad luck. If you want to add a little magickal candle aromatherapy, then go for spicy or coffee-scented candles. The aroma of coffee is an energy booster. It sharpens your other senses, and if you overdo it on the aromatherapy and you can't smell anything anymore, then taking a whiff of coffee beans can actually refresh your sense of smell!

Here is another little tip: look for carrot-cake-scented candles. (No, I am not kidding.) Carrots and spices are both associated with Mars, and the spicy scent of the candle corresponds with Tuesday and all of its passionate, daring qualities.

Hot Stuff Candle Spell

Want to drive your lover crazy? This candle spell is meant to entice and tempt. The whole point of it is to add a little spark back into your relationship and to make you irresistible. In this spell, you will be calling on Lilith, so prepare yourself for a good time. Please remember to be conscientious of this spell and only work this upon yourself, so you and your partner can have a little fun.

Gather a red candle, a black candle, and two candle holders. Sprinkle a dash of pepper and a pinch of allspice on the unlit candles. Arrange three snapdragons or three red roses in a vase. Repeat the following charm three times:

As I light red and black candles for a hot and sexy spell

I now call on Lilith for passion, and all will be well

Peppers and spice and snapdragons/red roses three

These will make me very enticing, so now must it be.

Close the spell with:

For the good of all, with harm to none

May my love and I have a little fun!

Now, go and find your lover, give him or her a bewitching smile, and see what kind of reaction you get.

Metals & Crystals

The metal associated with Tuesday is iron. If you have any black wrought-iron candle holders, these would coordinate with your Tuesday magick quite nicely. Iron has a projective energy and is associated with the planet Mars and the element of fire. Iron is protective, and old iron nails may be used in spells and charms to confuse your enemies, to guard your property, and to boost power. Also, cast-iron cauldrons, even though they are inherently a goddess symbol, by virtue of the metal they are created from, they fall under the planetary aspect of Mars as well.

The crystals and stones that are linked to Tuesday's fiery, passionate energy are garnet, bloodstone, and ruby. While two of these fall under the gemstone category, you can find low-grade rubies as a tumbled stone (I picked one up for about two dollars; it works out nicely in my Mars-themed spells). Since these stones all fall under the elemental correspondence of fire, then you may choose to empower them by passing them above a candle flame or by letting them sit in the sun's rays for a short while.

GARNET: The garnet is linked to the element of fire. This is the birthstone for January and is called "a stone of commitment." It is thought to enhance your strength and endurance. Deep red is the most popular color for garnets; however, they do come in a range of other colors too—pink, yellow, orange, green, and purple shades . . . just about every color except blue. This stone has a projective type of energy and is good to carry while you are doing any type of physical exertion. Once this stone was used to frighten away criminals, spooks, and ghosts. The garnet can help to pump up your self-esteem and strengthen your aura. Wearing garnet jewelry may help to give off a "don't mess with me" type of vibe. It is excellent for grounding your energy, warding off nightmares, and for magickal protection. According to folklore, the garnet is believed to reduce inflammation, improve your skin, and regulate the circulatory system.

BLOODSTONE: One of my favorite stones, the bloodstone is a beautiful deep green stone called chalcedony that is flecked with deep red. The next time you are at a shop that sells inexpensive tumbled stones, sort through the bloodstones and find one that speaks to you. Hold the stone in your receptive hand (opposite from the one that you write with) and then see if you notice anything. When you find one that gives you a little zap, makes your palm tingle, or makes you feel warmer, you will know you've found a keeper.

Bloodstones are associated with the element of fire and earth. They may be used in healing rituals and also to boost your courage, physical health, and endurance. It was also a talisman used to promote a healthy and safe pregnancy. This is a well-liked stone for athletes and for those of us who are on a fitness regime. A bloodstone can help you stay injury free, and it can also remind you not to overdo it, which I have found is the fastest way to getting a sports or workout-related injury in the first place. When you wear or carry a bloodstone, you will be more courageous, calmer, and even-tempered.

RUBY: The ruby is a stone of love, power, and wealth. This gem is the birthstone for July. The ruby is also from the corundum group of gems. However, only red corundums are called rubies. It is naturally linked to the element of fire due to its color. When rubies are worn, they increase personal protection. Some texts say that rubies make you invulnerable to unethical spells. Wearing ruby jewelry is thought to reinforce healing, promote happiness, and keep your outlook upbeat. The ruby is also thought to boost any magickal powers set into motion by spells and charms. The ruby's energy is believed to help push your spells to their best possible outcome in a timely manner. Folklore calls this jewel "the glowing stone," which describes the illuminated look that a fine ruby possesses. More stone legend states that the stone turns dark when danger is near, and that if a gardener or farmer dreams of rubies, that this is a sign of a bumper crop for the year.

Red Jasper: The red jasper is another stone associated with the planet Mars and the element of fire. This is a fabulous stone to utilize in protective and defensive magick. It encourages healing and is used in beauty-enhancement spells. Women can charm jasper beads or tumbled stones to boost their appearance—a very earthy type of glamour. Also, here is another little tip: wearing red jasper is thought to deflect any spells, negativity, or manipulation straight back to the sender. Today, red jasper beads are easily found in the jewelry-making aisle of the arts and crafts store. Pick up a package of the beads and some stretchy cord, and string yourself a bracelet for protection, magickal shielding, and personal strength.

A Bloodstone Protection and Courage Spell

The bloodstone, when worn or carried, brings courage and eliminates fear and anger. The bloodstone was often used as a talisman for athletes and warriors. When you need a little extra courage and bravery to face challenges and stressful, scary situations, give this practical Witch's spell a whirl.

For this particular crystal spell, you will need a few supplies: a red spicy-scented votive candle, a votive candle cup, three bloodstones (inexpensive tumbled stones are perfect), a photo of yourself or a small snip of your own hair, a small cast-iron cauldron, and matches or a lighter. Set up on a safe, flat surface.

Place the photo or snip of hair in the bottom of the cauldron. Now place the candle inside of the cup. Set this in the center of the small cauldron, on top of the photo or the hair. (If you are worried about the heat damaging the photo, then set the photo beneath the cauldron.) Next, arrange the three bloodstones around the candle cup. Ground and center yourself. Then, when you are ready, light the candle and repeat the following spell three times:

> On this Mars day, there is fiery energy to spare
>
> I call for courage and passion to know, to will, to dare
>
> Three green bloodstones and a burning candle of red
>
> I call for bravery and banish fear and dread.

Focus on the flame for a few moments. Believe in your ability to handle the situation, whatever it may be.

Close the spell by saying:

> For the good of all, with harm to none
>
> By Mars' energy, this spell is done.

Let the candle burn until it is consumed. If this is an ongoing problem or conflict, then repeat the spell every day for one week (in other words, from a Tuesday until the following Tuesday). Clean out the votive cup and light a new red votive candle for each day of the spell. When you are finished working this, clean up your setup and put away all of the spell components. If you like, you can carry those tumbled bloodstones with you to help reinforce your convictions.

POTIONS, PHILTERS & OILS

Tuesdays are the day to create philters and potions that work in harmony with Mars' planetary energy. As this is a warrior, take-no-prisoners type of day, today is the day to create a recipe for protection and to increase your courage. Sometimes we all need a bolster to our courage. This philter recipe will help you add some magickal valor and bravery into your magick.

Philter Recipe for Courage
- One small decorative glass bottle, red if you can find it
- Base oil, approximately ⅛ cup (sunflower or almond oil)
- Clean dropper
- 3 drops ginger oil
- 2 drops basil oil or 2 fresh basil leaves
- 1 drop black pepper oil
- 1 small fresh holly leaf
- Small red jasper chip
- 6 inches thin red or black satin ribbon
- 1 small metal protective charm or talisman of your choosing (such as a tiny pentagram, a star, or even the Eye of Horus)
- A label and a pen (to list the ingredients and to decorate and mark the bottle)

Pour the base oil into the bottle, enough to fill it three quarters of the way full. Add the essential oils one at a time. Next, add the crystal and the holly leaf. If you used basil leaves instead of oil, add those now. Close up the bottle with the lid, place your fingers over the lid, and carefully shake up the mixture. Hold up the mixture to the sunlight, and allow the light of Tuesday's sun to illuminate the philter within.

Wipe off the outside of the bottle. Use the label to list the ingredients and the use of this potion. Decorate the bottle by drawing protective symbols on the label or whatever else you think would add to the magick. Attach the label to the glass bottle and finish up by threading the metal charm onto the ribbon and then tying the red or black ribbon around the neck of the bottle.

As you finish tying on the bow, hold the bottle in your hands and concentrate on the visualization that your aura is pulsing a deep red, filled with vitality, courage, and protection. See it in your mind's eye and feel it all over your body. Now send all that energy straight into the bottle you hold in your hands. Take a deep breath, hold it for three counts, and then blow it out slowly. Now, repeat the charm below:

> Basil, holly, and ginger are associated with Mars
> Tap into a warrior's energy and you will go far
> Red and black are the Martian hues of power
> My spell begins in this enchanted hour
> This Tuesday philter will add valor galore
> I am courageous and strong forever more!

Set aside the bottle, and ground and center yourself. Clean up the supplies, then go for a quick walk and firmly reconnect yourself back to the earthly plane. Make sure to store the philter in a dark, dry place and out of the reach of young children.

Essential Oils

More essential oils that coordinate with Mars energy include:

- High John the Conqueror
- Ginger
- Pine
- Peppermint
- Pennyroyal
- Basil

The peppermint and pine oils will be easy to procure. Remember to be careful with the pine oil, as pine is a common allergen. Essential oils are not intended for direct contact with the skin. Typically, they are diluted in a carrier oil such as almond, olive, or sunflower oil.

TAROT CARD ASSOCIATIONS

The tarot cards that align with Tuesday and Mars energies are the Six of Wands for victory and triumph; the Five of Wands, which symbolizes the ability to handle life's little annoyances; and the Major Arcana card Strength (or Fortitude), which, oddly enough, stands for inner strength and self-control.

The tarot suit of Wands (or Rods, depending on your deck) is associated with the element of fire. The element of fire coordinates with the warrior-type planetary energies of Mars and Tuesday's passionate and feisty qualities. The suit of Wands is for folks who are fighters, dreamers, and rebels. The featured tarot cards in this chapter are both powerful and passionate symbols, so use them wisely.

Six of Wands

Six of Wands is often interpreted as a card of victory. This card often shows up in tarot readings when your hard work is finally being recognized, or when you feel as if you have just won a major battle of some kind in your life. If you take a good look at the image on this card, it typically shows a rider who is pale, perhaps a bit tired, but he is victorious nonetheless. This card clearly illustrates that if you are willing to work hard, then victory is within your reach. This card makes a great prop in magick. It gives you a very specific image of victory to focus on, and the image of a victorious rider helps to encourage the movement and energy that you want to promote with your spellwork.

Five of Wands

Five of Wands is an intriguing card. At first, when folks see this card, they see struggles and conflicts. What they often miss is that this card usually signifies a person who enjoys dealing with minor problems and day-to-day obstacles. This person loves to get in there and set things right again—you know, the type of personality you imagine as kicking butt and taking names? This is their card. This person adores challenges and revels in the excitement that only a good argument or debate can bring. This card encourages excitement and helps you to step up and face the average problems that life often throws your way.

Strength

Strength is usually depicted in one of two ways. Depending on your deck, it may show Hercules battling a lion or a woman who embraces a lion and gently holds the lion's head within her arms. The lion on the card is an illustration of powerful emotions under control. This may be a case of "you need to get your emotions under control" or "you have your emotions firmly under control," so think about it. When this card pops up in a reading, it always reminds you to suck it up and to stand strong. This card, used as a prop in magick, symbolizes self-control and the ability to handle things during a crisis by tapping into your inner strength. This is the card of quiet strength, conviction, gentle courage, heroism, and valor.

Here is a tarot card spell for you to try. This spell comes in handy during those stressful times of your life when you need a little extra courage and strength.

Victory Through Strength Tarot Spell

This tarot spell may be set up simply or more elaborately; it is up to you. Don't be afraid to make your magick personal and unique.

Either use the featured cards (Six of Wands, Five of Wands, and Strength) as your only props around a red candle or add the associated crystals for a Tuesday (ruby, blood-stone, and garnet). Try draping the workspace with a red cloth or scarf. Consider working this spell at sunrise or at noon, when the sun is directly overhead and bright. I suggest setting the candle and its holder in the center of your workspace, then arranging the cards and other accessories around it.

Another good idea would be to scatter those flat-bottomed, red glass marbles on the work surface. (You know, those pretty glass gems that are so popular for wedding-reception table decorations?) You can pick up a bag of those at most arts and crafts stores for a few bucks. Find some iridescent ones; wouldn't they look sharp? Use your imagination! How about holly leaves or red flower petals? Are you getting inspired yet? Good. Now psych yourself up and repeat the spell below three times:

> The lady holds the lion within her arms
>
> My strength comes from my soul and causes no harm
>
> I hold the power to succeed time and time again
>
> Honor and victory are mine, let the spell begin.

Meditate on the symbolism of the cards for a short time. Close the spell by saying:

> For the good of all, causing harm to none
>
> By fire and passion, this spell is done!

Let the candle burn until it goes out on its own. If you used stones in the spell, you may keep them with you for a few days in your purse or pocket to help reinforce the spell.

DAILY WITCH CRAFT
a witch's jar for protection

Today is a perfect day to create a Witch's jar. Classically, a Witch's jar is a lidded glass jar filled with broken glass, herbs, old nails, pins, thorns, and anything that is sharp and can catch something or prick something. For a modern spin on the Witch jar, I like to use those flat-bottomed glass marbles that are so popular for wedding decorations and in floral design. Check any floral section of the arts and crafts stores for lots of colors and options. (Also, they're safer to handle than shards of broken glass.) In this case, using the glass marbles reflects negativity all over the surfaces of the colored glass and keeps bouncing around inside of the jar until it gets smaller and smaller and finally dissipates.

- 1 medium-sized glass jar with lid
- 1 small bag red or black glass marbles
- Old iron nails or pins
- 3–4 holly leaves
- 3–4 thorns from a red rose
- A garlic clove (a Mars herb that will absorb negativity)
- A black permanent marker

Wash and dry the jar and the lid; set them aside. Begin by placing the clove of garlic in the bottom of the dry jar. Next, begin layering in some of the glass marbles, a few pins or a nail, a holly leaf, and the rose thorns. Add more marbles, then another nail or pins, the holly leaf, and the thorns. Keep going until you fill up the jar.

When the jar is full, hold your hands over the top of the jar and put some of your own protective energy into it. Visualize your need for protection filling up the jar and empowering all the supplies that are held within. Now screw the lid onto the jar, and draw a pentagram surrounded by a circle on the top of the jar with the black marker.

Now pick up the jar and hold it up to the sunlight. See all the light sparkling through the glass and bouncing around off those colored marbles? Pretty, isn't it? But in this case, pretty really gets the job done. Now, give the jar a gentle shake to start the magick. Hold the jar in both hands and concentrate on what you are doing. Then, when you are ready, repeat the spell:

> Tuesdays are the day for protection and courage
> This Witch's jar will remove any and all worries
> Garlic to keep emotional vampires at bay
> This jar is a magickal tool working night and day
> The thorns and nails catch any evil that may occur
> While colored pieces of glass will reflect and scatter
> This jar is now sealed with the sound of a Witch's rhyme
> The protective magick begins in this place and time.

Place the jar in the most-used room in your house. Tuck it in a corner, behind the living room couch, or under your desk. Allow the jar to absorb and to break up any negativity or spite coming your way. This spell may be renewed every few months or so by holding up the jar to the light and allowing the sun's light to burn out any lingering energy. If you wish, you may replace the old garlic clove with a fresh one. Then, please repeat the spell verse over the newly arranged, sealed, and freshened jar.

CUSTOM-MADE DAILY MAGICK

Now that you are starting to get into the passionate, courageous, and daring qualities of Tuesday, here are a few more spells for you to experiment with. Don't be afraid to adapt these spells to suit your needs. Add some tarot cards, herbs, scents, crystals, or essential oils to these Tuesday spells, and crank up the volume on your own witchery! As long as your intentions are honorable, I am sure they will work out beautifully.

The "Enchanted Evening" Elemental Spell

Looking to put a little passion back into your love life? How do you feel about working with the four elements and Lilith, our goddess of power and passion? There are times when even the most loving relationship needs a little *oomph*. So, if you simply want to spice things up with your partner in the bedroom, well, hey, Lilith's your best bet! But be careful; she has a wicked sense of humor. Calling on Lilith for some extra spark or desire works very well, and you may feel like you have a magickal hangover in the morning. A small price to pay . . . just don't say that I didn't warn you.

Let's get all of your senses involved. This spell is a sensual and sensory experience. To represent the four elements in this spell, light a few black or red candles to represent the element of fire. Burn dragon's blood incense to represent the element of air. To symbolize water, open a bottle of red wine and drink from the same cup as your partner. Finally, sprinkle the sheets with some crimson-colored rose petals to represent the element of earth.

And at the risk of sounding like a mom, while you're setting this stage for loving seduction, don't forget to practice safe sex! Ask for Lilith's blessings by using the following invocation:

Lilith, dark goddess, teach me to love, laugh, and be wise

Aid me in my witchery as you sail through the skies

By the natural magick of air, water, earth, and fire

I manifest the gifts of love, seduction, and desire

By the elements four, this spell is now begun

As I will, so shall it be, and let it harm none.

RITUAL FOR TUESDAY
mars' energy ritual

Try your hand at this fiery ritual for courage, passion, and winning battles. This ritual will take several days to complete, until the pillar candle burns all the way down. Also, personalize this spellwork by incorporating into it as many warm Marslike colors and other coordinating magickal correspondences as you can come up with. You just read an entire chapter devoted to Tuesday and Mars associations; here is your chance to flex your witchy muscles a bit and to show yourself what you have learned.

- 1 red pillar candle
- Coordinating-style candle holder (black wrought iron would be perfect)
- A nail or large pin to engrave the candle
- Any Mars-associated stones: red jasper, ruby, garnet, bloodstone
- A pinch of powdered garlic
- A pinch of allspice
- Your philter for courage and protection

- A lighter or matches
- A safe, flat surface on which to set up the spell

Take the nail and engrave the symbol for the planet Mars into the side of the candle. Take your time and make it look as nice as you can. Also, consider adding a bit of spice to this Tuesday ritual. Toss a pinch of powdered garlic in the candle holder to promote protection. Try adding a pinch of allspice to bring good fortune and success. You could also dig out a small hole in the top of the pillar candle and sprinkle the spices inside of it. Then, as the candle starts to burn, the hole will seal up with melting wax and eventually incorporate the herbs into the body of the candle. Or just place the candle on top of these powdered spices inside the candle holder, and you're all set.

In addition, think about using the philter recipe from this chapter, and dress the pillar candle with it for some increased power. Set a few Mars-associated tumbled stones next to a candle holder containing the pillar candle—try a ruby for power and a red jasper to encourage protection and defending yourself.

Another suggestion would be to work with those pretty red glass marbles again, and arrange them on your work surface to set an enchanting mood. Take the time to make the spell candle setup unique and attractive. Put some effort into it if you want good, strong results. Light the pillar candle, and then repeat the following spell verse three times:

> *Tuesday is the day for fiery, aggressive Mars*
> *Live with courage and passion, and you will go far*
> *Candle colors for today are midnight black and red*
> *These will draw success and deflect all harm and dread*

Help me to win my battles fairly, both great and small

While I show kindness and compassion to one and all

Candle burn and magick spin

Let my ritual now begin.

Close the spell verse by saying:

By all the power of three times three

As I will it, then so shall it be.

Let the candle burn until it is consumed; figure three to five days, depending on the width of the pillar. Make sure you have it in a safe place to finish burning, such as inside of an old metal cauldron or tucked into an unlit fireplace.

Please note: If you cannot leave the ritual candle safely burning, then snuff it out when you leave and relight it as soon as you are home. It may take a few days longer, but the magick will still turn out, especially since you are taking the time and energy to tend the ritual candle so carefully. As you relight the candle, say:

As this ritual candle relights, so does my magick once more ignite.

Happy casting!

Tuesday is the day to work any magick that falls in the category of increasing strength, courage, bravery, and passion. All of these intense emotions are linked to this day's energies, and spells designed around these themes will have extra punch when performed on this magickal day.

So, let's add a little passion and conviction into your life! Break out the daring red pieces of your wardrobe, and put a little pizzazz into your day. Work with Lilith, and see what she has to teach you about personal power and sexuality. Meditate on Tiw/Tyr and Mars, and see what those ancient warrior gods will show you about new tactics, strategies, and claiming personal victories in your life. Practice conjuring up that astral weapon from the meditation and use it wisely for protection and for courage.

Create a philter for courage and protection or handcraft your own Witch's jar to remove negativity from your home. See what other Witch crafts you can conjure up with Tuesday's magick. Create some kitchen magick on this Tuesday by whipping up a spicy stew—add in a few Mars-associated ingredients such as carrots, peppers, and garlic. Empower the stew for success, and then treat yourself and your family to a good, hearty meal. Try working with a little aromatherapy and burn some spicy or coffee-scented candles to increase your energy level.

Check the sky at night, and see if you can find the reddish planet Mars up in the heavens. Not sure where to look? Check an astronomy magazine or search the Web for more information.

Become a magickal warrior and move forward in your life with strength, courage, and compassion. Embrace the side of yourself that loves a good challenge and that is passionate and daring! Banish fear, and face your future with strength and conviction. Believe in yourself and in your dreams, work hard, and you will win every time.

Wednesday

EVERY SMILE MAKES you
a day younger.

Chinese proverb

At-a-Glance Correspondences

PLANETARY INFLUENCE	Mercury
PLANETARY SYMBOL	
DEITIES	Mercury/Hermes, Odin/Wodin, Athena
FLOWERS & PLANTS	Fern, lavender, lily of the valley, aspen tree
METAL	Quicksilver
COLORS	Purple, orange
CRYSTALS & STONES	Opal, agate, aventurine
ESSENTIAL OILS	Lily of the valley, eucalyptus, lavender, bergamot, sweet pea, dill
TAROT CARDS	Wheel of Fortune, Eight of Pentacles, the Magician
FOODS, HERBS & SPICES	Dill, lavender

DAILY MAGICKAL APPLICATIONS

To the Romans, this day was called *Dies Mercurii*, or "Mercury's day." Mercury was a popular character in the Roman pantheon. A messenger of the gods, he presided over commerce, trade, and anything that required skill or dexterity. The Celts also worshiped Mercury and eventually equated him with the Norse god Odin (some spelling variations on this name include Wotan, Wodin, and Wodan). In Norse mythologies, Odin, like Mercury, is associated with poetry and music. Interestingly enough, both Odin and Mercury were regarded as psychopomps, or the leaders of souls, in their individual mythologies.

Odin, one of the main gods in Norse mythology, was constantly seeking wisdom. He traveled the world in disguise as a one-eyed man with a long gray beard, wearing an old, beat-up hat and carrying a staff or a spear (which brings to my mind images of Gandalf from *The Lord of the Rings*). In the Old English language, this day of Mercury evolved into *Wodnes daeg*, "Woden's day," or Wednesday.

Wednesday carries all of the planetary and magickal energies and associations of the witty and nimble god Mercury himself. Some of these mercurial traits included good communication skills, cleverness, intelligence, creativity, business sense, writing, artistic talent, trickiness, and thievery. And don't forget all of those wise and enigmatic qualities associated with the Norse god Odin/Wodin, not to mention the goddess Athena's contributions of music, the arts, handmade crafts, and writing. Wednesdays afford excellent opportunities for seeking wisdom, changing your circumstances, and improving your skills, be they in trade and commerce, music and art, or in communication and writing.

Deities

Mercury/Hermes

Mercury is the fleet-footed Roman god of commerce, travel, self-expression, speed, and science. Mercury had a sacred festival day called the Mercuralia that was held in Rome on May 15. To the Greeks he was known as Hermes, and his symbols included winged sandals or boots and a winged cap of invisibility. There is a theory that the cap he wears can be a symbol for secrets and concealed feelings or thoughts. Mercury/Hermes also carried a bag full of magick, and he held a magickal healing rod with two intertwined, winged serpents called the caduceus.

While the Roman god Mercury's caduceus was a symbol of heralds and commerce, the caduceus of the Greek god Hermes became linked with medicine sometime during the seventh century BCE. As Hermes became connected with alchemy, the alchemists were called "the sons of Hermes." These practitioners of the Hermetic arts were also known as Hermeticists. Both Mercury and Hermes are known as the god with the winged feet.

This is a god of the crossroads, of travel; he is a guardian of commerce and anything that requires skill and dexterity. Mercury/Hermes is a multifaceted god and one of contradictions. He is also known as a patron deity of thieves for his sneaky, tricky, and cunning attributes. (According to mythology, as an infant he stole the god Apollo's cattle.) On the flip side of the coin, he can be both benevolent and helpful to shopkeepers and tradespeople as a god of profit and a guardian of merchants. This is a god of unexpected luck, happy coincidences, and synchronicity.

A familiar icon today, this Greco-Roman god is famous as the golden emblem for a major floral delivery service that advertises speedy and efficient floral delivery worldwide. Keep in mind, Mercury/Hermes was known as a joker and a clever, cunning magician. I'll just bet you that old Mercury or Hermes is secretly tickled at all of the attention that he receives from florists every day of the year.

Odin/Wodin

The name Odin tends to be more Norse in origin, while the name Wodin is Anglo-Saxon and Germanic. This hanged god is a god of wisdom and poetry, and his titles are many, including the All-Father. In some Norse mythologies, he is described as wearing a blue or black hooded cloak as he wanders the earth in the winter months, visiting his people. He has two raven companions, Huginn and Muninn, whose names translate to "thought" and "memory." These ravens circle the earth daily and then return to Odin to whisper to him the news of humankind. In Norse mythology, Odin willingly hung on the world tree, Yggdrasil, for nine days, seeking power. He gained several songs of power and twenty-four runes. Odin carried a spear that never missed its target. Trading one of his eyes for a drink from the well of wisdom, his sacrifice gained him immense knowledge.

Odin is a god of mystery, magick, shamanism, and rune lore. He also eventually became wrapped up in the mythology of Mercury and was called by many names, including Wodan, Wotan, and Ohdinn. Odin is associated with divine intention and the element of air. The horse, raven, wolf, and eagle are all sacred to him. Odin likes to challenge his followers, but he is always there if you need him. Legend says he may only be approached by those who know of him, but in particular by individuals who call his name.

Athena

Athena is a warrior/maiden goddess of wisdom, war, crafts, and poetry. In her war aspect, she is known as Pallas Athena. Some of the more familiar symbols for Athena are the javelin, spear, shield, and plumed helmet. She was usually depicted with an owl perched on her shoulder, symbolizing wisdom. There is some debate over Athena's origins. Traditional mythology says that she sprang full grown and ready to rumble from her father Zeus's head, while another school of thought believes that she may have been originally a Mycenaean goddess of home and hearth.

Athena was called "bright eyed" and was a patroness of women's rights and freedom. She also presided over craftsmen, potters, weavers, and spinners. To round things up, Athena was also associated with writing, music, wisdom, justice, and peace. In this aspect, her symbols are the owl and the olive tree. In a Homeric hymn to Athena, she is described as a "glorious goddess, gray-eyed, resourceful, and of implacable heart." The birthday of Athena was celebrated on March 23. Her sacred city was, of course, Athens.

WEDNESDAY'S WITCHERY

This meditation took me a while to get down on paper. No matter what idea I thought I had—my original idea had been to feature Hermes and Mercury in Wednesday's meditation—it just never seemed to gel. Plus, I was on a strict deadline. Since this fourth chapter refused to finish up and I could not get the meditation done, I sent in the introduction and the first three chapters and thought that in a worst-case scenario,

I'd simply move on to another chapter and come back and write this meditation later when it finally clicked for me.

Once I made that decision, dreams chased me—some of the most vividly clear dreams I had experienced in years. However, no matter what the theme of the dream, a quietly kind, wise, cloaked man was featured in all of them. It was easy to recognize Odin in the dreams, and apparently he had other plans for the theme of Wednesday's meditation. Even though I had taken a break on working on the expansion of this book for Thanksgiving weekend, it seemed the Norse gods, especially Odin, had other plans for me.

For some reason, I had always imagined Odin as stern and harsh. Imagine my surprise when I discovered that he is not like that at all. He actually has a wicked sense of humor, and he will challenge you in many ways until you open up your mind and your heart to his lessons. All he had to do was to get through to one stubborn and distracted writing Witch. And I'll admit that it took him a few days . . .

When I woke up early this morning, it was snowing. Where I live in the midwestern United States, snow is not that common on the first of December. Sure enough, when I staggered out of bed at five AM and looked out the windows, I saw a light and festive snowfall.

Cheered, I sat down at my computer, still in my pajamas and old gray hoodie, and prepared to dive back into this chapter. To get myself in the holiday mood, I was listening to my favorite holiday music on my iPod, and while I began to work, I was becoming very distracted, because my instincts were all screaming for me to *go outside.*

At five o' clock in the morning.

In the dark, while it was snowing.

Then I realized with a start that Odin was thought to visit his people during the winter months . . . okay, so technically December first is not yet winter—it would officially begin at the winter solstice, which was still three weeks away—but snowfall equals winter for me. So as quietly as possible, so as not to wake up the family, I quickly changed into a pair of sweatpants, grabbed my boots and gloves, and tossed an insulated vest on top of my hoodie. I left the iPod on, zipped up the vest, and pulled the hood over my head. Then I let myself out the door to stand in my snowy backyard gardens.

I walked away from the house and down the garden path so I could feel the wind, and then stopped and stood still. It was so quiet and gorgeous. Then, in an interesting quirk of fate, Loreena McKennitt's song "Snow" started to play in my holiday music playlist. Hello, synchronicity. So I stood outside in the pre-dawn darkness, softly laughing at myself. I swear I could hear Odin laughing along with me as he finally got through to me and told me what he wanted me to know.

I stayed outside for a little while and shivered pleasantly, tipping my face up to the snowflakes, listening to the music, and breathing in the sensation of winter. It was great feeling the cold, wintry winds and the sensation of the snowflakes bouncing off my nose. Inspired, I thanked Odin, who seems to be close to me these days, and reveled in his wintry magick and his wisdom.

Meditation

KNOWLEDGE COMES,
BUT wisdom lingers.

Alfred Tennyson

As we begin this meditation, I'd like you to visualize that you are walking through a winter woods at night. It is cold, but pleasantly so, and you are comfortable all bundled up against the weather. Sounds are hushed, and all you can hear is the crunching sounds that your footsteps are making. As you stop and take in the scenery, admiring the snow that is draping from the branches of the pine trees, the sounds of nature become magnified, and you can hear the snow softly falling around you. Up ahead, you see a light in the woods. Intrigued, you turn to follow the light. As you work your way closer, you realize that there is a small fire built in a clearing up ahead, and you decide to go check it out.

As you walk closer to the small fire, you see that there is an older, bearded man in gray tending it carefully. His back is to you as he turns to pick up another log to add to the blaze. As he turns to add the log, he sees you and then straightens, lifting his hand in greeting.

"Hail and well met," he says in a friendly tone.

You say hello and walk up to the fire and join him. You hold your hands out to the fire's warmth and turn to smile at the man. He looks like a cross between a wizard of old and a rustic, earthy version of Santa Claus. The Santa Claus analogy makes you smile a bit to yourself; it's the long gray beard, you think to yourself, and his aura, but he does exude a lot of kindness, good cheer, and charm. The two of you strike up a casual conversation.

He is dressed in a long gray cloak trimmed in black fur and has a hood raised against the cold. He has a staff with him, and as he stands there and chats with you about the snow, you realize that there are animals around the clearing. What you initially take for a dog is sitting at attention off to the far side of the fire. There are deer nosing through the snow, and also a couple of ravens perched in a tree behind him. They occasionally call out as if to punctuate the man's words.

The dog rises and walks over to sit with the man, and as it comes into the circle of light from the fire, you get a much better look at it. Whoa, that's not a dog at all—that is, in fact, a wolf, who seems totally disinterested in you. However, now you start to become a little nervous. You look carefully again at the man and at his companions. As if the birds have sensed you going on guard, the ravens really begin to make a racket.

"Yes, yes…" he waves them off and then turns to address them directly, "I know this is a seeker." He turns back to you with a twinkle in his eye and says in a conspirator's whisper, "Forgive them, they are pushy creatures."

He has one eye, you realize with a start. Ravens, the deer, a wolf, his gray cloak, staff…this is Odin you have met on your astral journey. You try not to sputter as you feel slightly embarrassed about the Santa Claus analogy. As if he knows your thoughts, he laughs out loud in delight.

"Where do you think that legend came from anyway?" He laughs uproariously at your embarrassment and thumps you on the back good-naturedly. "I'm a shaman, a traveler, and a shapeshifter, after all," he reminds you. "My legends and tales are many and varied. No need to be embarrassed." After a moment or two, you get over it and realize that he is not offended in the slightest. Companionably, you two stand at the fire and listen to the snowfall. After a time, he speaks again.

"So, you seek knowledge at this time," Odin says in a more serious tone. "Knowledge you will find if you learn to look within as well as without."

You nod your head in agreement, and he continues. "Wisdom, on the other hand, has to be earned, not unlike trust and love. So, my friend, are you willing to work toward gaining the knowledge of your craft and then keeping the wisdom that follows it?"

You answer that you are ready.

"Then look into the fire and see what you may." He gestures toward the fire, and you turn to look at the flames. Now you gaze into the flames and allow your mind to drift and to experience what wisdom Odin has for you. The images may come at this time or they may appear in your dreams for the next few days. When the images fade, you pull back, blink your eyes, and shake your head a bit to clear it. Feeling as though you are coming out of a trance, you turn to face Odin and thank him in your own words.

"If you would like to visit me again, call my name out loud and you can begin the astral journey back to me here in the clearing," he tells you with a smile. "Now I'd like you to return home and rest, and to think upon what you have seen this night." Smiling at the thought of being gently dismissed, you turn to leave, and he takes your arm with a smile and tells you that you are headed in the wrong direction.

Confused, you begin to argue that you remember well enough which way you came in, but as you look in the snow, you notice that all traces of the tracks you made are gone. You decide to acquiesce to his directions, and he escorts you out of the clearing and back along the path. After a moment, you gain your bearings and are confident in the path home.

You stop and take a careful look at Odin, and then you smile and say farewell. He pats you on the shoulder in a friendly gesture, and you turn and head out of the winter woods and begin the journey home.

Now take a deep, cleansing breath, and ground and center. Stretch and move your body around. If you like, find a journal and write down your impressions of Odin and anything you saw in the sacred fire. Keep open to the idea that you are on a quest for knowledge and wisdom today. Finally, take in a deep, cleansing breath, and slowly blow it out. Open your eyes and return to awareness.

MAGICKAL PLANTS & FLOWERS

Let's take a quick peek at some of the enchanting plants that have the planetary association of Mercury and that are connected with a Wednesday. For this tricky and changeable day of the week, we have the fern, lavender, lily of the valley, and the aspen tree. As you'll see, some of these plants are quite easy to link with the various deity information that's already been discussed in this chapter. Just like the multifaceted gods Odin and Mercury/Hermes, this bewitching day of the week and the following Mercury-aligned magickal plants can cover a wide variety of magickal uses.

Fern

The fern is a traditional Witch's garden plant. Ferns are herbs; they are perennials and prefer growing in the shade. There are over forty species of fern. Whether these are found growing in the wild or tucked into your backyard shade gardens, ferns are practical magickal plants. The fern has quite a bit of folk history behind it. It was thought that to grow ferns in the garden was lucky. Faeries were believed to jealously guard the fern, as ferns were thought to grant the power of invisibility. When a fern frond was carried on your person, it was thought to guide the wearer to hidden riches. On an interesting note, ferns are almost always used in fresh flower arrangements. Flower folklore tells us that adding ferns to a fresh flower arrangement increases the power and meanings of the individual blossoms, and it bestows protection on the recipient. In the language of flowers, the fern declares fascination and earnestness.

Lavender

Lavender (*Lavandula* spp.) is a popular aromatherapy flower. The scent of lavender is thought to reduce headaches, and it has a healing, calming influence that soothes the spirit.

Lavender is a protective herb. This herb is associated with benevolent Witchcraft. The lavender is a shielding and healing plant. It also has the qualities of banishing negativity and keeping negative thoughtforms at bay. Lavender is an herb of transformation, so it's a perfect addition to spells and charms for Wednesday, our unpredictable, changeable day of the week. In the language of flowers, lavender was believed to soothe a troubled heart, and this herb symbolizes devotion, luck, and happiness.

Garden Witch Tip

LAVENDER COMES IN many varieties. If it's classified as a "tender perennial," it may not survive cold winter climates. It grows best in full sun and along the edge of a sidewalk or driveway. It can be drought tolerant, but you'll still have to keep it watered occasionally so it will look and flower its best. Plant plenty of this wonderful-smelling herb—it's great for sachets and dried flower arrangements, and it's a powerful magickal herb that encourages the transformation of your dreams to reality.

Lily of the Valley

Lily of the valley (*Convallaria*) is an old-fashioned cottage garden plant. This fragrant, romantic flower is also associated with Mercury. These lovely scented plants are best suited for growing in the shade and will multiply rapidly if you do not keep them under control in your garden. Flower folklore warns against planting lily of the valley alone. Instead, plant other magickal shade-loving flowers such as columbine or foxglove along with them to keep the garden happy. Lily of the valley is toxic if ingested, so simply enjoy the blooms in small arrangements or just for their scent in the garden. The perfume of lily of the valley was thought to have the power to improve the memory and to lift the spirits. In the language of flowers, the lily of the valley speaks of a true platonic friendship and a return to cheerfulness and happy times.

Aspen Tree

The aspen tree (*Populus tremula*) is a tree of healing. It is associated with communication and the element of air. Also, aspen leaves were often used in spells designed to protect you from thieves. Well, it's not to hard to imagine why this tree ended up being aligned with Mercury, now, is it? Remember that Mercury was associated with speed, trickiness, and healing.

The aspen tree always appears to be in perpetual motion. The slightest breeze causes the leaves to tremble and shiver. A folk name for the aspen was the "whispering tree," due to the sounds that the rustling leaves seem to make while they dance in the breeze. In the old days, it was believed that the winds carried messages straight to the gods. The aspen then became associated with movement and communication, just like our pal Mercury/Hermes. According to folklore, aspen trees aid in communication with the faeries. They may also help you find your way into the realm of Faery itself.

Aspen Leaf Communication Spell

Have you been trying to get in touch with someone? Perhaps it's an old friend that you haven't been able to track down or a relative that you need to clear the air with. Perhaps it's a coworker who keeps "misplacing" your memos, messages, or notes. Then here is a clever natural magick spell to try.

For this herbal spell, you will need to gather three aspen leaves for movement and the positive reception of your message. This spell relies on the element of air and all of the qualities associated with this element, such as motion, contact, change, and intelligence. As stated above, the aspen is intimately connected with the element of air. So, unite these two enchanting energies and try a little natural magick to send your magickal message quickly on its way. Remember that this spell is designed to give the recipient a friendly nudge, sort of a psychic "Hey, I really need you to give me a call" type of energy.

Gather the leaves and hold them in your hands; at the third line of the spell (below), scatter the leaves to the breeze. Or, if you would prefer, simply try working with the aspen tree by sitting on the ground beneath its branches. Then repeat the spell three times while a nice breeze ruffles the leaves overhead.

> *Aspen leaves first are green and then in autumn turn to gold*
> *I call the element of air, for I am brave and bold*
> *As these aspen leaves catch the breeze, my spell to you will soar*
> *With the speed of Mercury and the help of the winds four.*

Close the spell with the line:

For the good of all, with harm to none

By leaf and breeze, this spell is now done!

Once you have made contact, the communication between the two of you is up to the spellcaster, but this spell should at least help you to get things moving in a positive direction.

COLORS, CANDLES, METALS & CRYSTALS

Colors

There are a few different ideas for colors associated with Mercury and Wednesdays. Honestly, did you expect anything else? Some traditions say that orange is the color for Mercury, while others claim that it's purple or a mixture of colors. So guess what this means? It means that you get to decide for yourself which color you'd like to use.

Personally, I don't see anything wrong with using both purple and orange for Wednesday spells, charms, and rituals. After all, both of these colors are secondary colors. Remember your color-wheel lessons from elementary school? In other words, it takes red to make each of them. Yellow and red make orange, while blue and red create purple. Are you following me here? Since both colors are produced with a base color of red, why not use them both?

If you wanted to wear the colors of this changeable and communicative day, then go with either purple or orange. If the thought of slipping on an orange shirt makes you cringe, then look for deeper shades in burnt orange or softer shades of melon to stimulate communication skills and to increase your productivity. Ladies, try looking for shades of cosmetics in coral and give that a try.

If purple is more your style, and it does seem to be a very popular color among magick users, then go for it! Whip out a violet-colored blouse. Slip on a deep purple tie or scarf. Maybe you have a favorite dark purple sweatshirt or casual pullover. Ladies, you can try wearing eye shadow in shades of plums and purples or nail polish in any tone from pale lilac to deep amethyst.

The energies and magick of Mercury are enigmatic and wild. Mercury is itself a mutable sign, which means that it is constantly changing. There are many magickal qualities to this day of the week. See what you can discover for yourself by working with a little Wednesday color magick.

Mercury's Color Candle Spell to Improve Communication

This spell reminds me of the line my two sons would often throw around the house in a deep and dramatic voice, complete with a cheesy foreign accent: "Yes, my brother, you are bold; but are you also . . . *daring*?" Well, are you? Are you ready to dive into the complex and varied moods and attributes of a Wednesday? I thought you might be. Give this little candle spell a whirl and see how it works out for you.

While gathering your supplies, try adding a bit of Wednesday aromatherapy while you're at it—see if you can find two lavender-scented purple candles. Don't forget that lavender is an herb of transformation and magick! Other supplies you will need are two orange candles, four candle holders, matches or a lighter, and a safe, flat surface to set up on.

This spell will help you to invoke, or call on, all of the clever and skillful attributes of this magickal day of the week. Expect to notice a difference within a day or so. But remember, if you are brave enough to work this spell designed to improve your communication skills, then you need to be daring enough to step up and use these gifts in a positive and productive way. Repeat the following spell three times. Allow the candles to burn until they go out on their own.

I light purple candles for power on a Wednesday eve

Now burn the orange candles for skill and dexterity

From these two colors spring magick on this fascinating day

Send wisdom, communication skills, and clarity my way.

Close the spell with this line:

For the good of all, with harm to none

By color and light, this spell is done!

Metals & Crystals

The metal for today is quicksilver, or mercury. It is both projective and receptive and aligns with the planet Mercury, just as you'd expect. The elements it is linked to are water, earth, and air. Why three elements? Because of the weight of quicksilver, it is tied to the earth; because it is a liquid, it corresponds to water; and the quick, rolling movements that it makes link it back to the element of air. I wanted to include this information into this Book of Shadows for you to have, but please keep in mind that quicksilver is intensely toxic and should not be handled. Its use in magick is not recommended today.

The stones and crystals that are associated with Mercury and Wednesdays are the opal, agate, and aventurine. Now, agates come in a vast array of colors and types. Make sure you keep a nice selection on hand for your crystal magick. Aventurines and agates are easy to find and affordable as tumbled stones. The opal will be more affordable in its rough form, but if you own any jewelry with opals, here is the perfect opportunity to work magick with them!

OPAL: The opal is a beautiful multicolored gemstone. This is the birthstone for those born in the month of October. It is associated with all of the magickal elements: earth, air, fire, water, and Spirit. It was thought that if you wrapped an opal inside of a fresh bay leaf that this would grant you the power of invisibility. I think it's much more likely that it may help you to remain unseen or safely in the background. The opal is also thought to increase psychic powers if worn. (Scott Cunningham's *Encyclopedia of Crystal, Gem & Metal Magic* suggests wearing opal earrings for this purpose.) Opals make a good subtle choice for magickal jewelry. They are thought to increase your self-esteem and bring out your inner beauty, or "sparkle." Opals may be used to aid astral projection and all psychic work. The opal is a stone of transformation and magick.

AVENTURINE: This stone is associated with the element of air and has a projective energy. Aventurine is a translucent to opaque variety of microcrystalline quartz. This stone contains tiny inclusions of minerals that give the stone its sparkle. It brings fast cash and good luck and is regarded as a gambler's stone. It is also associated with the god Mercury and has many of the same magickal attributes as that wily god. With all that Mercury energy, you just know it has to come in a variety of colors! Aventurine comes in creamy green, peach, brown, and blue colors. The common, inexpensive green tumbled stone of aventurine is perfect to carry in your purse or pocket to promote success and prosperity and to encourage good luck. The lovely green color of this stone was also believed to soothe emotional storms, to boost creativity, and to help speed up the healing process. Try adding aventurine to your own brand of witchery, and see what you can conjure up.

AGATE: The agate is a variety of chalcedony, and it comes in many different shades and colors. The overall magickal associations for agates are strengthening memory and bestowing stamina on the wearer. It also is believed to help you get a good night's sleep and will chase away bad dreams. Agates have a calming influence about them. However, each variety and color has its own enchanting meaning and, in keeping with the theme of this chapter, the meanings are many and varied. Here are a few examples of differ-ent agates and their elemental associations and magickal meanings:

Banded agate: Linked with the element of fire. Banded agates have a projective energy, and their power will radiate out and around you. Wearing jewelry made of agates is thought to keep the wearer energized yet also calm and centered. This is a beautiful, strong, protective stone that is readily available.

Blue lace agate: Associated with the element of water. This lovely crystal has receptive energies and is a good de-stressing stone. Try carrying a tumbled blue lace agate in your pocket or tuck a stone into your desk drawer at work. Excellent for use in any ritual to clear a home of negativity and psychic garbage. (You'll find a blue lace agate ritual a bit later in this chapter to help you do just that.)

Brown agate: Associated with the element of fire, this color of agate is a projective type of stone. Back in the day, it was used to ward off the evil eye, so this makes an excellent stone to carry for magickal protection. The brown agate (or tawny agate, as it sometimes called) is an amulet for wealth, success, prosperity, and accomplishment.

Green agate: As you would imagine, this green agate is associated with the element of earth. Classified as a receptive energy stone, it is a lucky stone for healing spells and fertility issues. According to folklore, the green agate is thought to help improve the strength of your eyes.

Moss agate: This receptive stone is also aligned to the element of earth. The moss agate is a gardener's stone. This is a complementary stone to utilize in green magick, garden witchery, and herbalism. If you wear moss agates, they will help to restore your energy and vitality after a long day or after you have worn yourself out by working in the magickal garden. In magick, the moss agate is used to promote luck, prosperity, and longevity.

Red agate: This projective stone is linked to the element of fire. It is a shielding and healing stone as well. A folk name is blood agate, as it was thought to remove impurities of the blood. Try working magick with this stone for health issues and to rid the body of infections.

Wednesday's All-Purpose Agate Spell

Try using tumbled agate stones for this Wednesday spell, as they are inexpensive and can be picked up at most metaphysical or magickal shops. Even nature-themed stores or arts and crafts stores often carry tumbled stones. This is a great spell for a friend or loved one who is going through a tough time. This crystal spell pretty much covers all the bases. The next time a friend asks for a little magickal help, you'll know just what to do.

Gather several different colors or varieties of agates (tumbled stones); four to six different-colored agates would be plenty. Ring the agates around a plain white tealight candle in a holder, and then repeat the following spell three times:

Lovely agates come in many colors and hues

May this charm grant luck and prosperity to you

Health, wisdom, and protection for you now do I call

In all seasons, winter to spring and summer to fall.

Close the spell with:

By all the powers of three times three

As I will it, then so shall it be!

Let the tealight burn until it goes out on its own. Then give the stones as a gift to your friend and tell them to keep the stones in a spot where they will see them daily for a month (or from one full moon phase to the next). They can either keep the agates or return them to you after the month has passed.

POTIONS, PHILTERS & OILS

Today is the time to create philters and potions that work in harmony with Mercury's planetary energy. Mercury has many moods and magickal qualities, including communication, movement, and precision, so I thought that today would be the most opportune time to create a philter for clear communication. This philter recipe will assist you in making your words heard and to get the correct message across loud and clear.

Clear Communication Philter

- One small decorative glass bottle
- Base oil, approximately ⅛ cup almond oil (almond aligns with Mercury)
- Clean dropper
- 3 drops lavender oil
- 3 drops bergamot oil
- 1 clover for good luck (another Mercury plant)
- Small chip of aventurine for creativity
- 6 inches thin orange or purple satin ribbon
- 1 small metal magickal charm or talisman that you feel coordinates with communication of your choosing
- A label and a pen (to list the ingredients and to decorate and mark the bottle)

Pour the base oil into the bottle until you have filled it three quarters of the way full. Add the essential oils one at a time. Next, add the crystal and the clover. Close up the bottle with the lid, place your fingers over the lid, and carefully shake up the mixture.

Hold up the mixture to the sunlight and allow the light of Wednesday's sun to illuminate the philter within.

Wipe off the outside of the bottle and use the label to list the ingredients and the use of this potion. Decorate the bottle by drawing the symbol of Mercury (☿) or even a winged foot. If you have other magickal symbols you would like to use, add these on the label. Attach the label to the glass bottle and finish up by threading the metal charm onto the orange or purple ribbon and then tying the ribbon around the neck of the bottle.

As you finish tying on the bow, hold the bottle in your hands and concentrate on the visualization that your aura around your throat and face is pulsing bright golden orange. Your words are unmistakably heard and your meaning is clearly comprehended; envision this outcome and nothing else. Now send all that energy from your visualization into the philter bottle that you hold in your hands. Take a deep breath, hold it for three counts, and then blow it out slowly. Now, repeat the charm below:

> *May the fleet-footed god hear my plea*
> *Grant clear communication now to me*
> *Empower this brew with magickal power*
> *I bless this philter in this time and hour*
> *Using a bit of Wednesday's witchery*
> *As I do will it, so mote it be!*

Set aside the philter bottle, and clean up the supplies. Ground and center yourself. Eat a few crackers or do something physical. Make sure to store the philter in a dark, dry place out of the reach of children.

Essential Oils

Here are a few of the essential oils associated with Mercury and Wednesday. As in other chapters, I chose oils that should be easy for you to find and purchase:

- Bergamot
- Dill
- Eucalyptus
- Lavender
- Lily of the valley
- Sweet pea

Try these oils on a candle or add them into potion or philter recipes of your own design. You could also use an oil diffuser and get some of that magickal fragrance wafting through your home. Use your imagination to customize your days of witchery.

TAROT CARD ASSOCIATIONS

The tarot cards that are associated with Wednesday and Mercury's attributes are the Wheel of Fortune, which represents good luck and chance events; the Magician, for skill, confidence, and communication; and the Eight of Pentacles (or Coins), for craftsmanship, skilled work, and pride in your accomplishments.

The Wheel of Fortune

The Wheel of Fortune is a Major Arcana card that literally means "chance." This is a card of fate. It symbolizes good fortune and an unexpected twist of fate. When the Wheel of Fortune card shows up, things are bound to change, possibly for the better. This is a card of good luck and happy coincidence.

The Magician

The Magician is a card of power, communication, confidence, and skills. The Magician is traditionally depicted as a man standing behind an altar that holds the four magickal tools—a wand, a pentacle, a cup, and a sword; one tool to represent each element. A master of the elements, one of his arms is raised while the other points downward; think of it as "As above, so below." This card characterizes a person who is quietly powerful and confident, charming, and articulate.

Adding this card as a prop in your spells will give you a big visual boost. Take a good look at the magickal images that are represented within this card. It's called "the Magician" for a reason, you know.

Eight of Pentacles

Eight of Pentacles is a card of the skilled craftsperson. It can represent a hobby or profession that you take pride in or a talent that you cleverly use to make a little extra money. Whether it's painting, weaving, sewing, pottery, or jewelry making, this is a craft that you create with your hands. This card indicates that you get more out of your talents than just a monetary bonus (although that can't be discounted). What this symbolizes is the sense of pride and personal satisfaction that you gain from using your imagination, creating the object, and working with your own two hands to produce something special.

A Tarot Spell to Increase Creativity

This spell is designed to give your creative juices a little boost. No matter how talented you are, everybody hits a creative wall now and then. I have two very artistic and witchy friends. Morgan is a mother, graphic designer, and talented artist. The other, Ravyn, is a full-time wildlife biologist and a part-time jewelry designer. And from time to time, they can both hit a little creative snag where something doesn't turn out the way they intended or a project just won't gel. Do they give up? Nope, they either look at the project from a different perspective or they let creativity take over and lead them to a different outcome than they had originally planned. The results are typically stunning.

So, with this thought in mind, let's look to our goddess for Wednesday, Athena. After all, Athena was a patron of the arts and of skilled craftspeople. How about using a little tarot magick and seeing what kind of imaginative and crafty things we can come up with?

- White votive candle (it's an all-purpose color)
- A votive cup/holder
- A representation of Athena's sacred bird, the owl (try using a picture or a tiny figurine)
- The Magician, the Eight of Pentacles, and the Wheel of Fortune tarot cards
- A sample of your project

- A few art supplies (if you are an artist, then set a couple of art pencils or paints on the workspace; if you sew, use a swatch of fabric; if you create jewelry, then set out a few beads, and so on—this is your item/items in sympathy)
- A safe, flat surface on which to set up the spell

Gather your supplies and then arrange your items around the candle holder. Set the tarot cards around the items of sympathy. Light the candle, and repeat the following spell three times:

> Gray-eyed Athena, patron of handmade crafts and the arts
> Send your divine inspiration, let it fill up my heart
> Throw in a bit of good luck and a dose of your wisdom
> Now, may my creativity take on a fresh, new spin!

Close the spell by saying:

> I thank the goddess Athena for her time and care
> I close this spell by the powers of the earth, water, fire, and air.

Keep an eye on the candle. Let the candle burn until it goes out on its own (a votive candle will take about six to eight hours). Allow the items of sympathy to stay where they are for a while, then take a little time off from your project. When the candle is consumed, take a fresh look at your project. Are you getting any new and innovative ideas? I bet you'll come up with something fabulous!

DAILY WITCH CRAFT
crafting magickal jewelry

Several years ago, I worked at an arts and crafts store as a class coordinator. On various weekends, I would sit in the front of the store and perform demos on various arts and crafts. The artsy-craftsy and floral design stuff was easy for me, as I was a trained floral designer, but when it came to jewelry making, I would invariably break a sweat.

Luckily for me, a fellow employee lent me a hand and taught me some basics. She was, at the time, a college student and a talented part-time jewelry designer. She saved my bacon on several occasions with on-the-spot lessons on simple bracelet-making with stretchy cord and various stone beads. Interestingly enough, she was also a Witch; the Goddess certainly works in mysterious ways. She and I became friends immediately, and several years later, though our lives have changed (I'm now a full-time writer and she's the wildlife biologist I mentioned earlier), Ravyn and I are still friends as well as covenmates.

The following spell can be easily adapted if you wish. For example, my coven all created ritual necklaces a few years ago. One of our members had a wholesale account with a jewelry design studio, and she ordered everyone a matching silver pentagram. We were lucky that the style we chose came in a few sizes and variations, but the overall design of the pentagram was the same. So everyone chose their pentagram, paid their money, and the order was filled.

On the first full moon of the year, when we gathered together, we created our necklaces. That January night, a few members brought over their jewelry-making supplies and tools and the rest of us brought our own cords, beads, crystals, and our coven pentagrams, and we all created necklaces. All of us sat down on the floor in a big circle and started laying out our necklaces. We traded beads and accessories back and forth and helped each other with the designs. In the end, we had very different necklaces, all with the same pentagram in the center. It was a lot of fun, though I will admit that I had a lot of help with mine. Then, when we were finished, we consecrated them all together in a ritual.

In the interest of keeping this simple (the mere thought of crimping beads and lobster-claw catches makes me shudder), we are going for uncomplicated bracelet-making directions here. Truthfully, the easiest jewelry to make is to string crystals, stones, beads, and metal charms onto stretch cord. Lay out your beads and baubles in a pattern that you like. Knot one end of the stretchy cord and begin to thread the beads and trinkets on one at a time. Enjoy the process—don't be in a hurry, and make the arrangement of stones and beads pleasing to your own taste. Measure as you go to get the correct length for your new bracelet. Don't cut the cord off the spool until you are about to tie the knot. When you have the beads strung long enough to fit around your wrist, snip the cord. Then carefully knot the ends with a double knot, and slip the bracelet on and admire your work.

Here is a spell to bless any magickal jewelry that you create. If you look at the third and fourth lines, you can adjust these to name the purpose of the piece and for the type of jewelry you have created.

> These beads and baubles, stones and metal findings
> I charm you all and make the magick binding
> Now enchanted for _____, this Wednesday jewelry spell begins
> May this bracelet/necklace bless its wearer with love, wealth, health, and wisdom.

Custom-Made Daily Magick

Originally, this chapter was a tough one to write. Mercury is such a varied planetary energy and there are so many different magickal qualities to a Wednesday that the subject can be more than a little overwhelming. When I wrote the original manuscript several years ago, I recall sitting at the computer for hours and wondering where to go with this chapter. I was getting frustrated and aggravated. The harder I tried to pin this day down, the less I actually had. Then my mother rode to the rescue. She called and asked me how my new book was coming along. I laughed and told her that I was seriously considering banging my head against the computer to see if that could get me anywhere. When she suggested that I get out of the house and meet her for lunch, I pounced on the offer. She advised me that the change of scenery would probably do me a world of good.

As I drove to meet her for lunch, I was sitting at a stoplight, waiting for it to turn green. It was then I noticed that the car in front of me had "Mercury" on the back of it. That gave me a little jolt. As a rule, I don't pay attention to the make or model of other cars while I drive. It's a blue car or a white truck to me, that's about as technical as I get. I smiled to myself and continued to drive.

In the ten minutes that it took me to drive to the restaurant where I was to meet my mother, I saw four different Mercury cars. Weird. When a floral delivery van pulled in front of me with that logo of a golden Mercury emblazoned across the side, I began to chuckle. Okay, so he was a god of synchronicity, after all. *Duh, Ellen* . . . communication, changeability, and cunning. Finally it dawned on me. Mercury was doing everything possible to get my attention.

I ended up laughing out loud. "Okay, thanks, I got it. Message received!" Mercury is a god of many faces, attributes, and guises, I reminded myself.

So that cinched it for me that the way to go with this chapter was to focus on the many varieties of magick that could be performed on this wild and wily day, as opposed to just picking one theme.

Now, several years later, I find Wednesdays to be one of the best for working witchery. There are so many options available to a clever Witch on a Wednesday. Look at all the different themes we've explored so far: creativity, communication, wisdom, knowledge . . . all you have to do is open yourself up to all the enchanting and ever-changing possibilities.

To wrap up this chapter, let's work a little fun, practical magick for good luck. Try this next spell out. It will require you to go on a hunt for one of the supplies, but honestly, that's half the fun!

Quick as a Flash Spell (for Good Luck)

This good luck spell will require you to locate a Mercury dime. A Mercury, or silver, dime was a dime minted in the year 1940. It does not actually portray the god Mercury on the coin. What it shows is Lady Liberty in a winged cap. However, it does look like Mercury, and many folks thought that's who it was, so the name stuck. How to find them? Check a coin dealer, or, if you have a family member who collects coins, see if they have one. I called a local coin shop and was told I could pick up a Mercury dime for about a dollar.

Occasionally, if you work retail or operate the cash register, you come across silver dimes. If you look at the side of the coin, the color is silver all the way through. Plus, it makes a different type of "clink" as it hits the change drawer. Happy hunting!

Take yourself, a tablespoon of dill (a Mercury herb used for prosperity and luck), and your Mercury dime, and go to the nearest crossroads early on a Wednesday evening. This can be anyplace where two streets intersect. Also bring the spell below, written on a piece of paper. Perhaps you'll want to do this while you're out walking the dog or taking a walk around the neighborhood with the kids. You can be subtle with this spell, as it is a quick one. It's not complicated, and it's fun! Read the spell below softly, repeating it three times:

Wednesday is for Mercury, that quick and nimble god,

A clever and canny soul, on winged feet he does trod.

Leave a Mercury dime at the crossroads tonight,

Quick as a flash, my good luck spell will now take flight.

Slip the paper back into your pocket. Make your wish for good luck, and then chuck the dime out there. (I caution you to stay away from traffic. I also don't want you to accidentally nail a car with the dime as you toss it out there into the middle of the street.) Sprinkle the dill at the curb. As you turn to walk back home, close the spell with:

By all the power of three times three,

As I will it, then so shall it be.

Note: If you perform this spell and you have your kids along, let them gently toss a penny along with your dime. They'll think it's fun, and that way they'll leave your dime alone. Good luck to you and yours!

Mercury is a mutable energy, and its moods and associations are many and varied. Take a good look at the spell worksheet on page 301 and get to work! What do you think you can come up with to personalize your magick? When in doubt, you can always try the tarot spell for creativity on page 132. Adapt the spell as necessary to suit your needs.

Perhaps you've got a yen to write. Well, go ahead—don't let anyone stop you. Mercury days are also for communication and, after all, writing is communication. It's the writer's way of communicating with their audience. They either tell the reader a story or they teach the reader something new. (This is the part where I really hope that I have managed to teach you something new—and maybe even inspired you to write your own spells.)

Not too sure about that yet? Maybe you should sit down and have a little chat with Athena, goddess of the arts, wisdom, and peace. Don't forget that the arts include writing and music as well. Try meditating on Athena, and see where that takes you. Here is a simple candle spell to help get you going.

Athena's Spell-Writing Charm

Light a purple candle for Athena and a white candle for peace. Now sit before the candles and concentrate on what variety of spell you'd like to write. Close your eyes for a few moments to center yourself. Now repeat the following spell three times:

Computer and printer, ink pens and paper

Send me inspiration sooner than later

Athena blesses me under a Wednesday-night sky

I can create my own spells, now let my magick fly

Using a bit of Wednesday's witchery

As I do will it, so mote it be!

Close this up by writing your own spell or charm. If you'd like to add a little herbal magick to this spell, add some lavender for transformation. It will help to transform your ideas into reality. Check your spice rack, and make use of some dill for good luck. Most of all, just have fun. Don't be afraid to try writing your own spells.

RITUAL FOR WEDNESDAY
clearing the air with blue lace agates

Here is a Wednesday-night ritual that will help clear the air after a nasty argument. This crystal magick will help to remove any family discord in the home. This is also excellent witchery to work if you think that things feel "off" or if you believe that the psychic energy in your home needs a good clearing out.

It happens to all of us—you think you have things all on track energy-wise and then you start to notice that things feel sour or that there are bad vibes lingering. Maybe you had a visitor who dumped their psychic garbage in your living room, or perhaps you had a coven meeting and all that energy is still boiling around in the house, making things feel frantic. Or maybe someone in the family just got over the flu, or the kids have just been wild and crazy lately…whatever the cause, let's clean house!

You can easily and quickly tap into Mercury's planetary magick of the day. Be clever and canny, like our featured gods Hermes/Mercury, and use some of that sense of speed and movement to send any negativity and lingering bad vibes on their way. Bear in mind that the planet Mercury has a mutable energy—it is always in motion and constantly changing, which is perfect for this type of witchery.

As you look over this ritual, you may realize that while you are working crystal magick, which is associated with the element of earth, you are also tapping into some water energy as well (the color blue from the candle and the blue lace agates). If you recall, this particular type of agate is connected to the element of water. Their cleansing energy is very complementary for this spell. In addition, you will be working with the element of air, because this is the elemental correspondence of both Hermes/Mercury the god and Mercury the planet. Finally, just to keep things nice and balanced, you've got yourself a dash of fire energy, too, from the candle flame.

Pretty clever, eh? What you thought was primarily crystal spellwork ends up being a much more advanced and involved witchery. Try it for yourself, and see the difference that it makes when you work magick in balance with all four of the natural elements.

- 1 blue votive candle
- 1 votive cup
- 4 blue lace agates
- A picture of your home and/or your family and pets (whoever lives in the house)

- Lighter or matches
- A safe, flat surface on which to set up the spell

Place the blue votive in the votive cup. Set the photos of your home and family on either side of the candle holder. Next, arrange the four blue lace agates in a small circle around the candle holder. As you place the tumbled stones one by one, say these lines:

Blue lace agates, lend me your power

Cleanse this home in this time and hour

Around this candle I create a ring

These four blue lace agates are just the thing.

Now light the spell candle and hold your hands out and over the stones and candle. (Not too close, we don't want you scorching your witchy fingers.) Finish the spell by saying the following verse:

I now call the four elements on this Wednesday night

On the wings of Mercury, I quickly set things to right

By blue lace agates and candle flame, this spell is begun

Now remove all negativity, and let it harm none.

Allow the votive to burn until it goes out on its own. (Most votives take four to six hours to burn completely out.) When the spell candle is consumed, take the four blue lace agates and place one in each of the four main corners of your home. This will keep the spell moving along quickly, and it will reenforce the cleansing. Clean up the rest of your spellwork supplies, and put up the pictures of your family in a prominent place so you can enjoy them.

Be bold and daring today! Expand your knowledge of the Craft by working with the planetary energies of Mercury on this multifaceted day of the week. Consider the Greco-Roman gods Mercury and Hermes and all of the many lessons they have for you. Embrace change and movement, and work on your communication techniques. Conjure up a little good luck for yourself with that Mercury dime spell. Call on Athena to inspire you to try magickal arts and crafts and to be more creative in your own spell-work and witchery.

Meditate on Odin and see what you can discover about him. I wonder what sort of fabulous and fascinating magickal wisdom you will uncover? Odin is a shaman, after all; he may appear in many guises and faces. I guarantee that he will make you laugh at yourself before he is through with you, but you will learn. It's up to you what you do with that knowledge. Will you let it shapeshift into wisdom?

Wednesday is the wild and wily day of the week, so try to go with the flow; don't fight the quirky energies of the day. Most importantly, follow your heart, and always keep a good sense of humor, because on Wednesdays, you will really need it.

Thursday

WOULD THAT YOU might pray
also in the fullness of your joy and
in the days of abundance.

Kahlil Gibran

At-a-Glance Correspondences

PLANETARY INFLUENCE	Jupiter
PLANETARY SYMBOL	♃
DEITIES	Thor, Juno, Jupiter/Jove, Zeus
FLOWERS & PLANTS	Honeysuckle, cinquefoil, mint, maple tree, oak tree
METAL	Tin
COLORS	Purple, royal blue, green
CRYSTALS & STONES	Sapphire, amethyst, turquoise
ESSENTIAL OILS	Clove, honeysuckle, nutmeg, sage
TAROT CARDS	Ten of Pentacles, Nine of Pentacles, Ace of Pentacles
FOODS, HERBS & SPICES	Cinnamon, nutmeg, wheat

DAILY MAGICKAL APPLICATIONS

Thursday comes from the Latin *Dies Iovis*, which means "Jove's day." Jove, or Jupiter as he was sometimes called, was the supreme god and patron of the ancient Romans. Jove/Jupiter is associated with wealth, leadership, thunder, and lightning. A lord of heaven, Jove/Jupiter was also a god of light, and his sacred color is white. In the Greek mythologies, this deity was known as Zeus.

This fifth day of our bewitching week was eventually turned into the Old English *Thursdaeg* or *Thunresdaeg*, which translates to "thunder's day" or, more simply, "Thor's day." This day of the week is named after Thor, the popular Norse god of thunder. Thor was the son of Odin. He carried a war hammer called Mjollnir, and it was this that made the thunder and lightning. All of these Thursday gods—Jupiter/Jove, Zeus, and Thor—were wielders of the thunderbolt.

Thursday has the planetary association of Jupiter, and this day of the week is associated with prosperity, abundance, leadership, and good health. Prosperity and abundance are the typical magickal concerns on a Thursday. However, the way people define prosperity can vary greatly between individuals.

Personally, I think prosperity and abundance aren't about owning the biggest house, fanciest wardrobe, or the newest car. It's about living within your means and living well. My definition of prosperity is having enough money in the checking account to cover the bills and to pay for the groceries; anything left over is gravy.

But with a family, there is always something. Just about the time you're feeling confident, something pops up. Somebody has to go to the doctor or the dentist, or someone needs work done on their car. Or my daughter calls from college with the classic "send money" request. It's enough to drive me bonkers! For instance, just this past month, I got hit up for sorority dues, book fees, dentist bills, a bit of car repair and, lest we forget, living money for my daughter while she is away at school. Ouch!

The aspiration to make your budget stretch and to find ways to cover extra expenses is a real need for just about everybody. So on this bewitching day, let's look at some practical, magickal ways to increase your prosperity and try out a few enchanting ideas designed to create a little abundance and, last but not least, good health.

DEITIES

Thor

This fifth day of the week is dedicated to Thor, for he was—and is—greatly loved. One of the most widely worshiped of the Norse gods, people called on Thor to protect them from evil and to bless them with both fertility and abundance. Thor is referred to as the "everyman's god." He is pictured with red hair and a red beard, and he is thought to be hearty and hot-tempered. He is married to a golden-haired goddess named Sif. Thor is the strongest of all the Norse gods. When he uses the hammer, he wears a belt, or girdle, that doubles his strength, and he wears magickal iron gauntlets. When Thor rides the earth in a chariot pulled by two gigantic male goats, he brings rain to germinate the crops and to make the fields fertile. The people believed that the turning of his chariot's wheels made the sound of thunder.

Even though he may seem a warlike god, Thor is not. His hammer is thought to be a symbol of the god's beneficence; in fact, the symbol was used to bless both infants and brides. (There are references to Thor blessing a bride by having her hold the hammer in her lap.) Yes, this is a macho-type god of storms and lightning; however, he is also associated with fertility and abundance. Thor is believed to be a guardian for the downtrodden and the frightened. He is both a compassionate friend and a fierce protector. Thor blesses us with stability and helps us to stay strong, grounded, and centered. He is worshiped as a benevolent god, one who protects both the other gods and humanity from evil and destruction. Thor brings fruitfulness to the fields and happiness to marriage.

Jupiter

The Roman sky god and ruler of their pantheon, sometimes called Jove, Jupiter is a god of justice and was originally a god of (believe it or not) agriculture; in that capacity, he was called Jupiter Lucetius. As the god Jupiter brought the rains that the crops needed to thrive, the older agricultural tie makes sense. As Rome developed over time, Jupiter became more of a dignified and stoic protector and the guardian of the city and state of Rome. In this incarnation he was called Jupiter Optimus Maximus, "the greatest god." The color associated with this Roman god of the heavens is white. Jupiter had a chariot pulled by four white horses, and his priests all wore white robes. The ram and the eagle were sacred to Jupiter. Foreseeing the future was also associated with Jupiter by ways of divining the signs in the heavens and by reading and studying the flight of birds.

Jupiter is often linked with Zeus in Greek mythology; many of the images of Jupiter are stylized after the Greek Zeus. He was later identified by the German people with their god of thunder, Thor. The Roman Jupiter/Jove was associated with hospitality (probably because he always rode herd on the squabbling gods and goddesses). Jupiter

Optimus Maximus, as the protector of Rome, was also in charge of laws and social order on earth. Oaths, treaties, and alliances were sworn in his name, which led to the custom of swearing in his name "By Jupiter!" or "By Jove!"

Zeus

The leader of the Greek gods and the head honcho of Olympus, Zeus was the god of the sky, and his weapon was the thunderbolt. Zeus was called the cloud collector and was typically portrayed either sitting on a throne or standing with one arm back, ready to hurl a lightning bolt. He was married to Hera and was known for his weakness for the ladies. Zeus had numerous children by scores of different lovers. His symbols include the eagle, oak tree, and lightning bolt. Zeus's image appeared on gold coins, and the sculptor Phidias carved a giant statue of Zeus made entirely of ivory and gold. (Though some sources suggest the core of the statue was wood, and it was then covered with ivory and gold.) This statue was built in Zeus's temple in Olympia. According to legend, the temple was spruced up for the Olympic games, as it was thought that the temple needed to be more grand to celebrate the deity that the Olympics were dedicated to. The statue of Zeus was fashioned to have the god sitting on a throne, holding a scepter of many metals in one hand while the winged goddess Nike (a goddess of victory) stood in the palm of his other hand. The statue of Zeus was believed to be forty feet tall and over twenty feet wide. Apparently the head of the statue almost touched the roof of the temple. The ancient statue of Zeus at Olympia became one of the most famous images in ancient times and was one of the seven wonders of the ancient world.

Juno

Juno was an ancient Roman great mother goddess. The mature and powerful Queen of Olympus, she was a powerful matriarch. Juno was a source of fertility, a goddess of marriage and childbirth, a guardian of women and children, and a goddess of money. She was known by many names, including Juno Augusta, the harvest mother; Juno Februata, the mother of Mars; and Juno Lucina, the mother of light. In this latter aspect, the goddess was pictured as carrying a torch, or scepter, of light.

Juno was associated with the lily, the cuckoo, and the peacock. In processionals, Juno's priestesses carried fans made of peacock feathers. The many "eyes" on the feathers were thought to watch over women, and they symbolized the fifty priestesses who served at Juno's temple.

To tie in with our Thursday theme of prosperity and abundance, Juno was also known as Juno Moneta. The word *money* actually comes from the word *moneta*. In ancient times, Juno's temples housed the Roman mint. Coins that were made there were considered to be blessed by the goddess herself.

THURSDAY'S WITCHERY

Today is the day for prosperity work of all kinds. It can also be used for healing work, whether that is a physical healing of an illness or an emotional healing. Also remember that you have to follow up your healing work and prosperity magick with physical action.

I can't tell you the number of times I have met new Witches who complain to me that their prosperity spell or "I need a better job" spell did not work out as they expected. They'll ramble on and on about how much time and money they spent working their magick . . . but, alas, they had no glorious manifestation of wealth or fabulous job that suddenly dropped out of the sky and landed in their laps.

Then, when I gently ask them, "Did you enchant your résumé or application when you filled it out? Did you do a little confidence-boosting spellwork when you went to apply for the job or went to the interview?" typically they give me a blank, confused stare.

Nine times out of ten, their response is, "You mean I have to go out and actually *look* for the job too?" Um, yes, my dear, you certainly do. Magick follows the path of least resistance, which means it's going to manifest along the simplest, quickest route. Get out there and hit the pavement. See what you can find. Times are tough and competition for good jobs is fierce, so you need whatever edge you can get. For folks like us, we're going to get the edge by using our magick and our spellcraft.

Thursdays have such a rich source of magick for us to draw upon that, honestly, the sky is the limit. This is the day associated with the gods of the sky and heavens, after all. Get to know these deities, and add their wisdom and magick into your days.

Meditation

> WHEN SHALL WE three meet again
> In thunder, lightning, or in rain?
>
> *Shakespeare*

For today's meditation, we are going to work with the Norse god Thor. I have found in my research that the Norse gods and goddesses are a friendly and welcoming lot.

Actually, I had Odin and Thor pay me visits in my dreams frequently while I worked on the Wednesday and Thursday chapters of this Book of Shadows.

At first, I thought that all the thunder and drama was Zeus or Jupiter trying to get my attention . . . and then I received a clearer impression of the being from my dreams who had been making all the commotion. He was warm, burly, and possessed a big-brother type of vibe—you know, the kind of guy you'd hang out with, drinking beer and watching a football game on television. That's the best way I can think to describe him. I'll admit it was a bit disconcerting, especially since he seemed very familiar to me. Maybe that connection is from the German and Danish side of my family tree?

Anyway, to punctuate the dream visit, his loud and laughing parting announcement of "Honey, I am not Zeus" was followed by a clap of thunder, and let me tell you, that woke me right up at three o'clock in the morning.

By the time I got to the actual writing of this meditation, Thor was suspiciously quiet in my mind. *Hmmm* . . . I started to work on the meditation several times, only to find myself stumped. What I had originally envisioned for this meditation never quite jelled. So, I decided to wait until a Thursday. It's his day, after all, and then I sat down and tried it again. After all, one of Thor's magickal qualities is the ability to persevere, and this writing Witch refused to give up.

Eventually, I decided to go for a walk to clear my head. So I bundled up and headed down to the riverfront woods. On a sunny December morning, when it was all of 24 degrees, I went looking for some inspiration. I repeat: Thor's gifts include *perseverance*. Walking along the Missouri River and listening to all the birds and squirrels in the woods really cleared my mind. I finally found that inspiration under some huge oak trees in the woods. (As you'll soon see, the oak is sacred to all of the gods listed in Thursday's chapter.)

Mission accomplished, I walked out of the woods at a fast clip and bustled back to my car. Amazing how fast you can move when you are freezing your *ears* off in the winter woods. So, enjoy your visit with Thor in the following guided meditation; just come as you are—you don't even have to freeze out in the woods like I did—and see what he has to say to you.

Visualize that you are sitting under an oak tree. It's a pleasant spring day, and you have your back leaning against the trunk of the old, sturdy oak. As you tip your head up to look into the crown of the tree, you enjoy the way the sunlight filters down through the new green leaves. The leaves are not quite to full size yet, and the tree is home to squirrels and various birds. Content, you settle in and let your mind wander as you contemplate the lessons you have learned about the days of the week so far. Now we are up to Thursday, Thor's day, and you consider how you can add to the healing and prosperity work that you already practice.

Around you are meadows and fields that have a mist of green color on them from the new crops just breaking the ground. Focus again on the sounds of the birds and the chatter of the squirrels. Enjoy the gentle spring breeze, and allow yourself to relax in the arms of nature and to open up your consciousness. Pay attention to the landscape around you and see if you recognize any of it.

A short time later, you start to notice that clouds are unexpectedly rolling in. The sunlight rapidly shifts as these new clouds are deep gray and moving into the area rather quickly from the north. As you watch, the breeze becomes stronger and the leaves on the tall oak are being whirled around as the storm moves in purposefully. You get so caught up in watching the advancing storm that not until some distant thunder rumbles through do you become aware of your predicament.

You realize that sitting under a tree during a thunderstorm is an invitation to disaster, and you decide to head for home before the storm cuts loose. As you rise to your feet, a loud clap of thunder crashes through. You jolt and cringe in automatic response at the volume, and instinctively you take a quick look up before leaving your shelter. Preparing to make a dash for it, you run instead smack into a man who has appeared from out of nowhere. You bounce off of each other, then you overbalance and land on your behind on the soft ground. Where did he come from? Shaken and aggravated, you look up, and your mouth falls open in surprise. This isn't your everyday type of person.

The man standing there, grinning down at you, has long, red flowing hair and a neat beard. He is wearing dark pants, boots, and a tunic of some type with a large metal and leather belt. Around his wrist are wide metal cuffs. His arms and shoulders are massive. The term "rippling biceps" seriously applies to this guy. He looms over you with his hands on his hips, looking incredibly buff and big as a mountain. He extends a hand out for you to grasp, and automatically you reach out. He hauls you to your feet with one effortless tug. Okay, so add *strong* to the list.

"Sorry about that. Excuse me," you say to him, and you begin to leave. He only holds up one hand to signal that he wants you to stay. You stop and look up at him as he asks where you are going in such a hurry. You reply that you need to get out of the storm.

"You are safe here with me," he tells you.

"Thanks," you say politely. "But it's going to cut loose here in a minute, so I'd better move indoors and away from the lightning." You give him a quick smile, and as you look up into his face, his gray eyes flash in synchronization with the lightning outside. Well, that confirms that.

"You're Thor, aren't you?" you ask him with a smile.

"You called, friend?" he says, smiling back.

"Ah, not really . . ." you begin. As you explain to him that you are merely working on getting more in tune with the daily magickal energies, he just stands there grinning at you while you talk. The rain begins to patter down, and he takes your arm and moves you back under the oak tree for some cover from the rain.

You begin to balk and you look up nervously, half-expecting lightning to come crashing out of the sky while you stand under the tree's sheltering limbs and branches . . . with a god of thunder and lightning.

As if he knows where your thoughts are headed, he lifts a red eyebrow at your impertinence. *Maybe I should just shut up now and not interrupt or argue with the big guy,* you think to yourself. With that, he throws his head back and laughs. As he does, the thunder booms along with him, and you do your best not to jump at the crash and rumble that it makes. After the noise dies down, you stand attentively and wait to see what he has to tell you.

In a lightning-fast change of mood, he now becomes more serious. "You called to me, and here I am." He looks at you intensely. You remain silent, so Thor continues. "I am everyman's god. I am the defender of the weak and comfort for the hopeless. I will bless you with victory and abundance. I am the spirit of courage and the power of perseverance. When you call on me, I bring a surge of strength, vitality, and valor."

From behind his back, he takes out a large metal hammer. He shows it to you and states that those who swear an oath upon it will be gifted with courage. He allows you to decide if this is something you would like to do at this time. If so, then state in your own words your oath and what you need help with. Listen carefully to his response and to how you feel physically afterwards.

You thank him for his wisdom and his words. He lets the hammer go back over his shoulder, and then he rolls his shoulders and it falls neatly into place. You notice that the rain is starting to lessen and the thunder has faded away.

"I will see you again, my friend," he tells you and claps a hand onto your shoulder. You do your best to stay upright, and his eyes twinkle in repressed laughter. You two share a smile, and then suddenly a ray of light beams out through the clouds and shines right into your face. You close your eyes briefly and turn your face away from the light so you can see again. Blinking, with your eyes watering, you wait for your vision to clear, then you begin to realize that Thor has left. Take a few moments and recall everything that he had to teach you during this journey. Remember that Thor is a compassionate, loyal, and fiercely protective god. If you ever need him, just call his name, and he will come and assist you.

Now take a few deep, cleansing breaths, and ground and center. Look around one last time at this scene under the old oak tree. See that the sun is now shining through the clouds and that the spring shower is moving on. Everything around you is renewed and refreshed, just as you are. Take in a final deep, cleansing breath, and slowly blow it out. Stretch gently, and return to awareness.

MAGICKAL PLANTS & FLOWERS

Honeysuckle

An old folk name for the honeysuckle (*Lonicera* spp.) is the woodbine. The honeysuckle grows wild where it can and is a popular plant for hedgerows. However, in the United States, we do have problems with a certain type of wild honeysuckle referred to as bush honeysuckle—the botanical name is *Lonicera maackii*, and it is classified as invasive. Bush honeysuckle is a sort of bully in the garden, and it will become a nuisance plant if you are not careful. It is spread by bird droppings and pops up in the garden when you least expect it. Typically camouflaging itself in the branches and foliage of other shrubs, it is easily identified in the late autumn–early winter by its bright green leaves and brilliant red berries. If you find it taking over your shrubs, be ruthless: prune it out of your other shrubs, then dig out the roots. (We had to do that ourselves this year.)

Now, the ornamental honeysuckle (*Lonicera japonica*), a lovely vine variety, is easy to find at local nurseries. It is also, unfortunately, very invasive. This is a hardy and heat-tolerant vine-type of honeysuckle and will easily train along an arbor or fence. This type of honeysuckle will attract many pollinating bees and butterflies as well as hummingbirds to your yard and garden. The foliage and flowers of the honeysuckle have long been used to promote prosperity. This fragrant herb is associated with the planet Jupiter and the element of earth. The scent of honeysuckle is also used to promote psychic abilities and to encourage abundance. According to tradition, if honeysuckle grows outside of your home or business, it is said that prosperity and good luck will always find their way to your door. And flower legends say that by bringing honeysuckle into the home, a wedding is sure to follow. This may have something to do with the old folklore behind the language of flowers, as honeysuckle represented a "plighted troth" and celebrates the ties of love and a deep and generous affection.

Cinquefoil

Cinquefoil (*Potentilla anserina*) is also known as five-finger grass. The five points of the leaves symbolize love, riches, good health, power, and knowledge. Cinquefoils are a popular garden perennial. A great variety of cinquefoil to try in your garden is called 'Miss Willmott'. This plant bears strawberry-pink flowers and does very well in sunny gardens. Cinquefoil is associated with the planet Jupiter and the element of fire. Old herbals declared the cinquefoil to be a plant with abundant healing energy, so this is the reason that this blooming herb is often worked into both prosperity and healing spells. In the language of flowers, this plant signifies a loving mother-daughter relationship.

Mint

The mint (*Mentha* spp.) is actually associated with the planet Mercury and the element of air. Surprise! However, it is a classic prosperity herb and readily available, so we are working with it on a Thursday. Mint is a much-maligned garden plant. The reason for its bad reputation in the garden is that it is classified as invasive—which means it will spread like crazy! Mint comes in an impressive array of varieties and scents: spearmint, apple mint, chocolate mint, peppermint . . . If you want to grow mint in the garden, then keep it corralled by planting it in pots or containers; try sinking that container into the ground so the roots and shoots will stay under control. Magickally, mint is worked into both money and health spells and charms. Add a few fresh mint leaves to a charm bag or tuck them into your wallet to promote prosperity. Also, taking a whiff of fresh mint can alleviate nausea and is thought to refresh you and to help clear your head. Pretty cool, huh?

Maple Tree

The sugar maple tree (*Acer saccharum*) is often utilized in both love and prosperity work (using its foliage and small branches). It is magickally associated with the planet Jupiter and the element of air. It is classified as possessing masculine energies, which I think is sort of cute, especially when you consider that the maple tree was once considered appropriate for planting in a "gentleman's garden." If you are looking for a way to "sweeten up your life," this is both a readily available and practical magickal tree to work with. Come on . . . think about it: maple syrup, sweetening up your life . . . are you following me here? Try creating a small wand out of a fallen maple branch and use that in your prosperity and loving abundance spells. Oh—and yes, you may certainly use real maple syrup in a pinch for those prosperity and love spells, too. After all, that syrup came from a maple tree!

Oak Tree

The oak tree (*Quercus* spp.) has a vast and colorful magickal history throughout the world. The oak's planetary influence is Jupiter, and the tree is associated with the element of fire. Many magickal cultures revere the oak. The oak is associated with the many sky-thunder gods, such as our featured gods Thor, Zeus, and Jupiter. Actually, the rustling of oak leaves in the breeze was thought to represent the voice of Zeus.

The foliage of the oak is celebrated as a happy, protective, and lucky symbol, and folks used to adorn themselves with garlands of its leaves. In modern-day folk art, it is common to see oak leaves in Green Man masks and worked into hex signs for protection and such. The oak tree also plays a major role in the winter and summer solstice celebrations, both in the decorations and in the symbolism of the Holly King and the Oak King.

Work magick with oak leaves and small fallen branches for prosperity, healing, courage, and luck. Try picking up a few fallen acorns and tucking them into your pocket like talismans. (This was thought to boost your fertility as well.) If you want a small natural representation of the god to place on your altar or workspace, then try adding a few acorns or a small twig covered in oak leaves.

Oak and Maple Leaf Spell for Prosperity and Abundance

Here is a Thursday-night spell to try. This is a quick and practical type of witchery that is based on the lore and magick of the trees. As discussed before, the maple and the oak are both linked to Thursdays and to Jupiter's influences of prosperity, abundance, and good health.

Gather a few leaves from an oak and maple tree ahead of time for this spell. If you can pull it off, this would be a great spell to work while it is thundering outside, but please work this spell indoors if safety is an issue. Arrange the leaves around a green votive candle in a pretty holder. Raise up your personal power and picture yourself vibrantly healthy and your life flowing with abundance. If this is difficult for you at the moment, then do your best to lay your fears aside and to focus on the improvements that you are trying to achieve. Now, repeat the following spell three times:

I call on Thursday's thunder gods to come aid me in my plight

Leaves of oak and maple tree I add to my spell tonight

Oak for protection and prosperity, and for courage true

Maple leaves for health and bounty, guard me in all that I do

This green candle spell brings abundance and healing galore

With a little help from the gods Jupiter, Zeus, and Thor.

Close up the spell by saying:

For the good of all, with harm to none

By leaf and thunder, this spell is done!

Let the candle burn until it goes out on its own. You may keep the leaves or return them to nature.

Colors, Candles, Metals & Crystals

Colors

The colors associated with Thursday are green and royal blue. Some magickal texts also list purple, as it is a color associated with royalty, leadership, and wealth. Royal blue is the traditional color associated with Jupiter. Green is a popular shade with magick users, as it represents the earth and nature. Today, green in its many shades is often utilized in prosperity and healing spells.

Now, if you take a look at the many different magickal books that are available today, you will see that just about everybody has their own opinion on which colors are assigned to which day of the week—which is why I listed three of them in this chapter. You should go with the color that seems right to you. Don't panic if the daily colors given here are not the ones that you have been working with. The best magick has personality and is tailor-made to suit your specific needs and tastes. Personalize your witchery! Don't be afraid to try something new or to experiment and have a little fun while working with color magick.

If you'd like to match up your outfit with Thursday's abundant and healing energies, then think of shades in blue and green. (Since we have already gone over purple in Wednesday's chapter, I will focus on our other Jupiter colors this time.) The various magickal shades of blue and green each have their own correlations, and they are just waiting for you to give them a try.

A soft scarf that bleeds from blue to turquoise to green would be a nice choice. Colors that blend from one tone to another invoke a feeling of harmony and well-being. Wear a deep navy suit for leadership and nobility, and a royal blue tie or blouse to correspond with Jupiter's energy and to get you and your hard work noticed!

How about a forest green T-shirt? That deep tone of green can invoke a little mystery, and it represents the element of earth. Feeling adventurous? How about a bright lime green blouse for energy and to ward off jealousy? Or how about slipping on a soft spring green sweater? That shade of green invokes fresh starts, new beginnings, and harmonizes with the burgeoning power of the spring season. Finally, you could try wearing a vibrant St. Patrick's Day green for prosperity and for fertility.

Candles

Candle colors for the day can be any or all of the above-listed shades of blue and green. Go with the color you like the best. If you're more traditional, you may choose to stick with the primary shades of blue and green. If you tend to be a bit more creative, then refer to those colorful suggestions above, and experiment with your candle magick and see how things develop.

If you want to add a bit of aromatherapy to your Thursday candle spells, then try out these bewitching fragrances: honeysuckle-scented candles for prosperity, pine fragrances for healing and abundance, and mint to refresh your spirits and to bring money. If the only mint candles you are able to locate are white, no worries; white is an all-purpose color. Perhaps you could use a Jupiter-colored blue or green candle holder. You know that old saying—adapt, improvise, and overcome! Be a practical Witch and try applying that philosophy to your own personal style of witchery.

An Herbal Candle Spell for Abundance and Health

Let's combine the herbal information with the color and candle information for a Thursday spell. You will need a few specific supplies for this spell, but the plants are common and easy to locate. You may not have to look very far—maybe not any further than your own backyard.

- 2 deep blue votive candles (you can switch these to purple)
- 2 green votive candles
- 4 votive cups
- A lighter or matches
- A sprig of honeysuckle (flower or foliage)
- A few leaves of fresh mint
- A small cluster of fresh pine needles
- A 6 x 6-inch square of green or blue fabric

- A 12-inch piece of ribbon (try a Jupiter color)
to tie the fabric up into a charm bag
- A safe, flat surface on which to set up the spell

Arrange the candles in their holders in a neat circle. Next, lay the foliage on the inside of the candle ring. Take your time and make this look as festive as you can; just make sure to keep the herbal ingredients well away from the flames. Then ground and center yourself, and repeat the following spell three times:

Jupiter's bright colors are in these candles four

Money and abundance they will bring to my door

Add some mint, pine, and honeysuckle to this Witch's spell

I call for health and prosperity, and all will be well.

Now, I want you to imagine yourself surrounded by a bright blue-green halo of light. Envision that this light protects you, encourages healing, promotes abundance, and invites prosperity into your life. Hold this imagery in place for a few moments.

Close the spell with this line:

For the good of all, with harm to none

By color and herb, this spell is done!

Let the candles burn until they go out on their own. When the candles are finished, the herbs will be empowered and ready to go. Tuck the herbal ingredients into the center of the blue or green cloth, and then gather up the edges. Tie the bundle closed with the ribbon. Ta-da! Instant charm bag!

Keep the prosperity charm bag with you, in your pocket or purse, for one week. If you care to re-empower the charm bag, repeat the spell on the following Thursday. Just place the bag in the center of the candle ring and you're good to go.

Metals & Crystals

Tin is linked to the planet Jupiter and the element of air. It has a projective energy and draws good luck and prosperity. Carrying a piece of stamped tin in your pocket is believed to draw money straight to you.

The stones and crystals that are associated with Jupiter and Thursday's energies of abundance and prosperity are the amethyst, the sapphire, and the turquoise.

AMETHYST: Amethyst is a variety of quartz and comes in several shades of violet, from a pink lavender to a deep purple with tones of red. Amethysts attract peace and spirituality. This is the classic birthstone for February. Amethysts correspond to both the planets Neptune and Jupiter. It is also aligned with the element of water. Some texts say that amethysts are connected to the crown chakra and to the fifth element of spirit; if you think about it, that makes sense. If it is a spiritual stone, then why wouldn't Spirit figure into the magickal mix? The amethyst can also enhance precognitive dreams, boost your witchy talents, and will strengthen any intuitive talents you possess. Amethyst is thought to protect you from drunkenness and is a healing stone. Also, it is thought to protect you from the manipulative magick of another practitioner.

The amethyst is also a great stone to wear or carry with you to help alleviate stress. (I have a pair of amethyst-point earrings that I wear specifically for that purpose.) When I take the earrings off at night, I either set them on my windowsill and let the moonlight fall on them or I run them under water to cleanse them of any residual energy. That way, the next time I wear them, the stones are all refreshed, happy, and ready to go. Amethyst is a popular jewelry stone with magick users, and you can't beat that gorgeous royal purple gem for all-around practical magick use.

SAPPHIRE: The traditional birthstone for September. This stone was featured in the Monday chapter as well, but I include it here again, as the sapphire is well-known for prosperity and wealth-increasing magick (which makes sense, as this semiprecious stone is pricey). So, if you happen to own any sapphire jewelry, Thursday would be yet another good day to work magick with it. Magickally, sapphires are protective and enchanting stones. This was the stone thought to be worn by powerful wizards and sorceresses in medieval times. Utilized in spells for both prosperity and healing, these deep blue stones pack a magickal wallop when worked into any positive witchery. Try enchanting your sapphire jewelry with this little charm:

Sapphire Charm

Sapphires, magickal stone of the deepest blue,
Aid and empower all charms and spells that I do.
By the power of your blue sparkle and bright fire,
Aid me in my witchery and grant my desire.

TURQUOISE: Turquoise is an ancient amulet to promote prosperity and to ensure wealth. It increases your intuitive talents and boosts your empathic qualities as well. Turquoise is a symbol of friendship and love, so it makes a great gift for a magickal friend or covenmate. This is a lucky, healing, and money-drawing stone. It also guards against disease and danger. (If the stone suddenly breaks, it's a warning to watch your back.) In addition, turquoise promotes courage. It is also one of the birthstones for the month of December and is associated with the element of earth. Turquoise comes in shades of greenish blue to a clear sky blue. Turquoise is easy to acquire as tumbled stone and affordable when set in silver rings and pendants, or as loose beads with which to make your own magickal jewelry.

I have a turquoise beaded bracelet that I wear when I feel the need to reinforce my personal protection. You know, when you have to be around folks that simply drive you up the wall? No matter how hard you try to be nice to them, they just give off an uncomfortable vibe? Try wearing turquoise next time you have to be around them; it should help.

Have you noticed anything about our stones for today? They are all the same colors as have been discussed in the color magick section: purple, blue, and bluish green. Don't you just love it when things fall neatly into place?

A *Turquoise and Amethyst De-Stressing Spell*

Stress and pressure are a nasty combination. Everybody faces stressful times now and again, even if things are going well at the moment. You know you worked so hard for that promotion or goal, and now that you've attained it, your workload increases—and with it comes new pressures, higher expectations (usually from yourself), and stress.

Yuck! Don't allow yourself to get swept up in the pressure. Stop, ground, and center. Try taking a walk or talking to your family and friends about what's bugging you. If you don't, you could wind up with high blood pressure and a lecture from your doctor about stress and what it can do to you physically. (I received that lecture myself a few years ago. And if you haven't figured it out by now . . . yes, I am a stereotypical Virgo.)

What's a person to do? Well, this Witch took a good look at herself and her life and dropped from her schedule whatever wasn't necessary. Next, I made my kids pitch in around the house more. My husband, bless him, picked up the slack, and I taught myself to eat more healthily, started taking walks and working out, and then I began to meditate on a regular basis. So did a miraculous, stress-free change happen overnight? Nope, I had to work for it. What follows below is the spell I created to help me learn to cope with my stress and worries, and then to let them go.

This spell uses a turquoise or amethyst tumbled stone or piece of jewelry. This Jupiter's day charm will work whether you are programming tumbled stones to keep in your pocket or enchanting jewelry to help keep your stress under control. Hold the stones or jewelry in the palms of your hands.

Take a moment to calm yourself down and to release all of your anxiety and fear. Call on the God and the Goddess to assist you. Now repeat the following spell three times:

> A turquoise will bring wealth and luck, this much is true
> Good fortune and health from a stone of greenish blue
> A purple amethyst for peace and to relieve nasty stress
> Now release all my anxiety and lay my fears to rest
> Peace, serenity, and health are the order of the day
> Help me to relax and let go, and to keep stress at bay.

Close the spell by saying:

> I release my stress and fears, they have no more power
> I close this spell by wind, flame, water, and flower.

Then tuck the crystals into your pocket or slip on the enchanted jewelry. Take time every day just for yourself, and do something that relaxes you—take a long bath, read a silly romantic novel, or rent a good comedy movie. Try working in the yard, planting flowers, or raking leaves into a big pile, then jumping in. You could take a nice stroll around the neighborhood park, or just sit outside in the fresh air and sip some soothing herbal tea for a bit. Relax in the sunshine and soak up this day's magickal healing energy.

POTIONS, PHILTERS & OILS

Abundance and Prosperity Philter

This recipe is designed to increase your cash flow and to bring abundance and prosperity to you in a beneficial way. This is great for adding to sachet or charm bags, or to dress prosperity spell candles with. You could even dab a tiny amount on your business cards, résumé, or a job application. When you use this philter, don't be surprised if you find yourself suddenly being offered more hours at work. This is practical magick; expect practical solutions to manifest. Basically what I am reminding you of is this: nothing is free; you have to work for your success.

- 1 small decorative glass bottle (green or royal blue)
- Base oil, approximately ⅛ cup
- Clean dropper
- 3 drops honeysuckle oil
- 3 drops mint oil
- 1 pinch dried sage or a fresh sage leaf from the garden
- Small turquoise chip
- 6 inches thin green or royal blue satin ribbon
- 1 small metal magickal charm or talisman that you feel coordinates with the prosperity of your choosing
- A label and a pen (to list the ingredients and to decorate and mark the bottle)

Pour the base oil into the bottle, enough to fill it three quarters of the way full. Add the essential oils one at a time. Next, add the crystal and the sage. Close up the bottle with the lid, place your fingers over the lid, and carefully shake up the mixture. Hold the mixture up to the sunlight and allow the light of Thursday's sun to illuminate the philter.

Wipe off the outside of the bottle. Use the label to list the ingredients and the use of this potion. Decorate the bottle by drawing the sigil of Jupiter ($2\!\!\!\downarrow$) or even a currency symbol. If you have other magickal symbols you would like to use for abundance and prosperity, then add those on the label. Attach the label to the glass bottle, and finish up by threading the metal charm onto the ribbon and then tying the green or royal blue ribbon around the neck of the bottle.

As you finish tying on the bow, hold the bottle in your hands and concentrate on the visualization that the aura around your heart is glowing with a brilliant emerald green color. See prosperity arriving in your life in the best possible way. Now send all that energy from your visualization into the philter bottle that you hold in your hands. Take a deep breath, hold it for three counts, and then blow it out slowly. Now, repeat the charm below:

> Potions and philters that are crafted on Jupiter's day
> Will bless me with abundance in many positive ways
> Sweet woodbine and mint now combine their enchanting scents
> While turquoise and the herb sage lend their bewitching strengths
> By Juno, Jupiter, Zeus, and Thor, this spell is spun
> To me success and prosperity will surely come.

Using a bit of Thursday's witchery

As I do will it, then so must it be!

Set aside the philter bottle, and clean up the supplies. Ground and center yourself. Eat a few crackers or do something physical. Make sure to store the philter in a dark, dry place out of the reach of children.

Essential Oils

All of these essential oils are associated with the planet Jupiter:

- Anise
- Cinquefoil
- Clove
- Honeysuckle
- Hyssop
- Nutmeg
- Oakmoss
- Sage

Most of these essential oils are easy to find at a metaphysical, arts and crafts, or home-decorating store. Use any of these essential oils to turn up the volume on the witchery you already practice. Add them to sachets or candles, or use an oil diffuser and let their enchanting aromas fill your home with a successful and prosperous vibe. Be creative, and see what you can come up with. Remember: you are only as successful as you believe yourself to be.

TAROT CARD ASSOCIATIONS

The cards associated with Thursdays all happen to be from the suit of Pentacles. The tarot suit of Pentacles (or Coins, depending on your deck) is associated with the element of earth, prosperity, comfort, and health.

Ten of Pentacles

Ten of Pentacles symbolizes completion and a group of people, typically your friends and family. This is interpreted as a card of security, spiritual riches, and the affectionate emotional support that comes from close friends and a loving family. This card reminds you to be thankful for your happy home—to be wise and look past the unimportant material things and to focus instead on what is vital: home, family, love, and life. Add this card to any spells concerning family issues or keeping a happy home, or where positive emotional support and encouragement are needed (like in the destressing spell).

Nine of Pentacles

Nine of Pentacles stands for material success and emotional well-being. In some decks, the Nine of Pentacles is portrayed as a woman standing contentedly alone in a beautiful garden. The number nine indicates protection, peace, and serenity. Combining the number nine—three times three—with the element of earth makes for a card that symbolizes beauty, creativity, and achievement that has resulted from your earlier efforts and experiences.

In other words, you have worked diligently to get to where you are standing. Relax; enjoy the benefits of your hard work and take the time to cherish these gifts. This tarot card is excellent to use in spells and charms designed for prosperity, abundance, and health, and also to protect what you have worked so hard to gain.

Ace of Pentacles

Ace of Pentacles signifies the undivided strength of the element that is associated with it. Since the element of earth is associated with material things, fertility, and

physical well-being, this is just the tarot card to work with on a Thursday. This is a card of generosity and the beauty of the fruitful earth. The Ace of Pentacles represents new opportunities, security, health, riches, and comfort.

It is a card to use when you feel good about yourself and your past achievements, and when you are looking to add a bit of a financial boost to your life. Are you looking for a better job, a promotion, or are you simply hoping to catch a little overtime? Try working a spell with this card. And in the spirit of the Ace of Pentacles, remember to be generous and giving to others when your prosperity starts to roll in.

Earthy Prosperity Tarot Spell

If possible, work this prosperity spell outdoors. You will be calling on the element of earth and all of its fertile and abundant energies. If weather prohibits you from being outside, then set this up so your work area faces north, because the northern direction is associated with the element of earth.

- A green votive candle
- A votive-cup candle holder
- ½ cup garden soil (you can use potting soil)
- A saucer or small plate to hold the soil
- The following tarot cards: Ace of Pentacles, Nine of Pentacles, and Ten of Pentacles (please note: the suits of Coins and Pentacles are the same thing)
- A lighter or matches
- A safe, flat surface on which to set up the spell

Place the green votive candle inside the cup. Snuggle the votive cup securely down into the soil. Arrange the cards next to the dish that holds the soil and candle. Take a few moments to center yourself. When you feel ready, light the candle, and speak the following spell three times:

Element of earth I call, ground and strengthen me tonight
May the gods now bless this green spell candle that burns so bright
The suit of Pentacles and Coins calls for prosperity
They will help to bring health and abundance quickly to me
Now together may all of these elements combine
And create opportunity for wealth at this time.

Close the spell by saying:

For the good of all, bringing harm to none
By the element of earth, this spell is done!

Allow the candle to burn until it goes out on its own. If necessary, move the candle to a safe location so it can finish burning, such as a shower stall, inside an unlit fireplace, or in the empty kitchen sink. Never leave a burning candle unattended, especially outdoors.

DAILY WITCH CRAFT
healing wreath

Here is another witchy craft from my Book of Shadows for you to give a whirl. You may decorate this wreath with either fresh or dried botanicals; it's up to you. Use whatever magickal healing plants you have growing at home in your garden or go to the arts and crafts store to peruse their selection of dried flowers. Should you decide to use fresh roses and allow them to dry naturally on the wreath, make sure you remove the thorns before you work with them.

Please note that I have the magickal attributes of the suggested floral materials listed for you in the supply section. So choose your herbal materials with intention and get to crafting!

- Fresh or dried sage (a Jupiter herb that encourages long life and wisdom)
- Fresh or dried feverfew (a healing and protective plant)

- Fresh or dried chamomile flowers (a healing herb that purifies and protects your health)
- Fresh or dried roses (roses speed up magickal workings and encourage a loving atmosphere in the home)
- Fresh or dried yarrow flowers (a beautiful and readily available "all purpose" magickal herb)
- Small 8- or 12-inch grapevine wreath
- Glue gun and glue sticks
- 1 floral wire paddle (16 gauge)
- 3 yards decorative green ribbon (green is a Jupiter color and one associated with herb magick, life, and good luck)

Gather small groups of your chosen herbs together and wire them into little bundles. Now lay a bundle on top of the wreath base, and start wrapping the wire around the wreath; go over the stems of the herbs as you do this. After you have the first bundle wired on, twist the wire together and snip off the ends, tucking any remaining wire down into the grapevine. Continue on to your left with the process, overlapping the stems from the first herb bundle with the flowers of the next. Work your way around the wreath until it is completely covered. If necessary, add a touch of hot glue to the herbs to make them stick to the grapevine wherever it is needed. Once you have the entire wreath covered, tie up a decorative bow and secure it with the floral wire, then attach it to the wreath. When you attach the bow, say these lines:

Witchy ribbon of green, now be for me
A charm for a life that's strong and healthy.

Use a twelve-inch length of ribbon for a hanger, if you choose. Once you are finished with the wreath, hold it in both of your hands and charge it full of healing energy. Repeat the charm below three times:

> By Jove! This wreath will radiate a healing light
>
> To ward and protect me and mine both day and night
>
> By the power of herbs, this Thursday Witch craft is spun
>
> Bringing healing energy to all and harm to none.

Now hang up your wreath and enjoy it. Clean up your supplies and straighten up your work area.

CUSTOM-MADE DAILY MAGICK

Well, let's see . . . abundance, prosperity, and good health has been our focus for this day. Now how about a little more information and ideas for working practical magick with one of our fascinating featured deities of the day?

Juno was the Queen of Heaven. As the matriarch of the gods, she guarded over women in every aspect of their lives. Juno was thought to have renewed her virginity every year. Similar to other goddess stories, Juno was a triple goddess—a virgin who belonged to no one; a mother and woman in the prime of her life, sexual and mature; and also a crone, powerful, wise, and sometimes vengeful (as she made her husband's many mistresses' lives either fairly unhappy or short).

There are references to an early all-female triad of goddesses known as the Capitoline Triad. This triad consisted of Juventas, Juno, and Minerva. To the Greeks, they would have been known as Hebe, Hera, and Hecate. Ultimately the triad became Juno, Minerva, and the male Jupiter. Jupiter, another of Thursday's gods, was Juno's consort.

As mentioned earlier, Juno, in her aspect as Juno Moneta, was the patron and protector of the Roman mint. The coins produced at her temples were blessed by Juno and imbued with her powers of abundance and prosperity. In another of her aspects as Juno Augusta, Juno was the goddess of an abundant harvest.

In addition, another of Juno's magickal correspondences is the semiprecious stone malachite. Malachite is a beautiful green-banded stone that was also called the "peacock stone" in Italy. The peacock was a sacred animal of Juno's, and the magickal energies of malachite encourage health and prosperity. So, guess where we are going with all of this information? That's right, a spell for prosperity and abundance.

RITUAL FOR THURSDAY
juno's prosperity elemental ritual

This spell calls for some natural magick supplies. Try working with affordable tumbled malachite stones. As for the wheat stalks, look at the dried flowers and fillers in the arts and crafts shops. Ditto for the feather, or peruse a fly-tying store; you can usually pick up a package of feathers for a few bucks. As to the green seven-day candle, if you look around, you can find green jar candles. I actually found some at the grocery store for a dollar apiece. They were in the ethnic food aisle and were called novena candles. I simply peeled the saint sticker off of it, and *abracadabra!* An instant seven-day candle for my witchery.

As mentioned before, all of these magickal supplies listed below correspond with the goddess Juno in two of her prosperity-drawing aspects, Juno Augusta (the harvest mother) and Juno Moneta (patron of the Roman mint).

- 1 malachite stone (to represent the earth element)
- A few peacock feathers (to represent the element of air)
- 3 small stalks dried wheat
- 1 green seven-day jar candle for prosperity
- 3 drops honeysuckle, peppermint, or clove oil
  (all of these oils encourage prosperity)
- A clean dropper (to add the oil to the candle)
- A long, thin screwdriver (to put holes in the candle)
- A dollar bill or coin
- Matches or a lighter
- A safe, flat surface on which to set up the spell

Carefully and slowly push the screwdriver straight down into the wax. Now pull it straight back up. Add two more holes for the essential oil. Now set the screwdriver aside; using the dropper, squirt a few drops of honeysuckle oil down into those channels that you just created.

Next, hold the green jar candle in your hands and transfer a little of your personal power and desire for prosperity into the candle. Then place the candle on your work area on top of the currency. Arrange the stone, wheat stalks, and feathers to your liking. Make your work area pretty, and enjoy the process. While you are doing so, you may chant the following (the chanting will help you raise some energy too):

By the power of three times three

Bring prosperity now to me!

When you feel that you are ready, light the candle and repeat the following verse three times:

Juno Moneta, Roman goddess of prosperity

Lend your power to this elemental spell that I weave

Juno Augusta, mother of the harvest, hear my plea

These three golden stalks of wheat are a gift to you from me

A peacock feather for air, and a malachite for earth

Lady, bless me with success, abundance, and rebirth

For the good of all, with harm to none

In Juno's name, this spell has begun!

Allow the candle to burn until it goes out on its own. It will probably take five to seven days for the jar candle to burn out. When I burn seven-day candles, I tuck them inside of my large cast-iron cauldron, then I place the spell components around the outside of the jar. That way, the candle can continue to safely burn, and even if it gets knocked over, everything stays contained inside of the fireproof cauldron.

Once the jar candle is finished, pocket the malachite stone and the bill or coin. Keep the money with you, tucked in your wallet or in your pocket. Tie up the feathers somewhere prominent where you will see them every day, like the rearview mirror of your car, your dresser mirror, or a chest of drawers' handle. Every time you see the feather, tell Juno thank you. Take the dried wheat and crumble the pieces apart. Sprinkle the seeds outside as an offering for Juno. Abundance and prosperity will find their way to you soon.

Please note: As I suggested to you in an earlier chapter, if you cannot leave the ritual candle safely burning, then snuff it out when you leave and relight it as soon as you are home. It may take a few days longer, but the magick will still turn out, especially since you are taking the time and energy to tend the ritual candle so carefully. As you relight the candle, say:

> As *this ritual candle relights, so does my magick once more ignite.*

Enjoy your ritual work, and may prosperity come to you in the best possible way!

If you have enjoyed working this final ritual, then take another closer look at the other natural correspondences that were listed in this chapter. What else do you suppose you could create for a little personalized magick? Are you feeling inspired? Flip back to the spell worksheet on page 301 and get busy crafting a spell or charm just for yourself.

Try wearing some honeysuckle-scented perfume to encourage prosperity. Bewitch someone by wearing deep royal blue or brighten up a dreary day by wearing lucky, prosperity-drawing green. Brew up a pot of mint tea to help increase your cash flow. Try adding a pinch of nutmeg or cinnamon to an unscented candle to encourage some fast cash. Bake up a loaf of wheat bread for the family, and celebrate abundance and be thankful for all that you have.

Conjure up a witchy craft and create a philter or two for your magickal needs. Work with the deities and the magickal plants featured in this chapter and experiment. How did the energies of the plants of Jupiter enhance your magick? What did you learn by working with Juno, Jove, or Zeus? The truth is that by adding these new techniques and information into your spellcasting repertoire, you will indeed advance your skills, thereby moving up in the ranks to become a more adept magickal practitioner.

Just by believing in yourself and working toward creating abundance, health, and prosperity, you have already begun to transform your outlook on life. Put your game face on; think positively. Work with Thor for perseverance and courage, and apply those qualities to your own prosperity spells and healing witchery. Break out the tarot cards; take a careful look at those images of the three featured cards in this chapter. How could you incorporate that symbolism into other spells of your own design?

Use your imagination, check Thursday's correspondence list, and see what other bewitching things you can conjure up for prosperity magick all by yourself. Call on the gods and goddess of Thursday and bring some positive change, abundance, health, and prosperity into your life!

Friday

A DAY WITHOUT love
is like a day without sunshine.

Familiar Saying

At-a-Glance Correspondences

PLANETARY INFLUENCE	Venus
PLANETARY SYMBOL	♀
DEITIES	Eros, Aphrodite/Venus, Freya/Frigga
FLOWERS & PLANTS	Rose, feverfew, violet, wild strawberry, apple tree, lady's bedstraw
METAL	Copper
COLORS	Pink, aqua green
CRYSTALS & STONES	Rose quartz, amber, coral, emerald
ESSENTIAL OILS	Apple, freesia, geranium, hyacinth, lilac, rose geranium, vanilla, violet leaf, ylang-ylang
TAROT CARDS	The Lovers, Two of Cups, the Empress
FOODS, HERBS & SPICES	Apple, strawberries, raspberries

DAILY MAGICKAL APPLICATIONS

Friday is named after the Norse goddesses of love, Freya and Frigga. There seems to be some debate as to whom the day is actually named after, so I thought I would share a little information so you can decide for yourself.

In Latin, this day is known as *Dies Veneris*, "Venus's day." In Greek, it's *Hermera Aphrodites*, which translates to the "day of Aphrodite." In Old English, this day is called *Frigedaeg*, or "Freya's day." This day has the Germanic title of *Frije-dagaz*, which, once again, could be Freya's day or Frigga's day.

Both Freya and Frigga were Norse goddesses of love and were the Teutonic equivalent of the Greco-Roman Venus/Aphrodite. However, Freya was one of the Vanir—the gods of fertility who supervised the land and sea—and she was the leader of the Valkyries. Frigga, Odin's wife, was the goddess of the heavens and of married love. She was one of the Aesir—the gods associated with battle, magick, and the sky. Freya and Frigga could be looked upon as different aspects of the same goddess. They both were called on to assist in childbirth and then in the naming of the new baby. Frigga represented the faithful wife and loving mother, while Freya, who really captured the hearts and imagination of the Norse people, was the passionate mistress and lover.

Fridays classically are days for love, fertility, romance, and beauty magick, as well as working for happiness, harmony in the home, and friendship. So let's take a look at some of the mythology involved with this loving, voluptuous, passionate, and luxurious day of the week, and see where it leads us.

DEITIES

Eros

Eros is the Greek god of love and desire. With a power as compelling as that of love and desire, it's really not a shocker that Eros played an important role in Greek myth and legend. Put aside your thoughts of a cute, naked baby boy playfully nailing folks with his bow and arrows. Eros *was* pictured as a winged god, but these would be strong and massive wings, not cute and dainty cherub wings. Eros is, instead, a handsome, sexy, virile man. I suppose in modern terms women would refer to him as a hottie! No one was supposed to be immune, unaffected, or able to defend themselves against his powers of enchantment. This is a compelling and irresistible god.

Eros is married to Psyche, and their story reads a bit like *Beauty and the Beast*, as in the early days of their relationship, Psyche never saw Eros—he only visited her and loved her by night. The story goes that Eros was so beautiful and compelling that he despaired of ever finding a maiden who would love him just for himself. So he set up Psyche in a palatial home in the mountains with invisible servants and made her promise that she would never try to see his face.

Besotted with her kind and mysterious lover, Psyche agreed and lived out her days in luxury. Her feelings grew, and she was content for a while. However, after a time, she grew lonely, as she saw no one during the day and missed her family. She asked for and was allowed to see her two older sisters, and they came to visit her. When her sisters visited, they were so jealous of Psyche's home and lifestyle that they told their impressionable sister that her wonderful lover was probably a monster. Why else would he hide?

After they left, doubt began to creep into Psyche's mind, so Psyche decided to find out for herself. The very next night, after their interlude, while her lover was sleeping, she quietly lit a candle and turned to take a look for herself. What she found was the gorgeous and winged god of erotic love, Eros, in her bed. Startled, her hands began to shake, and she spilled some hot wax onto his shoulder. Eros awakened and was upset that she betrayed him. He scolded her for not trusting him, and Psyche cried that she did love him but that her jealous sisters had tricked her and made her unsure.

After the fight, Eros was devastated and flew away feeling betrayed, leaving Psyche and going to his mother for some comfort. Aphrodite tended his burn and became angry at the mortal girl. (Aphrodite was not the goddess to piss off; for a goddess of love, she had a terrible dark side.) Eventually Psyche stopped crying and decided to prove to the gods that she was worthy of Eros and that she did love him. So she beseeched Aphrodite for her help, and in answer Aphrodite devised some brutally hard tests so that Psyche could attempt to prove her love and her worth. Psyche managed to pass all of them, almost killing herself in the process; however, Eros had been watching the whole time, and he swooped in and saved her at the last moment. They declared their love for one another, Eros presented her to the other gods, and Psyche was made immortal. They flew off into the sunset together. Psyche and Eros were happy together and had a daughter named Volupta (which means "pleasure").

According to some creation myths, Eros was thought to be one of first deities born into this world, along with Gaia (Mother Earth) and Tartarus (the Underworld). Over the centuries, Eros was a popular guy with the artistic set. He not only inspired desire in the common man but in the gods, goddesses, and heroes and heroines as well. Eros was believed to be held within the hearts of all the gods and men alike, so he is a perfect choice for Friday's witchery.

When I first sat down to write this section, I could not decide who I should focus on. After all, all of these goddesses are associated with Friday's theme of love, fertility, beauty, and desire. So, since they all seemed to be clamoring for attention, I decided not to pick and choose, and to just talk about all of them. It seemed like the smartest choice to me; remember your mythology? Freya was the leader of the Valkyries, Frigga is no pushover, and anybody who snubbed Aphrodite/Venus was usually just begging for trouble.

Aphrodite/Venus

Aphrodite was the Greek goddess of love, sexuality, and beauty. To the Romans, she was known as Venus. There is more to Aphrodite than meets the eye; did you know that she was a mother *and* a grandmother? Aphrodite was mother to several children by many different partners. Her most longstanding lover was Ares, the god of war. She produced three children by him. She also had a child with Dionysus and a child with Hermes. She also hooked up with mortals from time to time, and had a child or two with them as well. In some mythologies, she was also the mother of Eros (which is probably how the whole "cute baby" mixup started).

Aphrodite was, by all accounts, a celebrated goddess of her time. Her cult was popular throughout most of the Greek world. Interestingly enough, Aphrodite was not of Greek origin. Her followers came to Greece from Cyprus, where she was known as Kypris, or the Lady of Cyprus. Aphrodite was described in her day as being both an awful and lovely goddess, at whose feet grass sprang up and grew. She is a goddess of the sea and of gardens. The rose, all blue flowers, seashells, dolphins, and pearls are just a few of her many magickal correspondences.

Freya

According to Norse mythology, Freya was a deity of fertility, love, and magick. Considered the most beautiful of the Norse goddesses, she is the patron of agriculture and a goddess of battles, beauty, and sexual love. This is a goddess with depth.

Freya was the consort of Odur, or Od, another Norse deity who was a traveling god. While he was off rambling about, Freya mourned for him, and her tears fell into the sea and turned into golden amber. She rode in a chariot pulled by two huge gray cats, and her golden necklace, Brisengamen, was obtained by sleeping with four gold-working dwarves. She offered the dwarves anything they wanted if they would give her the necklace. What did the dwarves settle on? That each of them would get to spend the night with Freya, of course. Four nights later, the necklace was hers.

Brisengamen symbolized power, beauty, knowledge, and fertility—a gift from each element. Which makes me wonder: four dwarves, four elements, and four gifts, or magickal powers, of the necklace . . .

Freya is also associated with prophecy, rune lore, witchcraft, and magick. The lynx and the domestic cat are sacred to her. She also possessed the shamanistic ability to shapeshift. Legend tells that she could transform herself into a falcon with a magickal cloak made of falcon feathers. Freya is truly a multifaceted goddess. Besides the previous traits, she is, in addition, a goddess of war and death. She is the leader of the Valkyries, claiming half of all of the slain warriors for her great hall. In plant magick,

Freya is associated with the primrose, the rose, and the strawberry. Freya enjoys music and flowers and is very fond of nature spirits, elves, and the faeries.

Frigga

Frigga is called the "All-Mother" as Odin is referred to as the "All-Father." Frigga is married to Odin and is the mother of Hermod and Baldur. She is associated with spinning and the weaving of cloth. Some of her symbols are the distaff and the spindle. Frigga has an entourage of a dozen goddesses, including her sister, Fulla, who serve Frigga as her handmaidens and counselors. While Frigga is associated with childbirth and is a patron of married women, she is also thought of as a strong, wise hearth-and-home type of domestic goddess. It should be pointed out that Frigga is also a goddess of wisdom—because as anyone who runs a home and family will tell you, it takes a lot of effort and wisdom to keep things running happily, capably, and smoothly on the homefront. Frigga is a hearthkeeper and the guardian of the hearth and the kin. She is a mother goddess in the best sense of the word. Frigga is strong and steady, and she quietly boosts what some Witches refer to as sovereignty—that is, your divine sense of self. Frigga is associated with the perennial blooming herb lady's bedstraw.

FRIDAY'S WITCHERY

Love magick is a perennial popular topic. However, there is more to this topic than meets the eye. There are many enchanting layers here for us to explore on this day of the week. What about creating a loving home, or producing a loving and nurturing family? What about keeping your intimate relationships vital and on track? How about promoting happy, healthy, and enduring friendships? See, there is more to be considered than just the "You shall be mine…" type of fictional love spell. Don't forget that many of the deities associated with Fridays are also parents. So, yes, while this is the day to work on romance, sex, and love spells, there is additional magick to be considered here, which makes Fridays a more well-rounded and bigger opportunity for witchery than many folks ever truly realize. The truest, strongest magick always comes from the heart.

Meditation

> AND WHEN LOVE speaks, the
> voice of all the gods makes heaven
> drowsy with the harmony.
>
> *Shakespeare*

Begin this guided meditation by making yourself comfortable. Sit or lie back and relax. Visualize that you are sitting comfortably before a sturdy old fireplace with a warm fire. Around you is a rustic and homey lodge, and you are relaxing and watching people come and go throughout the hall. You are alone but not lonely as you enjoy the sounds of the other folks who are laughing, talking, and drinking in the hall. The fireplace you are sitting in front of is made of stone, and on its wide hearth, off to the side, is a set of fireplace tools and a large woven basket full of additional logs and kindling. The burning logs in the fireplace crackle and pop cheerfully, and you stretch out your toes toward the heat and snuggle deeper into your chair.

As you sit and watch the flames, a sleek gray cat hops up into your lap. The cat pads up your chest and begins to purr and to rub its face along yours. You reach down to give the cat an absent stroke, and it continues to purr lustily and to demand your attention. You shift your focus from the fireplace to the cat and give the smoky cat a face rub. You run a gentle finger under the cat's collar, and it tips its head back; you notice that a small polished amber stone hangs from the cat's collar. How cool. The cat is now purring loudly, and in pleasure, it stretches itself out on your chest and throws one paw out and up your shoulder as if to hug you. With a feline sigh, it closes its bright blue eyes. Amused, you chuckle to yourself, and then you both settle in, and you begin to drift off into a nice nap.

A short time later, you awake with a start and look around. The fire has gone out, and it is dark. You are cold, and the large hall is quiet and appears to be empty. Also, the friendly little cat that you shared a nap with is gone. You decide to get up and get the fire going in the fireplace again. You choose the smaller logs from the basket on the hearth and get to work. A few moments later, you have a nice fire burning away, and the flames are lighting up the area a bit. Tending the fire, you stay kneeling by the hearth and enjoy the light and the scent of the burning wood. As you look around you, you wonder where all the people that you saw earlier could have gone to. Perhaps they are off to dinner, you think to yourself. As you kneel by the stone hearth, a tall woman approaches and joins you at the flames. You look up and say hello in greeting, and in a friendly manner, she sits down in the chair that you just vacated and smiles at you.

You introduce yourself and ask for her name. In turn, she only smiles at you and flips her long blond hair over the shoulders of a soft, fuzzy gray sweater that she wears.

She replies mysteriously that she has many names. Her blue eyes are direct, and you start to wonder if you have met her before.

She stretches out her long, blue-jean-clad legs, and you realize that you won't be getting your chair back anytime soon. So you turn, sit on the hearth, and face her. As she crosses her ankles, you notice that she is wearing soft and elaborate leather boots. They appear to be handmade, and you observe that there are runes worked into the leather. You raise your eyes and look at her a bit more carefully, and you note a large amber pendant that she wears around her neck. Those blue eyes watch you carefully, and you think to yourself that they are the same shape and color as the cat that you shared a nap with earlier. Now you know for sure. "Hello, Freya," you say with a smile.

She nods her head in return and grins at you. "Did you not know me?" she questions you seriously with the lift of one blond eyebrow.

"Well," you confide, "the modern clothes sort of threw me off."

"My dear, you should remember that I am, after all, also a shapeshifter. Would you have been more comfortable if I would have visited you as a falcon or lynx instead of a domestic cat?" she inquires.

You reply no, while thinking to yourself that it would be tough to cuddle a bird of prey, not to mention a wildcat.

"There is more to me than you may realize," Freya states, leaning forward in her chair toward you. "I have many moods, many forms, and my magick is powerful." As if to punctuate her words, the fire blazes to life. You jump as the fire behind you gets larger. She looks at you intently and then explains to you carefully, "Yes, I am a goddess of love and sexuality, but I am also a goddess of war, death, divination, and witchcraft. I can be like a gentle loving pet, playful and full of fun . . . or I can be like a falcon, striking swiftly and without mercy. For any magick that works with love and the romantic feelings of another must be done precisely, with good humor as well as self-discipline." She lets you take that in and then asks, "Are you afraid of all the knowledge I possess, or are you up to my challenge?"

You tell her in your own words that you are up to the challenge that she presents to you and that you are willing to learn.

Listen carefully as Freya tells you about the magick of her special day, Friday. Pay attention to whatever images come to mind and what lessons she shares. When she is finished speaking, thank her for her time.

Freya smiles at you and says in a businesslike manner, "I have many things to attend to. You are welcome to return and to come visit me in my hall whenever you like," she tells you with a little smile.

"Thank you, I'll look forward to it," you say.

Freya starts to stand up and suddenly, in a blink, she is gone. Now perched in the comfortable chair is the blue-eyed gray cat that you took a nap with earlier. You grin at the goddess in her guise as a cat, and she hops down and waltzes over to where you are seated. She bumps against your leg, and you run a hand down the cat's back. In return, she reaches up toward your face, and as you lean over, she gives you a playful pat on the cheek. You smile and say goodbye, and then, with a flip of her tail, she strolls off.

Now, take a few deep, cleansing breaths, and ground and center. Hold the image in your mind of Freya's warm and inviting hall, the stone hearth, and the roaring fire. Know that you may return here on other meditative journeys anytime you choose to visit with the goddess again. Take in a final deep, cleansing breath, and slowly blow it out. Stretch gently and return to awareness.

MAGICKAL PLANTS & FLOWERS

The plants associated with the planetary influence of Venus and Friday's magick of love and desire are the rose, feverfew, violet, lady's bedstraw, and wild strawberry. The tree associated with today is the apple.

Rose

Very few flowers have so many ties and connections to folklore, mythology, and love magick as the rose. The rose (*Rosa* spp.) corresponds to the planet Venus, as you'd expect, and is linked to the element of water. In modern witchery, rose petals are typically added to spells and flower charms to "speed things up." Furthermore, just as in candle magick, the many different colors of the rose may be used for various magickal workings. Here is a nifty bit of floral mythology for you: did you know that it was originally thought that all roses were white?

The story goes that originally all roses were white. One day, the goddess Aphrodite accidentally scratched herself on the thorns of a wild rose, and her blood splattered on the petals. In apology, the rose then turned the petals of the flowers pinkish red. The goddess of love was so moved by the plant's remorse that she adopted the rose as her sacred emblem of love.

This fabulous, enchanting flower is well worth adding to your own various spells and charms. Try out a little flower fascination and see how it works for you. Here is a brief list of the various colors of roses and their magickal meanings:

RED   romantic love

RED AND WHITE   creativity, joy, solidarity

ORANGE   vitality, energy, stamina

CORAL   admiration, charm

PINK   friendship, beauty, elegance

GREEN   good luck, prosperity, fertility

YELLOW   joy, happiness

IVORY   romance and a steadfast, mature love

WHITE   new beginnings, innocence

PURPLE   power, passion

BURGUNDY   desire, ardor

It is also interesting to note that according to some plant folklore, a seven-petaled rose signified the seven days of the week, while a five-petaled rose is a symbol for the Goddess, as the shape and arrangement of the petals resembles a pentagram. In mythology, there are many goddesses with ties to the rose, including Aphrodite, Venus, Freya, Diana, Flora, Juno, Selene, and the Faerie Queen Titania.

Feverfew

The feverfew (*Chrysanthemum parthenium*) is a fabulous magickal flowering herb. It too has the planetary association of Venus and the element of water; however, its magickal energies are thought to be masculine. This is one of my favorite blooming herbs in my gardens. They are so cheerful, spunky, and fresh; plus, they grow and reproduce well, and I enjoy cutting them often for bouquets throughout the gardening season. The feverfew's tiny, daisylike blossoms make terrific fillers in arrangements. Herbalists recommend eating a few of the herb's green leaves to alleviate migraines.

The feverfew plant is a protective one and may be added to charm bags or worked into herbal spells to protect you from accidents, to boost a little cheer in your life, and to help you maintain good health.

Violet

The violet (*Viola odorata*) is also sometimes referred to as sweet violet or the wood violet. The wild violet corresponds to the planet Venus and the element of water. It is often used in magickal potpourri and charm bags to cure distress, encourage a romantic love, and to absorb negativity and manipulations. The violet is sacred to Venus/ Aphrodite, as are most of the true blue flowers. In the language of flowers, the blue violet signifies humility, while a white violet stands for the truth. If you gather violets in the spring and tie them together to form a chain, or necklace, you may wear this to protect yourself from deception and from the faeries' mischievous ways. This information may come in handy, especially on Beltane Eve.

Lady's Bedstraw

This particular variety of perennial is from the sweet woodruff (*Galium*) family. Lady's bedstraw (*Galium verum*) bears clusters of sweet-scented, yellow flowers. Folk names include Frigg's grass, bedstraw, and fragrant bedstraw. This particular flowering herb is sacred to the Norse goddess Frigga. This plant is also associated with the planet Venus and the element of water, and it carries feminine energies. Once, the fresh leaves were added to punches and wines for flavor as well as to fruit. The dried "new-mown hay"–scented leaves were added to potpourri as a fixative, meaning that it helped the other dried plant materials hold their own scents. Also, the dried leaves of the bedstraw herb were used to discourage insects and to perfume linens. In medieval times, this herb was stuffed into pallets (mattresses), as it smelled fresh and discouraged fleas. Because of this and its links to Frigga, the plant is also associated with childbirth. On an interesting note, the rhizomes of the plants in the Gallium family all produce a red dye, while the flowers produce a yellow dye that is actually used to color cheeses. According to florigraphy, the bedstraw symbolizes humility, birth, and new beginnings.

Wild Strawberry

In keeping with our planetary and elemental theme, the strawberry (*Fragaria vesca*) is also associated with the planet Venus and the element of water. The strawberry is considered to possess feminine energies. It is associated with love and good luck and is sacred to the goddess Freya. The foliage and small berries of the wild strawberry may be worked into floral fascinations and charms to encourage fertility and desire. (Which means that those wild strawberry "weeds" that you find in the garden may come in handy for witchery and natural magick.) Allow these plants a small spot where they can grow. I have a small patch that grows under my privacy fence. I leave the dainty berries for the birds and incorporate the foliage into hand-held bouquets, called tussie-mussies, or into various herbal spells and charms. In the language of flowers, the wild strawberry plant symbolizes perfection.

Apple Tree

The apple tree (*Malus* spp.) is a tree of ancient magickal lore and power. The apple is a sacred symbol of the goddesses Venus and Aphrodite and to many magickal cultures, including the Celts, the Norse, and the Druids. The apple is used in magick for love, healing, and inspiration; it is also linked to the Norse goddess Freya. Apple blossoms may be added to spells designed to encourage romance, or they may be scattered around your altar or circle to celebrate Friday and wisdom, love, and fertility.

Having trouble choosing between two lovers? An old apple charm tells you to take two apple seeds from an apple that you have just eaten. Then name the seeds, one for each lover, and stick one seed to each facial cheek. Here is a modern version of the apple seed charm:

> Apple seed, apple seed, I place you here on my cheek
> Show me the love that is true and will be faithful and sweet.

Whichever seed stays on your face longer denotes your true love and a faithful partner.

There are dozens of plant and flower associations for love, the planet Venus, and Fridays. However, I like to keep my witchery practical and write about easy-to-find flowers, trees, and herbs. So what do we do now? Let's take all of this herbal information and whip up a little Friday romance-inducing fertility spell.

The Apples/Strawberries and Roses Fertility Spell

Thinking about increasing your family or perhaps starting one? Call on the goddesses Aphrodite, Freya, or Frigga for a little assistance. These ladies can help you achieve your goal of a successful pregnancy and a safe delivery.

For this spell, you will need two ripe apples, one for you to snack on and the other for your partner. If you do not care for apples, then try strawberries. Strawberries are sacred to Freya, and let's face it—ripe, fresh, deeply red strawberries are a sexy food. (If you choose to go with strawberries, then adjust the spell's opening line accordingly.) You will also need a fresh red rose in a vase to symbolize your love for each other. If you choose, you may add a few rose pink candles to this spell for some atmosphere. How about scattering some fresh rose petals on the sheets? Listen to some music, break out the sexy lingerie, open up a little sparkling apple cider . . . and have a little fun. You know what sets a romantic mood for the two of you, so follow your instincts. For best results, work this fertility spell on a Friday during a waxing moon. You may say this charm together, silently or aloud:

> Symbols of the Goddess, apples/berries and a rose of red
>
> We call for fruitfulness to follow us now to bed
>
> A rose pink candle for love and to increase our fertility
>
> We call on Aphrodite, Freya, and Frigga to hear our plea
>
> Love and pleasure are their rituals, this much is true
>
> Goddesses, bless us with a child, make us parents soon.

Afterwards, allow the candles to go out on their own. Keep the rose in the vase until it starts to fade, then return the faded flower to nature by adding it to a compost pile or the recyclable yard waste. Gather up any rose petals from the sheets and let them dry out, then store them away and save them for other spells. (Goddess knows you have just imbued them with a lot of energy and magick.)

Finally, don't forget while you are working toward this goal to be romantic and have fun, relax, and let nature take its course. Trying to make a baby is sexy. Also, if you are shooting for a particular month in which to have your baby, or if you have been trying for a while with no luck, then consider getting those ovulation tests that let you know when you are ovulating. Then, when you are, go at it like bunnies! Or just do the old classic standby: have sex every other day for a month. (It really does work.) If you are ovulating, that should do the trick. Good luck and blessed be.

COLORS, CANDLES, METALS & CRYSTALS

Colors

The colors associated with Friday and the planetary influence of Venus are pink and aqua green. The color pink is often used to promote friendship and affection, and it can also be worked into children's magick.

In all of its shades, green promotes health and fertility. Aqua green works into Friday's magick nicely, as the elemental association for Friday is water—which makes sense, as Venus/Aphrodite rose from the sea, and this hue of sea green is sacred to her.

If you would enjoy incorporating a little color magick into your wardrobe, try pinks in shades from pale to rosy mauves—a silky shirt in a deep carmine pink, a soft sweater in pastel pink, or how about a floaty, flirty dress in bright pink? Ladies, you could coordinate your ensemble by wearing shades of mauve and rose for cosmetics. Men have the options of a pale pink shirt or tie, or go for that aquamarine blue color. If you aren't comfortable wearing pink, try strawberry red or look at various sea green colors. Use your imagination, and see what you can come up with.

Candles

Candle colors for this romantic day once again will be shades of pink and aqua green. If you'd like to experiment with a little magickal candle aromatherapy, then look to floral- and rose-scented candles. These scents will encourage love and romance and will promote a relaxed atmosphere. Also, see if you can find any pale green, apple-scented candles. The scent of apples is a good one to promote love and healing. It also dispels bad vibes and negativity. The apple has ties to our featured goddesses for the day. If you are petitioning one of these ladies, this should help to gain their attention and their help.

Drawing Love and Romance Spell

This candle spell is designed to draw a little romance and love into your life. Fridays are linked to the planet Venus and to all the love deities, and this is the most opportune day of the week to work your witchery for love and romance. Like always, remember not to target anyone specific here. We want to pull a little romantic fun and excitement into your life, not take away another's free will.

Gather the following supplies:

- 1 pink floral-scented votive
- 1 pale green, apple-scented votive
- 2 votive cups
- A rose and a bud vase or fresh, loose rose petals (match the color of the flower to your magickal intention: see pages 196–197)
- Lighter or matches
- A safe, flat surface on which to set up the spell

Arrange the candles and the flower or flower petals in a way that pleases you. Try scattering the petals in a circle around the outside of the votive cups or setting the flower in a bud vase off to the side. Please note that you can call on either the

Norse goddesses Freya and Frigga or you may petition the Roman Venus or the Greek Aphrodite with this spell—whoever you feel more of a connection to. Light the candles and repeat the following spell three times:

> Roses and candles, symbols of desire and love
>
> Venus/Freya, hear my call, send your help from above
>
> Send to me a lover who is fun, faithful, and true
>
> Guide my magick and assist me in all that I do.

Close the spell by saying:

> For the good of all, with harm to none
>
> By candle and rose, this spell is done!

Let the candles burn until they go out on their own. Keep the rose in the vase until it begins to fade, then crumble apart the petals and allow them to air-dry. If you used loose petals, allow those to dry out as well. After the petals have dried, you may add them to a charm bag and keep it with you to encourage loving vibrations or return them to nature as an offering to the Goddess.

Note: If you decide to reword this spell to suit your own needs, then please be very specific. If you go overboard on the "love me" theme and work for an existing spouse or lover to become more passionate or devoted to you, you could suddenly find yourself with an obsessive partner who never leaves your side. They may become jealous or never allow you any privacy. And no, I am not trying to spook you. Just think of this as a friendly reminder and consider yourself warned—and be very careful what you spell-cast for, especially when it comes to love.

Metals & Crystals

The metal for Friday is copper. Copper has the magickal correspondence of the planet Venus and the element of water. Copper has become an increasingly popular metal these days in magickal jewelry, so take a look around and see what you can find. Copper is a warm and receptive metal. It conducts electricity, which explains why wands made of copper tubing are so popular. It is a lucky metal and one that encourages and draws love into your life.

The crystals and stones linked to Friday and the planetary influence of Venus are the ones that draw love, healing, and power: the emerald and coral. We also have a few other rather obvious crystals to consider for our witchery: the rose quartz to encourage loving vibrations and warm fuzzies, and the amber, which is Freya's special stone. (If you recall, we went over amber's magickal properties in Sunday's chapter too.) Now, while these last two featured stones do not traditionally fall under the planetary influence of Venus, they certainly harmonize with our theme of the day. Both of these stones are fairly easy to obtain and are a great magickal link to the featured Friday goddesses.

EMERALD: The emerald is a green variety of beryl. The best emeralds are brilliant grass green in color and contain an undertone of blue. This is a receptive stone that corresponds to the planet Venus and the element of earth. Its associated metals are copper or silver, which works out beautifully, as copper is also linked to the planet Venus and love magick. Emeralds set in either one of those metals are rumored to be especially powerful. Emeralds are the birthstone for the month of May. They are thought to improve your memory and your clairvoyant talents. When any type of emerald jewelry is worn, it promotes love and happiness, which makes sense when you think about it. As the heart chakra is often depicted as an emerald green color, why wouldn't the emerald gemstone itself boost all those loving energies?

CORAL: Often referred to as "precious coral," this "gemstone" is actually a marine coral, the skeleton of deepwater branching corals called the cnidarians. Being an ocean organism, it's not too hard to figure out why it became associated with the goddesses Aphrodite and Venus. Precious coral comes in a range of colors, from a warm reddish pink to pale pink and deeper reddish tones. Coral has been worked into beads, jewelry, and deity statues for thousands of years. The ancient Romans believed that coral beads protected children from harm and could heal wounds. According to gem folklore, coral earrings were once worn to attract men; I don't see why that bit of information couldn't be used successfully today by any Witches who are looking to bring some romance into their lives. This is a gorgeous stone and one worth owning and working magick with. This gem's classic magickal correspondences are the planet Venus and the element of water.

AMBER: This a healing "stone" that is classically linked to the sun and the element of fire. Amber is especially sacred to Freya, which is why it is getting another nod in Friday's chapter. It promotes beauty and strength, and it is actually a fossilized resin from coniferous trees. Amber is typically warm to the touch and is a powerful natural treasure utilized for almost every magickal purpose. From love and fertility magick, to prosperity, to increasing personal power and protection, amber's got it all covered.

ROSE QUARTZ: This gorgeous pink stone is a type of quartz, and so it carries the classic correspondences of the sun and the moon and the elemental associations of fire and water. Rose quartz is considered to be receptive in its energies, which means that it helps to "draw in" and to attract. Rose quartz may be semitransparent or opaque, and it comes in many shades of pink. It is also used to open up the heart center, and it promotes joy, harmony, and a comfortable romantic relationship. The rose quartz crystal encourages a feeling that is best described as the warm fuzzies. The rose quartz is a perfect gift between two friends, and it also encourages the love of self, which is a wonderful thing, as it's hard to have someone love you if you don't even like yourself. So change your outlook! The rose quartz will boost your aura and make you feel more lovable and attractive. Check out this crystal ritual below and try it for yourself.

Aphrodite's Crystal Beauty Ritual

This ritual calls for an inner beauty—the sort of loveliness that just shines right through, sort of a magickal sparkle. With this thought in mind, Aphrodite can help you learn to love yourself just as you are, curvy and voluptuous or athletic and angular. Take a look at those old statues and paintings of the goddesses sometime. Notice anything different? They have curves! Real people have curves; learn to embrace yours, and don't worry so much about your clothing size. Beautiful, bewitching, and enchanting women (and men, for that matter) come in all different shapes, colors, and sizes. The Aphrodite image that is so popular depicts a woman with rounded thighs and a curved tummy, and she is a knockout. So take a hint from Aphrodite, and be voluptuous, sexy, and proud of who you are!

Start off this Friday-night ritual by taking a relaxing tub bath. Toss a few teaspoons of sea salt into your water for its cleansing properties. If you wish, you may light a few floral-scented candles and sprinkle a few rose petals on the water. After you've indulged in a nice long soak, step out of the tub and dry off. Slip on a robe or comfortable outfit. Gather together a few supplies, and settle down in your favorite magickal space.

The supplies to gather include a rose quartz tumbled stone, coral beads or a stone (an inexpensive coral beaded bracelet would work out great), a pink or aqua green candle, a few seashells (to represent Aphrodite, a sea-born goddess), a white flower in a vase, and a rose or other white garden flower (use whatever is handy).

Arrange the components of this witchery however you would like. Don't be afraid to personalize and set up this ritual however you prefer. Once you have things arranged, light the candles and visualize a rose pink aura sparkling brightly around you, making you smile. It shimmers and radiates warmth and joy. Feels great, doesn't it? Hold this image firmly in your mind for the next few moments. Feel that positive energy hovering an inch or two above your skin. Then repeat the following spell verse three times:

With seashells, candles, a rose quartz, and coral beads

Aphrodite, your assistance I do now seek

A white rose for magick and to boost my Friday-night spell

I now create a rose pink aura, and all will be well

Make my eyes sparkle and bring a glow to my skin
As I deepen the beauty that comes from within.

Slowly, allow the image of the expanded pink aura to fade. See your aura pulling in on itself and returning to normal. Now, close the ritual with this line:

By all the powers of land and sea
As I will it, then so shall it be.

When you are finished with your ritual, allow the candles to burn out in a safe place. Keep the stones, shells, or loose beads with you for one week. If you used a piece of jewelry, then wear it for the same amount of time. Try out that rose pink aura visualization whenever you need a bit of a boost. I think you'll be pleasantly surprised at the positive reaction you will receive.

Have fun with this inner beauty ritual, and may you walk through life as Aphrodite herself did, proudly wearing a magickal glow and with an irresistible inner beauty.

POTIONS, PHILTERS & OILS

Love Potion

Here is a philter recipe that works with three of the featured deities of this chapter. This witchery calls on Aphrodite, Freya, and Frigga; this enchanting trio will really give this philter recipe a boost of enchantment. This philter recipe and spell is more about the emotionality of love and less about the sexual act. Besides adding this to your basic romance spells and rituals, some other suggestions on how to use this love-imbued philter include adding it to candles to increase a positive, loving, and romantic vibe in the home. You may add a drop or two to any sachets or charm bags to bump up their positive, loving energies. Think about it . . . where else could your life use a little love, happiness, and charm?

- 1 small decorative glass bottle (look for a heart shape or go for red or pink glass if you can find it)
- Base oil (almond works well), approximately ⅛ cup
- Clean dropper
- 3 drops rose oil
- 3 drops rose geranium oil
- 1 drop vanilla extract or a vanilla bean
- Small rose quartz chip
- 6 inches each of thin red, pink, and aqua satin ribbon
- 1 small metal heart-shaped charm or talisman that you feel coordinates with love
- A label and a pen (to list the ingredients and to decorate and mark the bottle)

Pour the base oil into the bottle so it is filled three quarters of the way full. Add the essential oils one at a time. Next, add the crystal and the vanilla. Close up the bottle with the lid, place your fingers over the lid, and carefully shake up the mixture. Hold up the mixture to the sunlight and allow the light of Friday's sun to illuminate the philter within.

Wipe off the outside of the bottle. Use the label to list the ingredients and the use of this potion. Decorate the bottle by drawing the sigil of Venus (♀) or hearts. If you have other magickal symbols that you would like to use for love and romance, then add those to the label. Attach the label to the glass bottle and finish up by threading the metal charm onto the ribbon and then tying the three colored ribbons (the red ribbon for Freya, the pink for Frigga, and the aqua ribbon for Aphrodite) around the neck of the bottle.

As you finish tying on the bow, hold the bottle in your hands and concentrate on the visualization that the aura around your heart is glowing with a brilliant rose pink color (similar to the previous Aphrodite crystal ritual directions). Call on these three goddesses silently and ask for their assistance. See love and romance arriving in your life in the best possible way. Do not focus on any one person in particular; let the universe and the goddesses send who they see fit. Now push all that energy from your visualization into the philter bottle that you hold in your hands. Take a deep breath, hold it for three counts, and then blow it out slowly. Now, repeat the charm below:

> Dear Aphrodite, Freya, and Frigga, now gather 'round
> Bless this potion with Venus's energies that today abound
> Because the best day to work love magick is a Friday
> Encourage love and romance in the best possible way
> May this philter enhance my loving witchery
> For the good of all and by the power of three.

Set aside the bottle, and ground and center yourself. Clean up the supplies and eat a few crackers or do something physical. Make sure to store the love and romance philter in a dark, dry place out of the reach of young children.

Essential Oils

Of course, rose is the classic oil for love and Fridays; however, there are a few others that are easy to find and fabulous to work magick with. Some of the more familiar essential and fragrance oils for today include:

- Apple
- Freesia
- Geranium
- Hyacinth
- Lilac
- Rose geranium
- Vanilla
- Violet leaf
- Ylang-ylang

Please note: you may also occasionally run across synthetic violet fragrance oil. Before you go dumping it all over sachet bags with abandon, give it a testing sniff. Many folks find the scent of violets to be overwhelming—same thing goes for rose oil, hyacinth, or lilac. "A little dab will do ya" in this case! I know that for myself, too much rose oil makes me feel a bit nauseous. So take it easy on the oils until you learn how the fragrances make you feel. Essential oils and fragrance oils are potent. It only takes a drop to give off a very strong scent. See which scent you prefer and which is most harmonious with your magick. Any of these scents will nicely boost your loving witchery and add to the overall atmosphere of your area.

TAROT CARD ASSOCIATIONS

The tarot cards related to Friday and the qualities of love, fertility, beauty, and relationships are typically from the suit of Cups, which in some decks may be called Cauldrons. No matter what the title, this water-associated suit symbolizes love, fertility, intuition, dreams, and emotions. All of the following tarot cards link up with Friday's theme quite nicely. Remember that the suit of Cups/Cauldrons tends to focus mainly on family and relationship themes.

The Lovers

The Lovers is one card that even folks who only have a passing acquaintance with a tarot deck know about. The symbolism is fairly obvious. The Lovers card symbolizes an important emotional commitment may be in the future, perhaps a wedding. But what most folks don't realize is that while this card can signify a romantic relationship, it also represents choice.

This means that when this card shows up in a reading, there is a choice to be made. It may be between two individuals, or it could be between two opportunities. This card would be a good prop to add to the apple seed charm that was listed earlier in this chapter. The Lovers is a symbol of options, decisions, romance, sex, and emotional commitments.

Two of Cups

Two of Cups is a card that mainly deals with emotions and relationships. When this card pops up in a reading, it represents an upcoming engagement, a love affair, or a marriage. This card may also signify a close friendship, a mother and child, a good business partnership, or a reconciliation. This card is all about commitment. It shows that there is someone special in your life, someone you trust and to whom you turn for emotional support when the chips are down. This card is a wonderful tool to add to any spells designed to promote friendship, partnership, love, and marriage. It also makes a good prop for "let's kiss and make up" types of magick.

The Empress

The Empress card can represent the Mother aspect of the Goddess. This is a favorable and sensual card. This card represents the power to bring new life into the world. It is the classic motherhood card. It appears in readings when the client has pregnancy in their life (it might be their own or a loved one's pregnancy). The Empress card also celebrates the ability to be sexual and vibrant while also being nurturing, strong, and wise, all at the same time. While many believe it is strictly a card for women, that is not always the case. After all, the Goddess is not a single mother; she has a partner in the God. Don't forget that men can be nurturers and caregivers while also being strong, sexy, and wise too.

Classically, the Empress card depicts a woman in a ripe field of grain or in a natural and fertile environment such as in a forest next to a stream. The woman is surrounded by grains, flowers, and fruits; often she is shown as pregnant to denote her fertility. She has a "Mother Nature" look about her, and this card symbolizes a happy home, comfort, and a loving marriage. It also represents love, sex, fertility, pregnancy, childbirth, and parenthood.

Try adding the Empress card to the fertility spell that was listed earlier in this chapter. If you are already pregnant, set up this card next to a white candle and focus on the symbolism. Meditate on the idea of the Mother aspect of the Goddess, and ask her to protect you and your unborn child throughout the pregnancy. If you would like to work a spell to safeguard your pregnancy and to ensure a safe delivery, try this tarot spell below.

A Tarot Spell for Pregnancy and Childbirth

Frigga is the Norse goddess that is associated with childbirth, motherhood, and the home. She is a powerhouse of maternal energies and gentle wisdom, which makes her the perfect goddess to call on for this type of spell. Gather the following supplies:

- 1 green or white candle with matching holder or a plain seven-day candle
- The Empress and the Two of Cups tarot cards
- Grains (dried barley or stalks of wheat, or a bit of whole wheat flour)
- A cauldron, cup, or small bowl to hold the grains
- An item of sympathy for the baby, like a baby bootie or an ultrasound photo
- 12 inches pink and baby blue satin ribbon to tie around the candle holder

- An item of sympathy for the mother, such as a small lock of her hair or a photo of her or the two of you taken while she's pregnant
- Fresh flowers in a vase (use whatever is in season, in the garden, or affordable)

If your due date is fast approaching, you might want to set up this spell where you can see it every day—try the top of your dresser or on a shelf in the living room. If you prefer, try one of those large seven-day types of candles (you know, the kind that comes in a tall glass jar). That way, you can light and relight the candle as the mood suits you. If you are working this spell for your partner, make sure to get their permission and try working the spell together as a couple about to become a family.

Set up this spell in an arrangement that pleases you. Place the grains or the flour inside of the cauldron to keep the area tidy. Try propping up the tarot cards and photo against the candle, cup, or cauldron. During the pregnancy, I would repeat the spell once a month. As you get into the last week of the pregnancy, I would repeat it every day. (The seven-day candle will come in handy for that.) If you are working this together as a couple, then adjust the words accordingly.

> Frigga I do call, protect and watch over me today
> Bless this child that I carry as it grows stronger each day
> Tokens of fertility are the grains and the flowers
> Candles and cards are symbols of a new mother's power
> Guard us both during the labor and delivery
> Help me to be strong and to have a healthy baby.

Close the spell with this line:

By the Mother Goddess, the moon and sun
By the power of love, this spell is done.

Allow the candle to burn for as long as you wish, just be sure to keep an eye on it. Replace the grains and flowers with fresher ones as needed. Good luck to your family, and best wishes for a safe delivery and a happy, healthy baby!

DAILY WITCH CRAFT
attraction potpourri

Today's witchy craft is a sachet bag with an attraction potpourri recipe. By creating this recipe and by carrying this mixture, you are sending out a message to the universe that says, "Hey, I'm a fabulous and enchanting individual—don't you want to get to know me?" With the idea being that those folks who are intrigued by your sparkle may then be drawn to you of their own will, all you are doing is bumping up the package, so to speak.

- 1 organza favor bag in pink or red
- Fresh red rose petals
- Violet blossoms or leaves
- A crumbled head dried yarrow flowers (yarrow is an all-purpose herb)
- 1 small rose quartz stone for attraction and warmth
- 1 drop rose geranium oil
- 1 cotton ball
- A clean dropper

Stuff the little bag full of the rose petals. Put one drop of the oil on top of the cotton ball and tuck it down inside of the herb mixture. Put the rest of the herbal components on top. Add the rose quartz stone to the mixture, then tie the bag closed, knot it three times, and say the following verse while tying the knots:

> By *the magick power of three times three*
>
> I *enchant this sachet for love and beauty.*

Hold the sachet in the palms of your hands. Lean close and take a whiff of its fragrance. Visualize a bright pink energy radiating from the sachet bag. Now repeat the spell verse:

> *Fresh red rose petals for love and to boost attraction*
>
> *Rose geranium oil to encourage affection*
>
> *Witch's herbs bind the magick and keep it true*
>
> *A rosy quartz will bring warmth and kindness too*
>
> *The strongest magick does indeed come from the heart*
>
> *This spell is sealed by a rhyme and a Witch's art.*

Give the sachet bag a little shake and you are good to go. Keep it with you, in your pocket or purse, for one month. You may then either refresh the charm or return the herbal ingredients to nature and dispose of the cotton ball. When finished with this spell, wash the organza sachet bag out by hand and allow it to air-dry. This way, you may reuse the organza bag another time.

CUSTOM-MADE DAILY MAGICK

Here are a couple of spells for you to experiment with. These spells fit right in with our chapter's theme of love and romance. They feature two of our deities for Friday, Eros and Freya. The first spell works with the Greek god of passion, Eros. This spell is designed to bring a little more drive and passion into your life, and it is easy and simple, with few supplies, so you will be able to set it up and perform it quickly. It will help you get inspired, enthusiastic, and fired up to face your challenges and embrace life.

Eros's *"Passion for Life"* Spell

Gather a white feather (symbol for Eros and his mighty wings), a rosy pink candle, and a coordinating candle holder.

Carve a simple figure of a bow and arrow on the side of the candle. Place the feather off to the side, away from the heat of the candle flame. Picture the winged god Eros in your mind, and meditate on this image for a moment. Now, ask Eros in your own words to inspire you with passion and enthusiasm. Then repeat the following spell three times:

> *Eros, winged Greek god of passion and delight*
> *Aid me in my quest for inspiration tonight*
> *Passion is more than sexual, it conveys ambition too*
> *Help me face my challenges and succeed in all that I do.*

Allow the candle to burn out in a safe place. Close the spell by saying:

> *For the good of all, with harm to none*
> *By flame and feather, this spell is done.*

RITUAL FOR FRIDAY
freya's jewelry-cleansing ritual

Last but not least, here is a Friday ritual that works with the energies of the Norse goddess Freya. Freya was the mistress of cats and a supreme goddess of magick, sexuality,
and enchantment. The idea behind this Friday/Freya's-night spell is to empower and
to protect your magickal jewelry. Since Freya went above and beyond to obtain her sacred necklace Brisengamen, I think she'll work out beautifully for this ritual. (And no,
you don't have to sleep with any gold-smithing dwarves to get it to work, either.)

Most Witches wear special jewelry; usually that's how we identify each other in
public. Who needs a secret handshake? I mean, think about it. How many times have
you spotted a fellow Pagan or Witch by their necklace and commented with a smile, "I
like your necklace"—or my personal favorite, "Nice jewelry"—while you hold up your
own pentagram? Then you stand there grinning at each other.

Anyway, it's easy to forget to recharge those magickal pieces from time to time. Yes,
that goes for me too. I'm not a super Witch, and life happens. We all get busy and distracted, and the next thing you know, you're holding up that piece of favored jewelry
and looking at it with one squinting eye and wondering . . . *When was the last time I
cleansed and recharged my pentagram, or my magickal jewelry, anyway?* Well, here is just the
ritual to fix that.

You may work this Friday-night ritual during any moon phase. If it is a during a
waning moon, then banish and remove all negativity and strengthen your magickal
talismans. If it happens to be a waxing moon phase, then boost the magick of the jewelry and draw protection and happiness to you. After all, the whole point of this Book

of Shadows is to teach you how to work your witchery every single day. Yes, the moon phases are important, but we do not always have the luxury of sitting around and waiting a few weeks for the moon's phase to be where we want it. So learning about and working with the mysteries and energies of the days of the week is the most practical and powerful answer.

Look over the supply list carefully. Feel free to arrange the altar setup however you'd like. In case you haven't noticed, I have been harping on that individualizing and personalizing theme for quite a while now—so have fun, harm none, and be imaginative.

This ritual also employs a bit of feline fascination—in other words, cat magick. Cats have their own special magick, and they are sacred to the goddess Freya. This ritual calls for a small amount of loose cat hair. Now, if you are allergic to cats, don't panic; you can still work this ritual. Simply use a photo of a cat to focus on during the ritual instead.

If you have a pet cat and they enjoy working magick with you, then you can also invite your feline familiar to come and sit by you or stay in your lap while you work this ritual. Now, we all know you can't make a cat do anything. But if you treat them with respect and request their presence, your cat will probably lend you a magickal hand, so to speak.

Gather the following supplies:

- Your jewelry to be enchanted
- A few strands of loose cat hair—check the couch or their cat brush. Let's be absolutely clear on this ingredient: do not pull hair from a live cat. If you gently pet any cat, a few stray hairs are bound to shed off of their coat. You'll only need a few, and those loose hairs will work out fine. If you

work with shed hair, then place the cat hair under the candles and within the candle holders. Alternatively, you may use a picture of a cat.

- Amber-scented incense, cone or stick, for the element of air
- An incense holder
- A small bowl of water
- A small dish of salt to represent earth
- A pale green votive or taper-style candle for Friday and Venus's planetary energy
- One gold votive or taper-style candle for Freya
- 2 coordinating candle holders
- A small, clean hand towel
- Lighter or matches
- A safe, flat surface on which to set up the ritual

Place the jewelry on the work area. Tuck the shed cat hair under the candles, inside of the holders, or set the picture of the cat in a prominent place. Next, light the candles, then the incense, and then ground and center yourself. Take a few deep breaths, and let go of any stress or worries you are carrying around. Enjoy the flicker of the flames and the fragrance of the incense. If applicable, invite your cat to join you. Their presence in the work area is sufficient; they should not be on top of the altar. (For safety, always keep a curious kitty away from the burning candles and the incense.)

Cast a circle big enough to encompass your working area, including you and your cat. Start in the east. Point your index finger to the floor and visualize a blue circle of light forming around you. Now turn clockwise to the right. As you turn slowly around in a complete circle, say:

As above, now so below; the elemental powers spin and my circle holds.

Move to your altar. To begin, you will invite Freya to assist you with your witchery tonight. Say:

Lady Freya, Norse goddess of magick, enchant this jewelry of mine.

Pass the jewelry between the two candle flames. (Be careful not to burn your fingers.) Now say:

By the element of fire, its power will continue to shine.

Next, hold the jewelry up so it swings back and forth through the smoke of the incense. Continue with:

By the element of air, I remove all negativity.

Sprinkle a bit of water on the jewelry, and state:

By the element of water, I cleanse this magickal jewelry.

Dust the jewelry with a bit of salt, and say:

By the element of earth, I recharge the metal and freshen the charm.

Finally, wipe the piece of jewelry clean of water and salt with the towel, and slip the item back on. Then speak:

By the element of Spirit, may I wear it proudly and cause no harm.

Follow these steps and continue working on all your jewelry, one piece at a time. As you finish with them, place the items carefully to the side of the candles. When you have completed this and have blessed every piece, close up the ritual by repeating these lines:

> Now I seal this witchery right up with the sound of a rhyme
>
> I'll work magick with these jewels wisely, in all places and times
>
> Lady Freya, I thank you for your attention, time, and care
>
> I close this ritual up by earth, water, fire, and air.

Open the circle:

> This circle is open but unbroken
>
> Merry meet, merry part, and merry meet again!

Thank your cat for their assistance. Give them a kitty treat or some fresh catnip from your garden. Allow the incense to burn until it goes out on its own. You may snuff and then save the candles to reuse at a later time, if you wish. Tuck away your jewelry in your jewelry box or put it all back on. I would recommend recharging your magickal jewelry pieces once a month, no matter what the phase of the moon is.

Something else to consider if you really want to crank up the intensity of this ritual would be to work it on Friday the thirteenth. Since thirteen was a sacred number to Freya and Fridays are named after her, you can't get much better than that.

Fridays are days of loving enchantments and passionate emotions. Take a good look at this chapter, peruse that spell worksheet on page 301, and adapt or create a few spells of your own. See how many ways you could add a little loving enchantment into your life and the lives of your loved ones. If you wish to explore the topic of love and romance witchery even further, then check out my book *How to Enchant a Man: Spells to Bewitch, Bedazzle & Beguile*. If cat magick has tickled your fancy, then for further study read my book *The Enchanted Cat: Feline Fascinations, Spells & Magick*.

In the meantime, try sharing red berries with your partner some enchanted evening. Work that meditation, and see what other mysteries Freya has to teach you. Wear a Venus planetary color and call on the Goddess for a little inner sparkle. Burn some floral incense, light up some rosy candles, and set a romantic mood. Try wearing a little copper jewelry, and see how it affects you and your Friday magick. Get those potpourri and philter recipes going, and see what you can conjure up.

Advancing your magickal skills takes drive, ambition, and passion. Work with Eros to discover just how much enthusiasm, inspiration, and drive he can bring into your days, for the imagination is a place where dreams flourish and ideas come to fruition.

Call on these fertile and romantic powers, and create your own unique spells and charms. Just think of all the magickal information that you can now add to your repertoire of witchery. Lastly, remember this: when you combine imagination and a loving heart with magick, you'll succeed every time.

Saturday

How pleasant is Saturday night,
when I've tried all week to be good.

Nancy Sproat

At-a-Glance Correspondences

PLANETARY INFLUENCE	Saturn
PLANETARY SYMBOL	♄
DEITIES	Saturn, Hecate
FLOWERS & PLANTS	Pansy, morning glory, mullein, cypress tree, mimosa
METAL	Lead
COLORS	Black, deep purple
CRYSTALS & STONES	Obsidian/apache tear, hematite, jet, black tourmaline
ESSENTIAL OILS	Cypress, mimosa, myrrh, patchouli
TAROT CARDS	Temperance, Knight of Swords, Two of Swords
FOODS, HERBS & SPICES	Pomegranate, beets, thyme

DAILY MAGICKAL APPLICATIONS

Saturday, our final featured day of the week, gets its name from the Latin *Dies Saturni*, or "Saturn's day." In Old English, it was *Saeturnesdaeg*. The Middle English version was *Saterday*. Saturn, a Roman god of agriculture, was believed to have ruled the earth during an age of contentment and virtue. Saturn was a god who symbolized the passage of time and karma. He was not a harsh, judgmental god, either; he was a sower and a harvester. Interestingly enough, there is no Norse god associated with this day. It has remained under the province of Saturn. But if you think about what Saturn stood for, it does make a lot of sense.

Saturdays are traditionally days to work on protection, remove obstacles, bind troublesome or dangerous individuals, and banish negativity. Saturdays are like a magickal "let's clean house" day. Any magickal messes left lying around that need to be addressed, or any problems that need to be cleared up, are best dealt with on the day devoted to Saturn.

DEITIES

Saturn

An ancient Roman god also known as Father Time, Saturn was called the ruler of the Golden Age and the Father of the Gods. Saturn was considered the "great lesson giver," as he required people to learn their lessons through karma. Saturn was also a god of agriculture and fertility, and he was married to a fertility goddess named Ops.

There is a Roman festival named after him called the Saturnalia, which began on December 17 and ran until December 23. What was Saturnalia like? It was probably very similar to the rowdy and fun Mardi Gras celebrations of today. This seven-day midwinter festival was a time of gift-giving, feasts, and partying. Traditional gifts on Saturnalia were candles, clay figurines of the gods, and silver. Decorations included wreaths and fresh garlands hung above the doorways. With an "eat, drink, and make merry" type of attitude in place, the wine flowed freely, and the slaves were given the holiday off. Schools closed, and the military was given leave.

The god Saturn was described as a man with a half-bared chest, holding a sickle and a few ears of corn. This image of Saturn eventually evolved into our Father Time, a popular image at New Year's Eve. The sickle became the scythe, and the hourglass symbolized the passing of time and Saturn's control over it. Saturn is not a frightening god—he is a teacher, a spiritual influence that grants tranquility and calmness in your later years. Saturn is the guardian of time.

Hecate

Hecate was the daughter of Perses and one of the original Titans. Even after Zeus defeated the Titans, he kept Hecate in power to assist the mortals. Zeus honored Hecate greatly by granting her a share of power over the earth, the sky, and the sea.

Mortals who were favored by Hecate received great blessings, as she could increase the size of their herds or help the fishermen who prayed to her haul in huge catches of fish. Originally considered a generous and compassionate ancient fertility goddess, in later myths Hecate became associated with a darker and more frightening magick. She developed into the patron of sorcerers and became associated with the underworld, dark mysteries, crossroads, and graveyards. Hecate became known as the queen of the Witches and the guardian of the crossroads.

Hecate was frequently pictured as triple-faced deity. There are a few variations on her name as well—Hecate Trivia or Hekate. She is often part of another trio of Greco-Roman goddesses: Persephone the Maiden, Demeter the Mother, and Hecate as the Crone.

Hecate was thought to be all-seeing and wise. When Demeter searched everywhere for her daughter Persephone, who had been snatched by Hades into the underworld to be his bride, it was Hecate who finally told Demeter where she was.

Today, Hecate is a powerful and protective deity for Witches. If you feel the need to defend yourself, your property, or your family, Hecate is the one to call on. Associations for Hecate include three-way crossroads, black dogs, snakes, owls, ravens and crows, bats, and toads, who are a symbol of conception.

For herbal and plant correspondences, try the blooming cyclamen, dandelion, lavender, mugwort, mint, and poppy. Trees that are associated with Hecate and her magick are the yew, cypress, hazel, and willow. Festivals for Hecate include August 13 and November 16, called the "The Night of Hecate" in Greece, which began at sundown. Finally, there is Hecate's Day in Rome, celebrated on December 31.

SATURDAY'S WITCHERY

Saturday is a day filled with opportunities to clean up and clear out. So if you are wondering why I assigned Hecate to Saturday, take another look at what she symbolizes and the magick that is associated with her. That should answer your question.

Hecate was the oldest form of the Greek Triple Goddess, as she presided over heaven, the underworld, and earth. Crossroads where three roads met were especially sacred to Hecate, earning her the title of Hekate of the Three Ways. It's interesting to note that even after the worship of other goddesses waned, ancient people still worshiped Hecate as the queen of the underworld and the guardian of the three-way crossroad. It was also believed that if you left her an offering of food there, she would grant you her favors. As Hecate Trivia, her triple images were often displayed at these crossroads, where she was petitioned on the full moon for positive magick and on the dark of the moon for cursing and dark magick.

While this last bit of information sounds a little ominous, keep in mind that Hecate/Hekate was known by many titles and is a shapeshifter. Her appearance could and did change often. As a dark moon goddess, her faces are many. To some she may appear as a old crone, hunched over a smoking cauldron and draped in a midnight cape. To others she may appear as a dark, beautiful, mysterious, and mature woman wearing a shimmering crown. To some she may be perceived as a maiden priestess. She was called the "most lovely one," the Great Goddess of Nature, and the Queen of the World of Spirits. This dark goddess knows her way around the earth and the underworld. All the powers of nature, life, and death are at her command.

The following meditation is a favorite of mine. I felt Hecate guide me along when I penned this for her. I originally wrote a shorter version of this for an almanac article many years ago. It comes straight from my own personal Book of Shadows and is what I like to call an oldie but goodie. Enjoy the meditation, and have a good journey.

Meditation

THE EARTH BEGAN to bellow, trees to
dance, and howling dogs in glimmering
light advance, ere Hekate came.

Virgil

To begin this guided meditation, picture yourself walking safely along a dark, graveled path on a quiet, clear autumn night. It is late, and as you look to the east, you see a waning moon rising slowly over the tree line. The sounds of the night are quiet and calm, and you can hear the crickets singing off in the distance while the mournful hoot of an owl drifts to you. You walk confidently forward, enjoying your solitude and the companionable sound of the crunch of gravel beneath your feet. Your breath makes little puffs of white steam in the chill evening air.

Up ahead, you can see a flickering light. It is a torch mounted to the post marking the crossroads, and as you make your way closer, you can make out small offerings of food left neatly at the base of the signpost. Others have been here to honor Hecate before you. There is a small basket of apples, a plaque depicting the triple Hecate, and a few loaves of bread. Someone has left what appears to be a small jar of honey. Your hands tighten on the small wrapped bundle of homemade bread that you carry. It may be a humble offering, but sometimes simple is best. As you approach the crossroads, a breeze picks up, and a swirl of autumn leaves rushes through the crossroads. You stop for a moment to take in the captivating scene and approach the torchlit area as quietly as possible and with a calm reverence.

You prepare to leave your gift and offer up a quiet prayer to Hecate. While you are very aware of your surroundings and perfectly comfortable alone this night, there is something in the air that makes you stay on guard. You turn your head this way and that, trying to account for the sense that something is happening. Suddenly, the sound of howling dogs shatters the peaceful evening. The breeze that sent leaves playfully dancing has now whipped up into a much stronger force. A rush of dramatically colder air swirls past you, accompanied by a whirlwind of rustling leaves. Birds awaken and begin singing in the middle of the night; it is a beautiful but eerie song. As you push your hair out of your stinging eyes and look around you, a rumbling noise is growing in its intensity. You feel the earth tremble beneath your feet, and you instinctively make a grab for the signpost as you try to keep yourself upright.

As quickly as it began, the maelstrom fades, and the night falls to silence once more. Shaken, you right yourself and realize that you have dropped your offering. Concerned, you hunker down to pick up the little cloth-wrapped bundle and carefully brush a few dead leaves from the wrapping. As you look around, you realize that the other offerings once arranged so neatly are now in disarray. Without a thought, you immediately begin to straighten them back out. You lean the plaque against the signpost and return the apples quickly to their basket. A trio of old-fashioned keys catches your eye. Intrigued, you pick them up and admire their shapes and textures. Carefully, you place the keys on top of the little jar of honey. Pleased with the results, you look around for any missed items and prepare to rise to your feet.

A prickling at the base of your neck is the first indication that you are no longer alone. As you turn slowly to look behind you, a large black dog comes barreling out of the darkness and is running straight at you. There is no time to be afraid. Your eyes widen, and the next thing you know, the dog has knocked you flat on your back and is affectionately greeting you. Your initial shriek of alarm gives way to helpless laughter as you vainly attempt to get the dog off your chest so you can sit up. After a few moments of laughing struggle, you manage to collar the dog and sit upright again.

"Where did you come from?" you ask your new canine friend. As an answer, the large dog barks once and whips his tail back and forth. The dog barks again at you in a friendly way and sniffs you over. You sling an arm around your new friend and wonder who the animal belongs to. As you give the dog's ears a good scratch, he suddenly goes on alert and sits rigidly still, seeming to be at attention. You look up to see what has captured the interest of the dog and notice that a woman is silently approaching you. Her sandaled feet are noiseless on the gravel path, and she is draped from head to ankle in a richly textured, black hooded cape.

As she approaches, an owl swoops down from the tree line and lands gracefully on the top of the signpost as a sentinel. It blinks its wide eyes at you and ruffles its feathers. Your heart is hammering in your chest as you quickly rise to your feet to greet the lady. You bow your head and murmur a greeting. As she walks into the flickering light cast by the torch, you look upon her face to discover that she is a stately middle-aged woman wearing a glistening silver crown. The next moment, she appears as a young woman, dark and beautiful, then an elderly woman with a mass of wrinkles and a shock of white, wild hair. Back and forth, her image shifts and flows from one into another. The one thing that is constant is her eyes; they are ageless: a deep jet black, sparkling, and with a kindness and wisdom that radiates outwards. No matter which face she shows you, her eyes and the expression in them remain the same. Her hands raise to her hood, and she pushes it back so you can fully look upon her. Pay attention to how Hecate appears to you.

"Greetings," she says softly, in a voice that rustles like dry leaves. "I thank you for caring for my sacred place." She nods toward the items that you have just straightened out. You smile, and she looks at you carefully. "You have no fear of me." This is a statement, and it pleases her. She continues by saying, "Many who are unprepared for my mysteries are afraid. They believe that I am the one who brings death. But they are mistaken, for I do not. I am the midwife who assists you into this world and the wise one who escorts you into the next."

Hecate holds out her hand, and the three old metal keys that you were admiring appear in her palm. She silently hands them to you as her hair whips about in the cold wind. Honored, you silently close your fist around them.

"I leave you with three gifts, my child," she tells you quietly. "Knowledge, intuition, and magick. Hold these close to your heart, and if you ever have need of me, know that I will be there."

You clasp the keys to your chest, and a curious warmth emanates from the keys. Slowly they dissolve, and now the warmth is coming from inside your own body. You bow your head and whisper your thanks. Hecate holds up a hand, and the owl silently leaps from the signpost and flies over to circle over the goddess's head. With a single call, the owl swoops off and into the darkness. Hecate then pulls up her hood and smiles at you one last time. As she turns to leave, the dog leaps to her side and follows her down the path. A mist rising from the ground seems to swallow them up as they disappear from your view.

Look around you now, and focus on your image of the sacred crossroads. Keep this visualization in place; should you ever wish to return here, it will be waiting for you. Feel the warmth of Hecate's gifts of knowledge, intuition, and magick burning bright within yourself. Then take a deep breath, ground and center, and begin your journey home. Come to awareness, and stretch out. Now go and eat a light snack, and afterwards, take a brisk walk. Be sure that you are reconnected to the earth plane and are well grounded.

MAGICKAL PLANTS & FLOWERS

It should be noted that many of the plants that are classically associated with Saturn, and interestingly enough, the goddess Hecate, are indeed toxic—such as aconite (also known as wolfsbane or monkshood), deadly nightshade (*Atropa belladonna*), hellebore, hemlock, and yew. For more specific magickal information and folklore on these gothic and poisonous plants, please refer to my book *Garden Witch's Herbal*.

Some of the more common herbs associated with the planetary influence of Saturn are the pansy, morning glory, and mullein. The trees associated with Saturday and the planet Saturn are the mimosa and the cypress tree. The majority of the featured herbs, flowers, and trees for this chapter are easy to procure and are safe to work your spellcraft with.

Pansy

The pansy, or viola (*Viola tricolor*), is a common garden flower with a lot of magickal *oomph* behind it. Available in myriad colors, it is a happy, unassuming, protective flower that many magickal practitioners grow in their gardens but never put to work. Besides their qualities of healing a broken heart, they also speak of happy thoughts. The pansy has many folk names, including heartsease, Johnny jump-up, and love-in-idleness.

If you choose to work Saturday spells and protective charms with the pansy, then look for the dark purple and black ones. The deeper the color of the pansy, the more protective energy it will produce. (All colors of the pansy will work, but tap into a bit of color magick while you are at it and crank up the volume on your witchery!) There are black pansies that are readily available for you to work into your flower fascinations as well—look for the variety called 'Black Magic' or the 'Trick or Treat' varieties in the fall months.

I confess that I plant those witchy pansies every year; it's a readily available black flower that I love adding to my garden. This year, try it for yourself. Plant some of those deep, jewel-toned pansies in a container or add them to your semi-shady borders for a little mystery and drama in the magickal garden.

The classic magickal associations of the pansy are Saturn and the element of water. The pansy's definitions in florigraphy are many; for our cheerful friend the pansy, it announces "happy, kind, and loving thoughts."

You may also apply classic color magick correspondences to the many varieties and bewitching colors of the pansy: red for protecting your love and for passion; pink for children's magick and for friendship; white and purple mixtures for spirituality; baby blue for peace and tranquility; orange to increase energy and vitality; yellow for knowledge and sunshine. Lastly, don't forget to work with the deep purple and black pansies for banishing, bindings, stripping away a psychic vampire's power, and of course to remove negative magick or to break a spell.

Garden Witch Tip

PANSIES WILL PERFORM their best in the spring and fall months. They dislike hot weather. You can get pansies to winter over if they are planted in the ground—just mulch them well with fallen leaves in the late autumn, when temperatures start to dip toward the freezing point. Keep them covered up all winter and then, at the spring equinox, uncover them. They will bloom for you again even more heavily.

Morning Glory

The morning glory (*Ipomoea* spp.) is a favorite cottage-style plant of mine. These annual climbing vines can grow over fifteen feet in height in just one season. The deep-blue blooms open in September, and the vines, foliage, and flowers may be worked into protection spells and bindings. There are several varieties of morning glories available to garden Witches today. One of my favorites is a variety called 'Grandpa Otts'. This morning glory is dark purple with star-shaped markings on the flowers. It is very dramatic and witchy.

If you choose to work with morning glory vines for a binding, snip off a small section of the vine and wrap it around your item of sympathy. If this is a troublesome person, then you could wrap the vine around a photo or a sample of their handwriting. Or take an old, clean glass jar and put the item of sympathy inside, then stuff the jar full of morning glory leaves and vines. Bury or dispose of the jar off of your property.

In *Cunningham's Encyclopedia of Magical Herbs*, he suggests that "the roots of the morning glory plant may be used as a substitute for High John the Conqueror root."

Finally, the magickal associations for this blooming vine are the planet Saturn and the element of water. According to florigraphy, the morning glory conveys the message of being "sustained by your affections."

Mullein

Mullein (*Verbascum*) is a wildflower that grows in dry, rocky, disturbed ground. Folk names for mullein include graveyard dirt and hag's tapers. The latter name started because in olden times, the flower stalks were soaked in tallow and then set aflame to be used as long-lasting torches. The mullein is a biennial that produces large stalks of yellow flowers up to eight feet in height. The flower stalks bloom from the bottom up, and the large leaves are soft and fuzzy (sort of a gigantic version of lamb's ears). The leaves are so huge that the early American settlers used the leaves for diapers for their little ones!

I grew mullein in my sunny frontyard gardens once. As it is a biennial, the first year it sat there looking charming with those massive silver leaves. The second year, it grew into a monstrous plant. I'm not exaggerating, either—that plant literally stopped traffic. The blooming flower stalks were over seven feet tall. It got to be where folks would roll down their car windows and shout out, with a laugh, "What the hell is that plant?" My husband threatened to put a sign in the yard so people would stop asking. It went to seed shortly after the flowers faded, and I saved a few seeds and planted them in the back gardens.

In magickal herbalism, mullein leaves are thought to keep away all negative intentions and evil. Carrying a leaf was supposed to protect its bearer from attack and from harm. Finally, dried, crushed mullein leaves may be used as a substitute for real graveyard dirt, should you ever find yourself in need of some. In the language of flowers, the mullein stands for a "good-natured individual." The magickal correspondences include the planet Saturn and the element of fire. Mullein is classified as possessing feminine energies.

Mimosa

Also called silver wattle, the mimosa (*Acacia dealbata*) is a tree that can reach up to thirty feet in height and is indigenous to tropical climates. The acacia is native to Africa, Australia, parts of Asia, and the Mediterranean. It does grow beautifully in the United States in warm climates such as California. Its magickal uses are purification and protection, and its fluffy, fragrant flowers are typically worked into love spells. Having a mimosa tree growing on your property is thought to protect the entire household from hexes and curses.

The flowers of the mimosa are a golden yellow and are described as bearing the fragrance of violets. The evergreen foliage of the mimosa is silvery green, divided, and feathery. The best way I can think to describe the leaves is that they look like super-fine fern fronds. The planetary association is Saturn, and the elemental correspondence is water. In the language of flowers, the mimosa blossom symbolizes "a sensitive soul."

Cypress

The cypress tree (*Cupressus sempervirens*) is also known as Italian cypress. This tree is a symbol for immortality and eternity, and it has the startling folk name of "the tree of death." This may be because of its link to Hecate and darker magick, or it may simply be due to the fact that it is a tree often found in European graveyards and was once a popular wood with the Egyptians for building coffins. Some varieties of this grand evergreen may grow over 100 feet in height. The cypress has grayish-brown bark and small green foliage (needles). There is also a native cypress to the southwestern United States called the Arizona cypress. This tree has more of a silvery-blue color to its foliage. It is utilized to help stop erosion and is treasured for its ability to adapt to harsh climates.

Cypress oil is a popular ingredient in colognes and soaps, as its scent is bracing and clean. Carrying a piece of cypress wood is thought to bring you a long life, and when the tree is planted near the home, it bestows blessings and protection on the house's inhabitants. Cypress may be used to construct a wand for healing purposes or be used when working with the goddess Hecate. In the language of flowers, the cypress carries the definition of "mourning." It is classified as a feminine plant. Magickal associations are the planet Saturn and the element of earth.

Why not combine some of the plant folklore and magickal herbal information from this chapter into a protective spell with ingredients that you can probably find in your own gardens?

Garden Witch Protection Spell

This Saturday witchery is designed to stop bad feelings and harsh words between two friends. It's tough when a person that you consider your friend turns against you for whatever reason. Perhaps you quarreled or you have simply grown apart. In these situations, however, now that the feud is on, your defenses are low. Emotions can be raw, and feelings may be hurt very easily on both sides. Why? Probably because you know each other well enough to know exactly which buttons to push. If you feel that you've hit your limit on what you can handle, then try this protection spell designed to end the fight and let the both of you heal and move forward in a positive way.

Gather the following supplies:

- A single stem of blooming snapdragons (if you recall from Tuesday's chapter, snapdragons break manipulative energies and are very protective magickal flowers)
- A few dark purple pansies—a bloom or two will suffice
- A black satin ribbon
- A 6 x 6-inch square of cotton or silk dark purple or black fabric (it's best if the fabric is natural)

Take a few of the snapdragon blooms and a pansy flower, and place them in the center of the cloth square. Repeat the spell below three times, and on the final saying, gather up the sides of the bag and tie it closed with the black ribbon.

Snapdragons, snap back at hostility

End the quarrel between my friend and me

The bewitching colors of purple and black

Remove hurt and keep negativity back

Pansies are a sure cure for the brokenhearted

Let us both move on and our relief get started!

Knot the bag three times. Close the spell by saying:

For the good of all, with harm to none

By Saturn's energies, this spell is done.

You may keep the charm bag on your person for as long as you need to. Allow yourself some time to mend. It won't be instantaneous, but you can reinforce this spell every Saturday as needed. Perform in a waning moon phase to push away the hurt and in a waxing moon phase to pull healing toward yourself.

When you feel that you don't need the herbal charm bag anymore, open it up and give the floral components back to nature. You now have two options with the fabric square and the ribbon. You may wash them by hand, allow them to air-dry, and save them for another use. Or you can dispose of them in a garbage can well away from where you live and work.

Colors, Candles, Metals & Crystals

Colors

The colors linked with Saturn and Saturday's protective magick are black and dark purple. Yes, I agree that purple has shown up all over the daily color correspondences, perhaps because it is a very popular color with magick users. There is just something mystical about it. However, for today's spells and color magick, we need the deepest, darkest purple that we can find.

Black is the classic Witch's color. This midnight hue is a traditional color to work with and to wear on a Saturday or anytime you want to appear in control and confident. Whether you go trendy, dramatic, and gothic or more subdued, such as wearing a classic tailored black jacket and slacks, black is a seductive, attention-getting color for clothes.

Now, typically magick users adore all colors, but we tend to save our all-black ensembles for special occasions. Honestly, doesn't everybody? No matter your religious preference, almost every woman owns a "little black dress"—something she saves for when she really wants to turn a few heads or make a confident statement.

Candles

Black is also the traditional candle color for protection magick. There is something extra intriguing and witchy about black candles. Sometimes these may be hard to locate throughout the year. Your best bet is to watch for black candles during the fall months (especially around Halloween) and stock up on them.

If you check out a few specialty or trendy candle shops at the mall, you will be able to find black jar candles and votives. It always makes me smile to see a classy jar candle labeled something like "Midsummer's Magic" or "Midnight Spice." Typically these are patchouli scented, which is perfect to use in candle magick, as patchouli is associated with Saturn and protection. Work with either of these dramatic and dark-featured colors for Saturday candle spells designed to protect, neutralize gossip, and deflect harm.

A Black Candle Uncrossing Spell to Deflect Negativity

Have you had one ghastly week at work? Is bad luck plaguing you, or does everything seem to be going wrong? Maybe you simply feel that you are surrounded by everyone else's psychic garbage. Before you start to panic, stop and consider your options. Here is a candle spell to break up those bad vibes and to deflect the negativity that seems to be surrounding you. Technically, this would be referred to as an uncrossing. A crossed condition is somewhat like a low-scale hex, but a crossed situation typically happens from a combination of events and influences. Uncrossing spells and rituals focus on making the magickal problems leave for good, as opposed to focusing on where it all started from.

All this time you've been waiting for the perfect excuse to get all vamped up and to break out the black candles. This dramatic spell is a favorite of my friends and students, as many of them love to have any excuse to be as theatrical and witchy as possible. For this spell, you'll need to go all-out: black clothes, dark makeup (if you wish), and several black candles. Play your favorite magickal music—Native American drums, haunting Celtic tunes, or a dreamy synthesizer piece—whatever you find particularly inspiring or magickal.

When should you work this spell? Set it up late Friday night and, as the clock strikes midnight, signaling the start of a new Saturday, light the altar candles and begin the spell.

Gather the following supplies:

- A black piece of cloth or scarf to drape over your work area
- 2 black votive candles (you will use the votives
  as altar candles for illumination)
- 1 black taper candle to represent the negativity you are fighting
- 3 coordinating candle holders (2 votive cups, 1 candlestick holder)
- Matches or a lighter
- 1 brown paper lunch bag
- A black permanent marker
- A safe, flat surface on which to set up the spell

One of these candles must be a taper, as you need to be able to easily snap the candle in half during this spell. This is a quick sort of witchery, but it's very effective. Ground and center yourself before you begin this spell, and remove all hatred from your heart. Put yourself into a determined and practical state of mind, and then get to work. Begin speaking the charm as the clock strikes twelve:

As the clock strikes midnight, this candle spell now takes place

Fear and dread, begone—I banish you from time and space!

Light the black taper. Take a few moments to calmly visualize all of the negativity and problems that you need safely removed from your life, and say:

This black candle represents all the negativity

With magick, I break the bad luck that is surrounding me

With Saturn's power to bring all problems to an end

These crossed conditions will now surely begin to mend.

Pinch out the candle and then snap the taper in half, and say:

By the powers of the moon, the stars, and the sun

As I will, so mote it be, and let it harm none.

Place the broken taper candle into the lunch bag. Fold the bag closed and drip a bit of the votive candle wax on it to seal the spell. Now, draw the symbol for the planet Saturn (♄) on the bag with the black marker. You may allow the votive illuminator candles to burn until they go out on their own or save them to reuse for another Saturday spell.

Take the paper bag holding the candle and remove it from your property. This represents the negativity that has been surrounding you, so let's get rid of it. Take a drive— or better yet, a walk—and toss the brown bag into a public garbage can, somewhere away from your house and away from where you work. Once it's been disposed of, turn your back and don't look back. Put all of this garbage behind you.

Metals & Crystals

The metal associated with the planet Saturn is lead. Lead is very toxic, as I am sure you know, and this metal is aligned with the element of earth. Lead is considered receptive, probably due to the fact that this material is so malleable. It was once used to ward the thresholds of the home, and the metal is complementary to protective and defensive magick. While I find the history to be fascinating, this metal is not recommend for magickal use today.

The following crystals and stones that are connected to Saturday and the energies of Saturn are useful for grounding, centering, protection, and for absorbing negativity. Three of these featured crystals are easy to find as tumbled stones; the black tourmaline is sold in its raw form. Keep a good supply of crystals and stones in your home. They will come in handy for all sorts of protective witchery.

> OBSIDIAN: Obsidian is a naturally occurring glass. It's lava that cooled so quickly that the minerals inside of it did not have time to form. Its elemental association is fire, and its planetary correspondence is Saturn. Sometimes this black, translucent stone is called an apache tear, and you may also find obsidian with white patterns in it—this variety is called snowflake obsidian. No matter what variety you discover, this is a great

stone to help you ground and center. An excellent choice to add to any Saturday spell, obsidian is a popular stone to utilize in protective spells and magick designed to fight negativity and break bad luck. Check out a few stores that carry inexpensive tumbled stones and pick up a few to have on hand.

HEMATITE: Hematite is a solid, heavy-feeling silvery-black colored stone. This stone is popular for its grounding and calming properties. Hematite is a stabilizer, and you may often find rings carved out of it. I always felt light-headed whenever I wore a solid hematite ring. I can and do work with the tumbled stones of hematite successfully, and with no side effects, but in my research, I discovered why this type of jewelry affected me so. Wearing or carrying hematite will calm you down and open you up to impressions and the feelings of another (think of it as having similar qualities as moonstone).

Not everyone may experience this; in fact, if you need to be more receptive and levelheaded, then this stone is the way to go. Hematite claims the elemental correspondence of fire and the planetary association of Saturn. Hematite may be also used in types of emotional healing rituals, so if you wanted to, this would be a great stone to add to any spells designed to help feuding friends or romantic partners heal, forgive, let go, and then to move forward.

JET: Jet has the folk name of Witch's amber or black amber, probably due to the fact that many high priestesses wear beads of amber and jet to denote their rank. Jet is ancient fossilized wood, which explains its compatibility with amber. Jet has links to many crone goddesses, such as Hecate. Its elemental associations are earth and Spirit. This black stone, like the other featured crystals in this chapter, also claims the planetary correspondence of Saturn. The jet will clear your aura, boost your psychic abilities, and allow you to see things as they truly are.

Jet becomes electronically charged when it is rubbed. It is a sympathetic stone and will absorb pessimistic or negative energies. It can be placed in a heavily trafficked room in your home to absorb bad vibes or to absorb anger. If jet is placed in the bedroom, it promotes a good night's sleep and guards against nightmares. Try placing jet around a candle and then focus your intentions on creating a happy and argument-free zone in your home. Set the candle and the stones somewhere in the most-used room in the house and silently let them do their work. On an interesting note, today some magicians suggest that female Witches work with jet for issues regarding menopause and perimenopause.

BLACK TOURMALINE: This has the magickal associations of the element of earth and the planetary correspondence of Saturn. It is a receptive stone and a powerful tool for protection, as it absorbs negativity and magickal manipulations. Black tourmaline will help seal your aura, and it also reflects and pushes out psychic pollution. Think of it as a clever little secret to defend yourself from needy emotional vampires and the occasional psychic vampire. The black tourmaline stone is sold in chunks and comes in its rough crystal form, which I personally enjoy. This stone is considered to be brittle, and it does shatter easily, so handle it carefully.

The nifty thing about black tourmaline is that it creates a psychic barrier. If you are inside the boundary, then black tourmaline helps you to make quick decisions. When someone is on the outside of the tourmaline barrier, the stones reflect any unbalanced energy right back to them like a mirror. For the exact reasons listed previously, I use this bewitching crystal often when I do back-to-back clairvoyant or tarot readings for several hours with the general public. Because I have to tell you, you do get some wild and sometimes even unbalanced folks in for readings.

About half of readings are fun. People are happy, in a good mood, and really enjoy their readings. But the other half . . . the client is typically wound up emotionally and their auras are leaking all over the place. They have no qualms about dumping all that on you. After all, in their mind, that's what they are paying you for—your time and attention. So unless you want to wade through all that emotional muck and mire, you need some psychic protection on hand, because, my witchy friend, if you don't shield against that, you will be carting it home with you at the end of the day.

It's a delicate line to walk. You do want to remain open to the psychic impressions; however, you don't want to get bombarded with all that swirl of negative emotions and anxiety either. Personally, if I do not protect myself, I have found that I will become overloaded very quickly.

For me, that's a bad situation, since when that scenario does occur, all of my mediumship abilities will come roaring out to play—it's sort of like, "Hey, we are all psychically warmed up. Let us out so we can show off and do our thing!" And I am merely along for the ride.

Honestly, while that sounds super-cool to some folks, in reality, it's a gigantic pain in the ass. Yes, sometimes I have no choice in the matter, and the messages from the other side of the veil will pop through. But typically these surprise visits from the client's dearly departed don't last too long, and it's usually pretty mild. However, if I choose to do the medium thing on purpose, then I want a controlled environment so I can begin and end the session when I decide.

I mean, think about it—would you want a bunch of folks' deceased relatives talking your ear off night and day? 'Cause once they find you and figure out that you are open to the messages, it can be tough to turn them off, so to speak.

In an effort to help me combat this problem, a coven sister and jewelry-designing friend, Ravyn, made me a bracelet out of black tourmaline chunks, and it works like a charm. And it's the strangest thing, but the bracelet goes on vacation and disappears from time to time. My theory is that it needs to recharge and to purify. So when it is ready to go again, it always shows back up somewhere in my home.

Black Tourmaline Boundary Spell

If you are the sort of person who really wants or needs a fast crystal protection spell that is no muss, no fuss, then try out this Saturday witchery while working with your black tourmaline. Hold the black tourmaline jewelry piece or the raw chunks of stone in your hands. Visualize what it is that you want them to do. Then repeat the following spell verse three times:

> Lovely tourmaline crystal so chunky and black
> Reflect all negativity right out and back
> While I am inside of this magickal boundary
> I am protected from any psychic vampirey
> By the element of earth, keep me free from the mire
> May this crystal spell grant the outcome I desire.

Now go ahead and work with the black tourmaline. I bet that you will notice a huge difference.

POTIONS, PHILTERS & OILS

Magickal Protection Oil

In keeping with our theme of the day, here is a recipe for you to create your own magickal protection oil. Add this to candles or dab a bit onto a talisman or a sachet bag filled with protective herbs. Put a bit on a cotton ball and rub it on doorframes and thresholds to ward your home or office. (Don't go overboard, now—we don't want to ruin the woodwork or cause someone to slip on a oily surface.) Just a small amount will work beautifully. As with all philter and potion recipes in this book, do not apply it directly to the skin.

- 1 small decorative glass bottle
- Base oil, approximately ⅛ cup
- Clean dropper
- 3 drops myrrh or cypress oil
- 3 drops patchouli oil
- 1 pansy flower (dark purple or black is best)
- 1 small morning glory leaf or tiny bit of the vine
- A small chip of black tourmaline
- 6 inches each purple and black thin satin ribbon
- 1 small metal pentagram charm or talisman
  that you feel coordinates with protection
- A label and a pen (to list the ingredients and to
  decorate and mark the bottle)

Pour the base oil into the bottle; fill it three quarters of the way full. Add the essential oils one at a time. Next, add the herbs and the crystal. Close up the bottle with the lid, place your fingers over the lid, and carefully shake up the mixture. Hold up the mixture to the sunlight and allow the light of Saturday's sun to illuminate the philter for a moment or two.

Wipe off the outside of the bottle. Use the label to list the ingredients and the use of this potion. Decorate the bottle by drawing the sigil of Saturn (♄) or pentagrams. If you have other magickal symbols that you would like to use for protection, then add those to the label. Attach the label to the glass bottle, and finish up by threading the metal charm onto the ribbon and then tying the two colored ribbons around the neck of the bottle.

As you finish tying on the bow, hold the bottle in your hands and concentrate on the visualization that your aura around your entire body is glowing with a deep and sparkling purple color. Silently call on the god of karma and time, Saturn, and the triple goddess Hecate to ask for their assistance. Visualize that protection is swirling around you, your home, and your loved ones in the best possible way. Now pull all that energy from your visualization into the philter bottle that you hold in your hands. Take a deep breath, hold it for three counts, and then blow it out slowly. Now, repeat the charm below:

> Hecate, I call upon you now
> This philter with your magick endow
> Saturn's strong energy will circle around
> With this potion, only protection is found
> Witches' herbs and crystal add their power
> Begin the magick in this hour.

Set the bottle aside, and ground and center yourself. Clean up the supplies, and eat a few crackers or do something physical. Make sure to store the protection philter in a dark, dry place out of the reach of young children.

Essential Oils

In this final chapter on the days of the week, here are the essential oils associated with Saturn:

- Cypress
- Myrrh
- Patchouli
- Mimosa
- Tamarisk

Some of these essential oils, such as the myrrh, may be on the pricey side. Personally, I always have regular old essential patchouli oil on hand for protection spells. I just enjoy the scent of it. Plus, if you need to watch your budget, go for the patchouli. It's available everywhere—just make sure you are purchasing essential oils, not fragrance oils.

Tarot Card Associations

The tarot cards that correspond with Saturday's protective and troubleshooting energy are Temperance, the Knight of Swords, and the Two of Swords. The suit of Swords often represents conflict, power, decisions, and judgment. The Major Arcana card featured in this final chapter is Temperance. This card symbolizes moderation and patience, a way of maintaining a sort of inner balance. These are the qualities we will want to tap into for our Saturday spellwork.

Temperance

Temperance is a Major Arcana card that typically shows a winged female figure pouring liquid from one cup into another. While some folks assume that this is an angel, this winged figure has probable Pagan origins. (Think of Isis and her sister Nepthys—both of these goddesses had wings.) The Temperance card may be used in spells designed to help you find the right balance. This symbolism can assist you in finding a way to harmoniously blend all of the aspects of your life. It may also mean that you need to work harder to pull things and situations back into alignment in your own life. When the Temperance card appears in a tarot reading, it means that the person has a mature and balanced personality, and that they can handle difficult situations with diplomacy and competence. This is the sort of tone or imagery that we want to invoke for Saturday spells.

Knight of Swords

The Knight of Swords can be summed up in two words: no fear. The Knight of Swords symbolizes a person who is fearless. They ride into situations and handle even the most difficult things in a spirited and competent fashion. In a reading, this card symbolizes a direct, honest, and open person. This is the tarot card to work with when dealing with a conflict or argument with another person. This type of energy comes in handy when you need to make a quick and wise decision, are working to overcome obstacles, or if you are breaking negativity or attempting to deal fairly with a difficult person.

Two of Swords

Many of the cards in the suit of Swords represent struggle or conflict. However, the Two of Swords stands for balance and restored peace. This card speaks of two equal forces that have maintained a balance. Neither is better than the other; they are both just as strong or as right. In magick, this card invokes a truce and a cautious peace. Work with this card when you are trying to create a peaceful resolution to a problem and when justice is the issue. This card will help ensure that the magick turns out fairly for everyone involved. Now, with that idea in mind, here is a tarot spell to try when you need to call for justice and harmony.

Tarot Spell for Justice and Peace

Here is our final tarot spell, and it's a doozy. Remember to work your spells honestly and ethically, especially when you call for justice. Justice is a neutral force. It doesn't take sides or play favorites. The scales will be weighed for you as well. So be honest and fair in both your magickal and mundane dealings. You may use whatever style candle you prefer—taper, votive, or pillar. Even those little mini taper candles would be fabulous for this spell.

Gather the following supplies:

- Temperance, Two of Swords, and the Knight of Swords tarot cards
- 1 black candle
- 1 white candle
- 1 gray candle

- 3 coordinating candle holders
- Mullein flowers or leaves to banish negativity
- An item of sympathy
- Matches or a lighter
- A safe, flat surface on which to set up the spell

Arrange the herb and cards to your liking between the white and black candles. Set the gray candle, symbolizing neutrality, in its holder, in the center and directly behind the cards. The white and black candles symbolize balance and represent the two opposing forces that are at work.

If you choose, you can personalize this spell by adding an item of sympathy. If this is a legal matter, perhaps you could add a letter from your attorney. If it's personal, you could add an item that was given to you as a gift by the other party. Be creative! Take a few moments to ground and center. Calm yourself, and hold the idea in your mind for the fairest and best possible outcome. Repeat the following spell three times:

> The Knight of Swords, a symbol for courage under fire
> Hear my call for protection; it's justice I desire
> The Two of Swords settles conflicts and does invoke peace so fair
> Add Temperance for balance, and a bit of personal flair
> Lord and Lady, hear my cry, defend and watch over me
> Help me settle this fairly; as I will, so mote it be.

Close the spell by saying:

> In no way will this tarot spell reverse
> Or place upon me or mine any curse.

Allow the candles to burn until they go out on their own. When finished, straighten up your work area and tuck the Temperance card into your wallet, purse, or day planner. Carry it with you until the following Saturday, then return it to your tarot deck.

DAILY WITCH CRAFT
poppets

The poppet is one of the most misunderstood tools in witchcraft today. If you even mention poppet work to people, they get very nervous, very quickly. Personally, I don't see what the fuss is about. Using a poppet in protection magick is a practical and powerful way to bind a troublemaker. A poppet is a small cloth doll in the rough shape of a human. To me, it always looks like a gingerbread-man shape. It is sewn up by hand, leaving the side open to stuff the doll with natural materials, such as cotton batting or sphagnum moss. A simple face is drawn on to the doll, and then sympathetic items are added into the stuffing of the doll to link it to the individual who needs to be bound.

These items of sympathy may be shed hair, nail clippings, or a sample of the person's handwriting. This item creates a physical link to the miscreant. The doll is sewn closed, and then you ceremonially bind up the doll with white ribbons or a cord. You wrap the ribbon around the arms and hands, and then around the feet and legs, to symbolically restrict their movements. If the person who is causing all the trouble is running their mouth, then wrap the ribbon around the head and right over the drawn-on mouth too, effectively keeping all parts of the person bound from causing any more harm.

Some modern books on the Craft today recommend that you keep the doll very small so that you can keep it with you and keep an eye on it at all times. While I like the idea of a travel-sized poppet, hauling it around with you all the time, in my opinion, is a bad idea. Think of how much explaining you'd have to do if for some reason that bound poppet came out of your purse or pocket, or if someone else accidentally found it. Instead, I recommend tucking away the poppet somewhere safe in your home, where no one will find it and it's well out of the way.

Never Piss Off the Witch

A *Poppet Magick Tale*

So, if you are wondering when have I ever used poppet magick, I have a story for you. Many years ago, I had a boss at a little boutique where I worked who was the moodiest, craziest, meanest woman I have ever met in my life. She could be sweet, charming, and kind one moment, and the next she was screaming at you and accusing you of all sorts of things. She was an interesting and unpredictable character. She would be on a tear for a few days and make all the employees a nervous wreck . . . and then she'd be fine for a few weeks or so. Just about the time you had convinced yourself that you must have exaggerated how bad she was, things would flare up, and off she'd go. There was no rhyme or reason to her behavior; one day she treated you like family, the next she was hell on wheels.

Why did I stay? Well, the hours were great, it was close to home, and the pay was good. It was one of those situations where I needed to keep the paychecks coming in, so I kept working there while I started searching for a new job. However, I still had to deal with her and all her tantrums until I landed that different job.

One especially brutal day, I went to the bathroom to calm down and, yes, to get away from my boss and her screaming fits for a few moments. I had reached my limit, my nerves were shot, and my temper was up. I was literally shaking, I was that angry. That very morning, I had started to mentally plot and plan just what I could do, magick-wise, to quiet down the psychopath. I truly did not want to cause her harm, I only wanted the verbal abuse and screaming to stop.

While hiding out in the bathroom, I tried to ground and center and calm myself down. I leaned my back against the door, took deep breaths, and considered my witchy options. It was then that I discovered my boss's makeup bag was open and lying right out and on the bathroom counter. It was definitely hers—she had top-of-the-line cosmetics in there and her name was embroidered on the bag. Inside of the makeup bag was her hairbrush, and it was full of hair.

I just stood there and grinned. I pulled a big wad of hair out of her brush, wrapped it in tissue, and tucked it into my pocket. Armed for the coming battle, I managed to quietly finish out my shift at work. That evening, I sewed up a small gingerbread-man-shaped doll, stuffed it full of cotton batting and that chunk of my boss's hair, and sewed it shut. I then tucked the little doll inside of a cloth bag and put it in the bottom of my purse. It made me a nervous wreck the day that I took it into work with me, but I disguised it as best I could and worked a charm to made my purse less noticeable.

The following Saturday when I went to work, I did my best to act nonchalant. The first chance I got, I took my purse into the bathroom with me and found the boss's makeup bag lying open and out on the counter again. So I locked myself in the bath-room, took out the little poppet from my purse, and fished out the eyeliner and lip-stick from my boss's makeup bag. Using her own cosmetics, I drew eyes and a nose on the face of the doll, and then used her lipstick to draw a mouth on the doll. I was damn near cackling to myself. Think about it: these were her own cosmetics, so you know that they carried her saliva and skin cells. Now that's what I call a link to the troublemaker.

I carefully wrapped up the doll, stashed it in the bottom of my purse, put back all of my crazy boss's cosmetics in her makeup bag, and left the bag looking untouched. Then I went back to work. When I went home that night, I cast a ritual circle, took the poppet out of the cloth bag, and got busy working protection magick. That little poppet was bound up good and tight. And it worked like a charm. Not only did my boss stop the verbal abuse, she even stopped coming in on the days that I was scheduled, which made me very happy and made for a much more pleasant working atmosphere.

A few months later, I found a better job and turned in my resignation. Once I was happily employed at the new job, I unwrapped the doll that I had stashed in my house, removed all the stuffing, and burned all the components—the ribbons, stuffing, and hair—to end the spell and to release the magick.

So, yes, poppet magick can be safely used to stop troublemakers and abusive people. All you have to do is be creative and keep yourself calm and focused on the goal at hand. Here is the spell and the directions that I used.

- 2 pieces plain cotton fabric, 12 inches square
- Cotton batting to stuff the doll; cotton balls will work in a pinch
- White thread to sew the doll closed
- Items of sympathy
- A permanent marker to draw a face on the doll
- 1 yard of white ribbon or cord
- A black candle to stop the negativity and to end any harm that the troublemaker is causing

- A candle holder
- Lighter or matches
- A safe, flat surface on which to set up the spell

Draw a rough gingerbread-man-looking shape on the fabric, cut it out, and sew it together by hand with simple stitches. Leave a small section of one side of the poppet open for stuffing. Next, stuff the poppet full. Add any items of sympathy to the inside of the doll and sew the doll shut. Then, draw on eyes, a nose, and a mouth. Move to your work area. Set up the poppet, the ribbon/cord, and the candle. Take a few moments, and make sure you are calm and ready to go.

Light the candle. Cast a circle in whatever style you prefer. Now pick up the poppet and say these lines:

I now bind you, [Name], from doing any more harm

I halt your negative actions and words with this charm.

Wrap the ribbon or cord around the doll's arms, legs, and over its mouth. Continue with:

White ribbons and cords now tie your legs, mouth, and hands

Quickly bringing protection to me without end.

Set aside the poppet on the work surface. Place one hand on the poppet and focus your attention to the spell candle. Now say:

When you have learned your lesson, this spell will fade

Leaving us both free to enjoy better days.

I recommend closing up this poppet spell with a tagline. The tagline reinforces that the magick you are doing is for the highest good and that it will not turn around and bite you in the magickal behind. Say:

This protection magick is just; now I close this charm

It will not reverse nor place upon me any harm.

Allow the candle to burn out in a safe place. Then pick up the poppet and wrap it in a plain piece of fabric or a paper bag. Put it in an out-of-the-way place and let the magick work itself out.

CUSTOM-MADE DAILY MAGICK

Protection, removing negativity, justice, and balance have been the theme of this chapter. As we have just seen, you can indeed perform a binding and not cross the ethical line. Bindings are a more ethical route than cursing someone. But are there other options? Why, of course. I know of some Witches who, when they see a criminal's face on television or read about them in the paper, mentally paint a white X over a criminal's face while they say the phrase "I neutralize that person" with intention. This neutralizes the power and harm that the stranger causes.

If there is someone that you personally know who is causing you or your family harm, it is possible to use a photograph of the destructive person. Simply wrap white ribbon around their photo to symbolize you binding them up as you say, "I neutralize any physical or emotional harm that you are causing."

But if you feel magickal bindings are the way to go, then perhaps your best course of action is to remove all emotion from yourself and the spell when you perform the binding. Just as I stated before, justice—like magick—is a neutral force. For lack of a better term, be businesslike. Wild swings of emotion only make for an uncontrollable magickal energy. Therefore, your best bet is to be neutral. If there was ever a time to be calm and in control, this is it. If you are not sure that you can pull off being neutral, then I suggest that you leave magick alone. It is essential to be in control. How much karma drama are you willing to pull into your life?

Bindings: A Commonsense Guideline

If you don't like the idea of poppets and have decided to work a binding, and you have a handle on your emotions, then here are some commonsense guidelines that I suggest you follow:

- Bindings are best performed on a Saturday.
- Work the binding at sunset and you pull into the spell the closing energies of not only the day, but of the entire week.
- Work with black candles; they coordinate with Saturn's energies and they are the classic magickal color for this type of witchery.

Finally, to be crystal clear, a binding is the act of psychically restraining a harmful person or criminal so that their actions cannot harm anyone else. The goddess to call on is Hecate, and she is a mighty magickal force. Consider your words and actions carefully when you call on her. How you choose to work a binding is up to you. At this point, I strongly suggest that you take a moment and draft out your binding spell on paper. Refer to the spell worksheet on page 301; it will help you. Go carefully, and remember to harm none.

You may experience some dramatic special effects when working with Hecate. Don't be taken aback if the wind picks up . . . if your candles flicker and snap . . . or if you begin to notice barking or howling dogs. The animals sense when Hecate is near. Yes, we have gotten very serious all of a sudden. That's because a binding is a serious matter. Surprised? Don't be. Just because I tend to look at things from a humorous perspective doesn't mean I am not serious when the situation calls for it.

This invocation includes some of the correspondences for Hecate. If you choose, you can add these to your spellwork. (This would also be a fine addition to the opening of the poppet magick spell.) A general invocation for Hecate follows.

Invocation to Hecate

Cauldrons, three keys, and black dogs that bay at the moon

Grant me wisdom and strength, pray hear this Witch's tune

Goddess of the crossroads, Hecate, I call on you

Come lend your magick to mine; my need is strong and true.

Note: Remember to thank Hecate for her time and attention when you are finished with your witchery.

Ritual for Saturday
four crystals of saturn protection ritual

Try this final Saturday ritual to work for protection and a little help in boosting your personal shields. Sometimes we all need to boost our auras, or our personal energy shields. Whether you have a case of the magickal "blahs," are recovering from being sick, or are just feeling emotionally vulnerable at the moment, this enjoyable witchery for a Saturday ought to do the trick.

For this ritual, the phase that the moon is currently in does not matter. If the moon is in a waxing lunar phase, then pull protection toward you. Consequently, if you are in a waning moon phase, then push away all negativity and bad vibes. If it happens to be a full moon or the new moon, then go for it and take advantage of all that extra magickal energy that's out there!

Remember, we are working to make you in sync with the daily planetary energies for your magick. That has been the theme of the entire book! There is always a way to work things out, no matter what phase the moon is in. It's up to you to use your witchery in a creative way and to work your magick successfully with what you have, and with what energies are currently in play.

Gather the following supplies:

- One each of the four crystals associated with Saturn: hematite, black tourmaline, jet, and obsidian
- A plain white tealight candle
- A coordinating fireproof candle holder (a tiny metal cauldron would be a nice touch)
- A current photo of yourself

- A lighter or matches
- A safe, flat surface on which to set up the spell

First things first: take a shower or a bath, and imagine that all of the negativity you've been carrying around is being washed away by the age-old cure of running water. Step out of the shower, dry off, and slip on a favorite comfy outfit or robe.

Find a good spot on which to set up this ritual—try a shelf or a fireplace mantle. Maybe you'll want to use your nightstand. Just make sure you are setting the candle in a safe place, away from small children or pets.

Situate the photo of yourself off to the side of the candle and holder. Surround the photo with the four protective stones.

Cast a circle in the way that you prefer or use this elemental circlecasting verse; if you speak this deliberately and with magickal intention, it works wonderfully:

> The elements four, I call you here
> Earth, air, fire, and water so dear
> Now circle around and create a ring
> Your energies and strength to me please bring.

Now visualize yourself surrounded by a dazzling white light and a strong, protective energy. Repeat the following verse three times:

> Crystals and stones of protection and power
> Lend your strength to me in this magick hour
> Tealight candle that is burning so clear and bright
> Lend your magick to mine on this Saturday night

Safety and security this ritual now yields

As I increase my energy and boost my own shields.

Close the spell by saying:

For the good of all, bringing harm to no one

By flame and crystal, this witchery is done!

You should know the drill by now—open your ritual circle. I personally like the following classic line:

The circle is open but unbroken

Merry meet, merry part, and merry meet again.

Allow the candle to burn out. Keep an eye on it while it does so. Once the candle is out, pocket the four protective crystals and keep them with you, on your person, for a week.

Well, we have just about wrapped things up with this chapter and the individual days of the week. Before we move on to the final chapter, here are a few more quick and practical ideas for magick on a Saturday. Feel the need for a psychic cleansing in the house? Light up some patchouli- or myrrh-scented incense, and wave the smoke around your house or apartment. It will help to break up any lingering negativity or bad feelings. Crumble up a few dried mullein leaves and create a circle around your home, or scatter it across the thresholds, to keep prowlers away.

Burn a few black candles to repel manipulative intentions or unwanted advances. Add a few protective herbs to your dinner such as thyme or basil. Try growing a blooming cyclamen plant in your kitchen to ward the family and to encourage Hecate's blessings. Grow deep purple and black pansies in window boxes to encourage the planetary vibrations of Saturn. Let ivy grow up the walls of your home for even more bewitching security.

Saturdays are the particular day of the week for protection and for dealing with more serious magickal matters. Go back over the at-a-glance list and see what components you can add to your spells for today for a little more *oomph*.

Don't forget to check out the daily spell worksheet on page 301. Write down some ideas for your own individual and custom-made magick. For example, what other plants, crystals, and stones do you enjoy working with that were not listed in these chapters? How do you imagine you could creatively integrate them? Try creating even more tarot spells just for you. Craft your own quick candle spells, and write your own colorful charms and daily incantations.

Meditate on Hecate to learn her lessons and include some dark goddess wisdom into your Craft. As a Witch, you already know that you have power—the power to effect real change in your life. Working with Hecate can teach you how and when to best use this power for the greater good.

If you want to expand your magickal skills, then start learning how to incorporate all of this information on the days of witchery in a whole new way. This includes the knowledge you already have and the new day-by-day correspondences and witchcraft that were presented in this Book of Shadows. Put your own unique spin on things. Decide what your enchanting specialties are, then apply them to your Craft each and every day with wisdom and style.

Full Moon Witchery

Now that you understand the daily energies that are in play for each of the days of the week, what do you suppose happens, witchery wise, when full moon energy gets added into the mix? Short answer: the full moon magick actually becomes influenced and intensified by the theme of the particular day. After working your way through the last seven chapters, I imagine your brain is buzzing with fresh magickal correspondence information and you are all ready to blurt out what you know.

Oh, and I could not be prouder. So now I am going to ask you to stop for a moment and think about the next full moon. Check what day of the week it will fall on in your time zone. Okay, now that you have that information, what magickal possibilities pop into your brain?

What have you learned, Grasshopper? No, I won't go into a "When you can snatch the pebbles from my hand…" riff, though I admit I am very tempted. At this point, think of me like a sort of witchy cheerleader, but without the megaphone. I know you can do this. I am only trying to fire you up and encourage you to enthusiastically dive in there and see what else you can accomplish.

Magick is all about possibilities. There is something thrilling about knowing down in your very soul that you have the opportunity to create positive change at any time. However, we don't want to turn up our witchy noses at the other days of power that cycle through the bewitching year that will add depth to the days of witchery—for example, the full moons.

There is something awe-inspiring about watching a full moon rise. Whether you watch it rise above a metropolitan skyline, through the trees in your neighborhood, over the desert canyons, or over shimmering waves of water, a rising full moon just stops us in our tracks and tugs on our witchy hearts. There is power there. Imagine what sort of fabulous things you could accomplish with that. We have explored the bewitching characteristics of the individual days of the week in our previous chapters. Now we are taking what we know and building on that with full moon magick.

There are, on average, twelve full moons per calendar year. Classically, many Witches will call the full moon date an esbat. Also, every few years we get thirteen full moons in one calendar year. (That second full moon falling within one calendar month is referred to as a blue moon.) If you are curious about working with blue moon magick, you might wish to check out my book *Natural Witchery* for a few blue moon spells and charms. A blue moon is a lot of fun to work with; it is a time for miracles.

For a general lunar cycle reference, please check the bibliography in this book for an excellent website that lists lunar calendars until the year 2025. But as a quick reference, I can tell you that the years 2009, 2012, and 2015 will each have thirteen full moons in the Eastern Standard Time Zone for the United States.

If you take a look at lunar calendars, you will see that throughout the year we hit each day of the week at least once for a full moon. Some days of the calendar week will get a full moon twice, so you will have the opportunity to try this unique witchery out for yourself over the course of the next year.

So, what do you say? Why don't we expand on what witcheries you have already learned from this Book of Shadows? Let's explore the concept of full moon magick to coordinate with the unique energies of the day of the week that the full moon takes place on.

Full Moon on a Sunday

It takes the moon for this. The sun's a
wizard by all I tell; but so's the moon a Witch.

Robert Frost

Sundays are for success, fame, and wealth, so imagine all the extra *oomph* you can add to those spells if a full moon occurs on a Sunday. Success directly stems from your own creative drive and ambition. However much effort you are willing to devote to your own success directly influences the results that you will achieve. This includes both magickal measures, such as spells and charms, as well as following up those magickal actions with physical actions such as filling out job applications, sending out résumés, or doing an outstanding job so when promotion time comes up at work, you are noticeably the best candidate. You only get out of things what you put into them, whether that's a creative project like writing or drawing, or working in an office, a retail store, a factory, or doing construction work or landscaping.

If your idea of personal success is about getting in shape or losing weight, then the same basic principles apply. You can do all the magick you want for weight loss, but until you start physically doing something—such as changing your diet, exercising, and making healthier lifestyle choices—then nothing will happen. You are the fuel that makes the success spells go. Magick is a powerful boost to your success and an influence to the situation. It speeds things along and smoothes the way. But it will not do all the work for you. You really do hold the power to influence these positive changes in your life. So be prepared to work hard, put your heart into it, and then work your witchery for the best possible outcome.

Sunday Full Moon Spell for Success

- Golden candle
- White candle
- 2 coordinating candle holders
- A pin or nail to engrave the candles with
- A fresh yellow carnation in a bud vase
- Matches or a lighter
- A safe, flat surface on which to set up the spell
- Items of sympathy
- Yellow envelope or sachet bag

You may incorporate whatever size and style of candle you personally prefer: taper, votive, mini spell candle, whatever you like. Add the sun's astrological symbol (☉) to the golden candle, and the carve the moon's astrological symbol (☽) into the white. Arrange the candles in their holders. Place the bud vase holding the carnation in the center, back from the candle flames.

Now add an item of sympathy to this spell to help strengthen the spellwork. The item that you add should be in sympathy with what you are casting toward. For example, if you are going for a promotion or applying for a new job and you want to be successful at it, then add your company letterhead, the ad, your business card, résumé, or the description of the job.

If you are dieting and working toward being healthier, then work with a nice picture of yourself, with a realistic and healthy goal weight written on the back. These items of sympathy then supply the energy link between the spell and the goal. Take a few moments to ground and center.

Light the candles, and repeat the following spell verse three times:

> I *combine the full moon's magick with the day of the sun*
> *For a winning combination, now this spell has begun*
> *My goals will come to fruition beginning today*
> *These two bright candle flames will illuminate the way*
> *This Sunday night esbat brings rich power to spare*
> *Success is mine as my words flow out on the air.*

Close the spell with these lines:

> *May the full moon's light bless all the ways*
> *I'll work my witchery on this day.*

Allow the spell candles to burn out in a safe place. Keep an eye on them. When the candles are finished, gently take a few of the carnation's fragrant petals and gather up any remaining wax and the item of sympathy. Tuck the petals, wax fragments, and your item of sympathy inside of a yellow envelope or cloth bag, and keep them together and on your person, magickal working space, or altar until the next full moon. Allow the flower to stay in the vase until it begins to fade, then neatly return the flower to nature.

FULL MOON ON A MONDAY

> BY NIGHT ONLY crazy things
> like the full moon and the
> whippoorwill and us are busy.
>
> *Charles Olson*

Way back in the beginning of this book, I mentioned that if a full moon phase occurred on a Monday, then this would create a double dose of lunar energy, power, and magick. Here is where we are going to explore this idea with the following spell. For our full moon witchery that falls on the day of the week that is dedicated to the moon, we are going to work with the Egyptian god Thoth. Thoth's symbol is a crescent moon resting on its curved back, on top of a full lunar disc. Thoth is a god of wisdom, magick, and mystery, and he acts as a guide for those who are seeking wisdom.

We will also be working again with the Moon card from the tarot deck. As far as props go, the Moon tarot card is an especially appropriate one for a full moon on a Monday. This Major Arcana card is a symbol of intuition, instinct, and the conscious and the unconscious minds. When this card pops up in a reading, it is a warning of delusion and deception. It is a caution that things are not as they appear. It tells you to look carefully at what you think you know, and to then consider what is real and what is not before you proceed down your path.

There is a trail illustrated on this card, flanked by a wolf on one side and a dog on the other. This symbolizes a pathway to another land and the astral journey into your own inner wisdom and vision.

This full moon spell is perfect for those times when you feel that something is afoot. Maybe you can't figure out what is wrong, but something seems too good to be true or your intuition is trying to get you to pay attention. This spell will help you brush away illusions to see things as they truly are and help you to get back on your path.

Breaking Through Illusions Spell

- Fresh white flower petals (pop into the local florist and pick up a stem or two of white flowers—try the petals of the white chrysanthemum or the daisy, as these are inexpensive to purchase and will work well in this spell; or, if your garden is blooming, then work with any white flower petals from your own garden)
- 1 silver candle, whatever style or shape you prefer
- A coordinating candle holder
- A pin or nail to engrave Thoth's symbol on the candle
- A few drops of jasmine or sandalwood essential oil (use whichever scent you prefer; both of these oils are associated with the moon)
- 1 clean eye dropper for the oil
- A small cloth to wipe your hands
- The Moon tarot card
- Matches or a lighter
- Your altar or magickal workspace; make sure it is a flat, safe surface to set up on

To begin this spell, try to set this up where you will have a view of the rising full moon. If weather permits, this would be fabulous to do outside on your porch or deck.

Gather your supplies, and set up your working area. Carefully and reverently strip the petals from the white flowers. Now scatter the loose petals across the work surface and in a circle around yourself. Take your time, and make the area festive and pretty. When that's done, take the pin or nail and gently carve Thoth's symbol into the side of the silver candle.

Hold the candle in both your hands for a few moments and then raise the candle up to the light of the moon to imbue it with more lunar energy. Place the candle in its holder, and then anoint the candle with the essential oil. Use an eye dropper to add the oil, or if you use your fingers, take a moment and wipe your hands clean with the small towel.

When you are all set, prop up the tarot card in the center of your working area. Take a few moments to ground and center yourself. When you are ready, light the silver candle and repeat the following verse:

> Thoth, help me to break through illusions on this night
> For things are not as they seem under the moon's light
> I ask for your guidance as I walk my path
> May the wisdom you grant to me truly last.

Take a few moments and study the images on the tarot card. Meditate on the symbolism for a time, and see what the moon god Thoth has to tell you. When finished, thank Thoth with these lines:

Thoth, I thank you now for your time and gentle care

Your wisdom enlightens me with this lunar prayer.

Look up at the full moon and blow her a kiss. Then close the Monday night spell with these lines:

Blow a kiss to the lady moon when she is round

Then insight and witchery will surely be found.

Now, you may sit outside and enjoy the moonlight. I would suggest moving the candle indoors when you are finished, so you can keep it under observation and allow it to burn out in a safe place. Clean up the rest of your magickal supplies. Return the card to the tarot deck and enjoy the rest of your evening. If you worked outdoors, leave the flower petals where they fell. If not, gather them up and return them neatly to nature in the morning.

Finally, pay attention to and write down any dreams you have for the next few nights. Thoth may very well choose to communicate with your subconscious mind, through your dreams. Happy esbat!

FULL MOON ON A TUESDAY

BUT SCREW YOUR courage to the
sticking-place and we'll not fail.

William Shakespeare

For this Tuesday night full moon spell, we are working with fire magick and warrior energy. This spell incorporates one of the court cards from the tarot deck, the Knight of Swords. If you recall, the Knight of Swords can be summed up in two words: no fear!

This card symbolizes people who have moxie and determination and who refuse to take no or "I can't!" for an answer. It also symbolizes situations that require you to dive in, to show no fear, and to bravely tackle any issues and challenges with intellect and courage. It is one of my favorite cards in the entire deck. This is a card of movement, bravery, and decisive action, which makes it ideal for this full moon spell.

If it helps you to visualize the god Mars with you while you work this spell, then do so. One of my covenmates, Ravyn, suggested picturing the Spartans from the movie 300. Whoa. Tuesday is a Mars day, after all; this is a day of passion. Ahem.

But you know, I kind of like the idea of a troop of rough-and-ready soldiers standing with me. The fact that they all look great is just icing on the cake. I trust that you can focus your energies toward your magickal goal, so do whatever works best for you.

If visualizing buff, tough, gorgeous men in loincloths, crimson red capes, and tufted bronze helmets helps, then go for it.

The "No Fear" Spell

This spell is best worked outdoors. Supplies are as follows:

- 1 red taper illuminator candle
- 1 black taper illuminator candle
- 2 coordinating black metal candle holders (use wrought iron, if possible)
- A pin or nail to engrave Mars's symbol on the candles (♂)
- The Knight of Swords card from your tarot deck
- A fireproof small metal cauldron
- A sheet of paper, no larger than 6 inches square
- Black ink pen
- Rubbing alcohol
- Wooden matches
- An outdoor working area—make sure it is a flat, safe surface to set up all of the spell supplies on (you need to be outside for this one, otherwise you will set off the smoke alarms while you are burning the paper in the cauldron; talk about blowing the magickal mood!)

You have to be careful with the fire. Anytime you have an open flame inside of a cauldron, fire pit, or fireplace and you add magick and intention, things tend to be unpredictable with the flames. Also, just a few drops of alcohol will help that paper burn. So don't go overboard and singe yourself. Safety first! The spell fire is symbolic. A little fire held within a metal cauldron that is lit with intention does pack more power than you realize, so please be smart and safe and work this full moon spell with care.

Arrange the outdoor setup as follows. Engrave and then place the candles in their holders, and set them toward the back of your working area. Position the metal cauldron in the center. Leave a small area to place the Knight of Swords card in front of the cauldron, where it is easily visible. Set the rubbing alcohol, the matches, and paper and pen to the side and within reach.

To start, take up the paper and pen and write down what it is that you fear. Keep it short and to the point. Then, fold the paper in half and drop it into the cauldron. Sprinkle a bit of rubbing alcohol on the paper. Close up the bottle and set it off and away to the side. Now put your game face on. Call up whatever courage you can muster. Visualize those Spartan soldiers or the god Mars standing strong and right alongside of you. Come on, tap into that warrior energy. Growl. Get tough, and raise up some courageous energy. Hold your hands out and over the cauldron. Now repeat this verse with intention:

> Mars energy is bolstered by the full moon light
> I remove anxiety and stress on this night
> Mighty warrior energy now defeats the shadows and fear
> As I conjure bravery and courage to reside with me here!

Move your hands away from the cauldron. Step back from the work area and strike the match. Carefully drop it on top of the paper inside of the cauldron. If necessary, you can hold the match to the edge of the paper and encourage it to completely burn.

If you need to use a couple of matches, that's fine. Just drop the spent matches inside of the cauldron. Keep going until the paper is ash. Then close the spell with these lines:

Ashes to ashes and dust to moon dust

My courage soars and my magick is just

I work boldly with the days of witchery

This lunar spell is sealed; set the magick free!

You may snuff the black and red illuminator candles and take them inside with you. If you wish, use them again for other Tuesday spells or to repeat this spell if necessary. Allow the contents of the cauldron to cool completely, then take a little garden spade and bury the ashes in the garden. Pour water on top of the spot to make doubly sure nothing is smoldering. Tap your fist on the ground on top of it, and say:

So mote it be!

Now, go and clean out your cauldron. Keep the tarot card with you for a week to bolster your courage. To close up this full moon magick, go do something positive. Take a jog or a walk under that enchanting moon. Play some music and dance, or go find your partner and make love. Just do something positive, life-affirming, and physical. Any of those activities will help you to ground and center.

FULL MOON ON A WEDNESDAY

KNOWLEDGE COMES,
BUT wisdom lingers…

Alfred Tennyson

For this Wednesday night esbat, we are working magick with the Norse god Odin. Odin is a trickster god, and in his search for wisdom he gained deep magickal knowledge. This spell also works with the images of the tarot card the Hanged Man. This illustrated card has many links to the god Odin, as Odin hung on the tree for nine days to gather wisdom and was eventually rewarded with the runes.

The Hanged Man card tells you to look at things from a new perspective. It speaks of a time of a transitional period, astral travel, and meditation. If you look carefully at the Hanged Man card, you will see that while the fellow is hanging upside down from his foot, he looks pretty peaceful about the whole situation. This card symbolizes letting go of that which no longer serves your highest good. This card's image illustrates the quiet search for inner wisdom and knowledge and the gaining of a new perspective on your current situation. Wednesdays are all about movement, communication, and change, so let's take this energy and put it to good use. Combining this with the light and influence of the full moon only sweetens the deal and turns up the power of the witchery.

Insight and Gaining New Perspectives Spell

This spell works with the runes as one of its props. If you have a set of runes, this is definitely the time to break them out. If not, no worries. The runes are a nice link back to the god Odin, but in a pinch you could also draw a few rune sigils on a piece of paper and set that on your work area. Improvise and be creative. What do you think you could also add to this full moon spell?

- 1 purple candle (purple for spirituality and to align with the energies of Mercury)
- A coordinating candle holder
- A nail or pin to engrave the candle with Wednesday's planetary symbol of Mercury ($\u263F$)
- A black feather or a picture of a raven (this bird was sacred to Odin, and the raven represents mystery and magick)
- The Hanged Man tarot card
- Your tarot deck, set off to the side
- Runes scattered across the work surface or a drawing of a few runes
- A lighter or matches
- A safe, flat surface on which to set up the spell

Carefully engrave the Mercury symbol on the candle. Place the candle in its holder and then arrange the rest of the spell components to your liking. You may certainly embellish this spell by adding a statue or image of Odin, if you choose. This full moon spell is designed to help you look at things from a new perspective and to receive some inspiration, so put on your thinking cap and be imaginative. Take a few moments to ground and center yourself. Then light the purple candle and speak the following verse:

> Odin, hear my call on this full moon night
>
> Grant me wisdom and improve my insight
>
> May I gain a new perspective at this time
>
> Bless me with peace and inspiration divine
>
> I now release that which no longer serves
>
> This change begins with the sound of my words.

If you choose, this would be an excellent time to meditate and see what Odin has to tell you. Lay your hands on the card, feather, and runes. Take a deep breath and relax. Now let your mind open, and see what you learn. When you are finished, close the spell with these words:

> By the power of Wednesday's witchery
>
> This spell is sealed; I set the magick free!

Allow the candle to burn out in a safe place. Clean up your other spell supplies. Save the feather or raven picture for future magick. Return the card to the tarot deck, and gather up all your runes. If you like, now is the perfect time to do a simple reading with your runes or your tarot cards. Ask for clarity and for insight, then draw three cards or stones and see what Odin has to say.

Full Moon on a Thursday

A FAMILY IN harmony will
prosper in everything.
Chinese proverb
༺ঽৡৡৡঽ༻

The full moon's energy really adds intensity to all of these daily spells. If you work this magick wisely, you will notice a difference in the level of the results. When it comes to our families, many of us become passionate. When you are a parent, your emotions become even more involved. Whether you have an infant in your arms, toddlers or grade-school children running amok, teens adding their drama into your life, or college-aged children insisting they are adults but still running to you to fix their crises, being a parent is not a job for the faint of heart.

Let's not forget that you have to keep your marriage or personal relationships loving and vital too. No matter how you look at it, it's a lot of work. And for those of you who are pet parents, we want our beloved pets to behave themselves and to be happy and healthy too.

This full moon spell is designed for your entire family. In this day and age, it certainly is a good idea to work for the strength, happiness, and prosperity of your family and home. Running a home is a lot of work. Add your job, your spouse, the kids, and assorted pets into the mix, and you've got your hands full. So on a Thursday full moon night, you have a golden opportunity to work with all those complementary energies and whip up a little witchery designed to boost the entire family's health, happiness, and abundance.

This spell works with the red-bearded Norse god Thor. This Norse god is a defender of those he loves, and that theme makes it perfect for this type of magick. Also, the tarot cards the Ten of Pentacles and the Ten of Cups/Cauldrons are incorporated. These two cards are about all the emotional support of the home and family. The Ten of Pentacles is aligned to prosperity, success, and family support, while the Ten of Cups/Cauldrons is linked to emotional support, a good home life, and the loving bonds of a family unit.

Happy, Healthy Family Spell

- A green 7-day jar candle (green for prosperity and to align with Jupiter's energies)
- A permanent marker to draw Thursday's planetary symbol of Jupiter (♃) and the names of each household member
- A photo of your entire household (make sure all of the members are in the photo; if necessary, use a couple of photos to get your kids, spouse, and your pets)
- 3 oak leaves gathered from a living tree (oak leaves are linked to Thor as well as the planet Jupiter)
- 1 tumbled turquoise stone for prosperity and protection
- 1 small tumbled moonstone for loving emotions
- The Ten of Pentacles and Ten of Cups tarot cards
- A 6 x 6-inch square of green fabric or a green sachet bag
- 12 inches white satin ribbon
- A lighter or matches

If possible, set up this spell on a safe, flat surface where the light of the full moon illuminates your working area. If weather permits, this would be a nice spell to work outdoors—just be sure to move the candle indoors when you finish the spell. To start, take the marker and draw the planetary symbol of Jupiter on the jar candle. Next, add the names of all the members of your household; this includes pets!

Place the candle and the other components of the spell on your working area. The stones can nestle around the jar candle. Lay the photo(s) of your family in the center of your altar, with the two tarot cards, the Ten of Cups/Cauldrons and the Ten of Pentacles, one on each side of the photos. Place the oak leaves above the photos and the cards. Keep the sachet bag or fabric and ribbon within reach.

Light the candle, and place your hands on the photos. Then repeat the spell verse:

Abundance flourishes on the night of the full moon

May the deities of Thursday heed this Witch's tune

Thor, hear my call and bless my family

Bring us love, support, and prosperity

Keep us healthy, happy, and secure, come what may

As we stand strong together through all of our days.

Gather the photos, one of the oak leaves, and the two tumbled stones, and place them in the center of the fabric. Gather up the edges into a small bundle, and use the ribbon to tie it closed, or place the items inside the sachet bag and pull the drawstring closed. Knot the ribbon three times, and say:

By *all the power of three times three*
This magick strengthens my family.

Finally, close the spell with these lines:

May the full moon bless all of the ways
I work my witchery on this day.

Allow the candle to burn out in a safe place; it will take about a week. I typically put jar candles on my brick hearth, inside of a large cast-iron cauldron, so even if it somehow got tipped over, the flame would stay contained in a fireproof area.

Clean up your other spell supplies. Save the two oak leaves and keep them for future magick. Return the cards to the tarot deck. Keep the bag with the photos, stones, and leaf together in a safe place until the next full moon. Then, on the night of the following full moon, open it up. Keep the photos and the crystals, and return the oak leaf to nature.

FULL MOON ON A FRIDAY

LOVE, THE STRONGEST and
deepest element in all life…

Emma Goldman

Love is in the air … especially on a Friday full moon. For this bewitching recipe, we combine all those ripe, full, mystical, and inspiring lunar energies of a full moon mixed together with the special day of the week aligned with the planet Venus. Now sprinkle in a dash of love and romance, add a teaspoon of flower and color magick, and you've got yourself one powerful formula with which to work loving and romantic theme spells.

This full moon spell works with a common variety of houseplant, which is also a magickal flower: the African violet. This hearth-and-home spell is designed to increase the loving vibrations and the feelings of the fullness of love in your home. Just like the common violet, the African violet falls under the planetary influences of Venus. These little blooming houseplants make a lovely addition to your Friday full moon spells. Basically, this spell is a floral fascination. A floral fascination is a term that I coined years ago, and it means practical and powerful magick worked with a flower or a blooming plant.

Making Love Grow Spell

- 1 African violet plant—a pink blooming variety is best (if for some reason you cannot find a pink blooming violet, go with a white variety; white is an all-purpose color)
- 1 pink votive candle
- 1 votive candle cup
- A pin or nail to engrave the candle with the symbol of Venus (♀)
- A small tumbled rose quartz stone to increase warm, fuzzy feelings
- Lighter or matches
- A safe, flat surface on which to set up the spell

Again, I would suggest working this spell out under the moonlight or at least near a window that allows you a view of the full moon. To start, set the African violet and the rose quartz stone in the center of your working area. Take the pin and gently carve the planetary symbol of Venus into the side of the votive candle. Drop the votive inside of the cup, and set it to one side. Take a few moments to visualize the spirit of love blessing your home. Feel the fun and the joy of love, and let it fill up your heart. Now light the candle, and place your hands on either side of the potted plant. Repeat the following verse:

Under the light of Friday's full moon
I ask the Goddess to grant me a boon
By the energy of a Venus flower
Mix with this a rose quartz's warm, fuzzy powers
Bless this home with love and your grace
Let it expand out and fill up this place.

Close the spell with these lines:

> *By flower petal and moonlight, this spell is begun*
>
> *For the good of all, this witchery brings harm to none.*

Pocket the rose quartz stone and keep it with you. Care for your houseplant, and enjoy the richness of love that is sure to bless your days and your home.

FULL MOON ON A SATURDAY

> EVERY EXPERIENCE IN life enriches one's
> background and should teach valuable lessons.
>
> *Mary Barnett Gilson*

Well, here we are at the last day of the week on which we can explore full moon magick. A full moon that occurs on a Saturday brings interesting energies into play. As a matter of fact, as I finish up this book I am only a few days away from the first full moon of 2009, and coincidentally it will fall on a Saturday in my time zone. When this type of magickal Saturday/full moon scenario occurs, what you have is a big old karmic lesson theme to work with. This is a fabulous time for introspection and to consider the life lessons you are presently working through.

Saturn, the deity classically associated with this day of the week, is a figure with staying power. In today's world, he has been recast a bit as a gentle Father Time sort of figure, holding a sheaf of wheat and a tall sickle, and having a long, flowing white beard. Nevertheless, do not underestimate him or his magick.

The bottom line is Saturn can be a noble, wise, and, yes, a loving mentor-type of figure. But when the situation calls for it, he has no compunctions about firmly whacking you over the head with the handle of his sickle. Saturn teaches you about karma, and sometimes we all have to take our lumps. That's his job. And trust me, he is damn good at it. After all, he's only had all of time to perfect his technique.

So while you are sitting there and wondering why you are experiencing whatever drama you are currently going through, he'll be standing back, waiting for you to accept, to deal, to grow up, and then to learn from those life lessons that he has for you.

Saturn was originally a god of agriculture, so he knows all about the various cycles and seasons of our lives. This god can teach you to take responsibility for your actions, both mundane and magickal. He's not the deity to turn to when you want to run around and point the finger at someone else for your current situation. Instead, he can teach you perseverance and will grant you knowledge and the wisdom of self-acceptance if you only open up your heart and mind and allow his teachings to come into your life.

Understanding Karmic Lessons Spell

The following spellwork is very personal. Again, this spell is not meant to be used to place the blame on another person for your current predicament. Instead, it is a way to learn from the lessons that life likes to hand out to all of us. Sometimes we all wonder how we got sidetracked from our plans, how we got pulled into someone else's drama, or how we were misdirected from our own magickal path.

No matter who you are or how long you've been a Witch, we all will face times when we are unsure about how we got into whatever situation we are currently dealing with. The good news is that if you are willing to take an honest look at yourself and the situation, then the god Saturn will grant you some of his own wisdom. Best of all, he can truly help you to learn not to repeat the same mistake.

Regardless of how long you have been practicing your Craft, you will always have more to learn. The most powerful coven leaders, elders, and high priests and high priestesses that I know in the community are all individuals who are human. They make mistakes too. The difference is that they learn from their mistakes—and then they admit them and move forward.

The final spell of this Book of Shadows is, in fact, one of the more important ones in the entire book, because it gives you a great opportunity to grow a little as a practitioner and to gain some real understanding about yourself, the lessons of life, and your witchery.

Supplies:

- 1 black candle
- 1 white candle
- 2 coordinating candle holders
- A representation of the god Saturn (use a picture from the Internet or a drawing of a sickle and a sheaf of wheat)
- 1 stick or cone of patchouli incense (patchouli is associated with Saturn)
- An incense holder
- Matches or a lighter
- A safe, flat surface on which to set up the spell

Arrange the candles and the incense and the holder on your work surface. Set the picture of the god Saturn flat on the table, in front of the candles. Light the candles and the incense. Wave some of the scented smoke over yourself and around your working area. Return the incense to the altar. Take a few moments to ground and center yourself. This is a very important step in this spell, so don't skip this part. Take your time to become grounded and calm.

When you feel peaceful and centered, repeat the following spell verse:

Saturn's karmic lessons are enhanced by a full moon's light

Lord of Time, please grant me clarity and insight

As the moon illuminates Saturday's nighttime sky

The answers become clearer as time passes by.

Close the spell with these lines:

Let this full moon wisdom come swiftly to me

Causing no distress or harm; so mote it be.

Allow the candles and the incense to burn out in a safe place. Pay attention to your dreams and to your intuition for the next few days. See what Saturn has to teach you. Now move forward with grace, purpose, and a sense of magickal accomplishment. Blessed be.

Closing Thoughts

EACH DAY COMES bearing its
own gifts. Untie the ribbons.
Ruth Ann Schabacker

༼྾༽

Every day is a magickal day. Just how bewitching of a day it turns out to be is completely up to you. As we've seen, there is always a way to work your magick. *Book of Witchery* is meant to inspire you and to pump you up. Get in there and try out new magick for yourself. Shake things up! Personalize and work a few new spells. Get to know the featured deities, add some tarot cards to your spellcraft, and work those daily meditations.

Dive into herbal lore and check out crystal and color magick. Make copies of the spell worksheet, and get busy! Advance your skills by teaching yourself new daily enchantments. There are plenty of magickal arts and crafts, spells, philter recipes, and advanced techniques here for you to add to your repertoire.

Now, take these daily correspondences and original ideas from this Book of Shadows, and fly with them. Be creative, and stand out as the talented magickal individual you are. Just imagine what fantastic things you can achieve every single day of the bewitching week.

You can advance your magickal skills all on your own. The longer you practice your Craft, the more experience you will gain. Half of the fun of being a Witch is growing and living with your magick. Break out a notebook, and start working on creating your own spells and charms. Take a good look at all the information that is in this book, and let it inspire you to write your own enchantments. It's a great way to learn, and it's an awesome feeling to see your own magickal skills evolve and grow. So enjoy the journey, and embrace all the life lessons you learn along the way.

Brightest blessings and best wishes on your spellwork and witchery!

DAILY SPELL WORKSHEET

DAY: _____

GOAL: _____

DEITY INVOKED: _____

HERBS USED AND THEIR MAGICKAL APPLICATION: _____

_____

_____

CANDLE COLOR: _____

CRYSTALS OR STONES: _____

_____

COORDINATING TAROT CARDS: _____

_____

CHARM: _____

_____

_____

SETUP (EQUIPMENT SUCH AS CANDLE HOLDERS, A VASE, A CAULDRON,

ETC.): _____

_____

_____

RESULTS: _____

_____

DAYS OF THE WEEK
in old english and gaelic
❧❀❧

This list is simply for fun; I thought it would amuse you!

Gaelic Days of the Week (and Pronunciation)

SUNDAY	Domhnach (*dow-neg*)
MONDAY	Luan (*loo-in*)
TUESDAY	Máirt (*martch*)
WEDNESDAY	Céadaoin (*kay-deen*)
THURSDAY	Déardaoin (*jeyr-deen*)
FRIDAY	Aoine (*hayn-ya*)
SATURDAY	Satharn (*sa-harn*)

Old English Days of the Week (and Their Meanings)

SUNDAY Sunnandaeg, "day of the sun"

MONDAY Monandaeg, "day of the moon"

TUESDAY Tiwesdaeg, "Tiw's day"

WEDNESDAY Wodnesdaeg, "Woden's day"

THURSDAY Thunresdaeg, "thunder's day" or "Thor's day"

FRIDAY Frigedaeg, "Freya's day"

SATURDAY Saeturnesdaeg, "Saturn's day"

WEEKDAY HEPTAGRAM

The heptagram is a seven-pointed star that is to be drawn in seven strokes. It is used to represent the magickal days of the week. I am sure you will find many ways to incorporate it into your days of witchery.

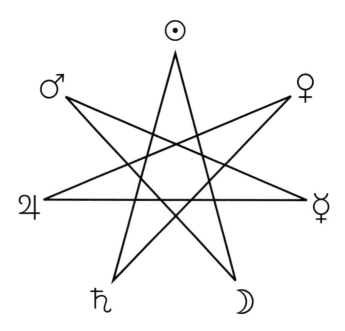

Bibliography

THE TRUE UNIVERSITY of these
days is a collection of books.

Thomas Carlyle

Almond, Jocelyn, and Keith Seddon. *Understanding Tarot: A Practical Guide to Tarot Card Reading.* London, UK: Aquarian Press, 1991.

Aswynn, Freya. *Northern Mysteries and Magick.* St. Paul, MN: Llewellyn, 1998.

Biziou, Barbara. *The Joy of Ritual.* New York: Golden Books, 1999.

Bowes, Susan. *Notions and Potions: A Safe Practical Guide to Creating Magick & Miracles.* New York: Sterling Publishing Company, 1997.

Bremness, Lesley. *Herbs.* New York: Dorling Publishing, Inc., 1994.

Budapest, Zsuzsanna. *The Goddess in the Office.* San Francisco, CA: HarperSanFrancisco, 1993.

Cabot, Laurie, and Tom Cowan. *Power of the Witch.* New York: Delta Books, 1989.

Conway, D. J. *Moon Magick.* St. Paul, MN: Llewellyn, 1995.

Culpeper, Nicholas. *Culpeper's Color Herbal.* Edited by David Potterton. New York: Sterling Publishing, 1983.

Cunningham, Scott. *The Complete Book of Incense, Oils and Brews*. St. Paul, MN: Llewellyn, 1992, 1998.

———. *Cunningham's Encyclopedia of Crystal, Gem & Metal Magic*. St. Paul, MN: Llewellyn, 1992.

———. *Cunningham's Encyclopedia of Magical Herbs*. St. Paul, MN: Llewellyn, 1996.

———. *Magical Aromatherapy*. St. Paul, MN: Llewellyn, 1993.

Dolnick, Barrie. *Simple Spells for Success*. New York: Harmony Books, 1996.

Dugan, Ellen. "Aphrodite." *Llewellyn's Magical Almanac 2004*. St. Paul, MN: Llewellyn, 2003.

———. *Autumn Equinox: The Enchantment of Mabon*. St. Paul, MN: Llewellyn, 2005.

———. *Elements of Witchcraft: Natural Magick for Teens*. St. Paul, MN: Llewellyn, 2003.

———. *Garden Witchery: Magick from the Ground Up*. St. Paul, MN: Llewellyn, 2003.

———. "Hecate." *Llewellyn's Magical Almanac 2004*. St. Paul, MN: Llewellyn, 2005.

———. *Herb Magic for Beginners*. Woodbury, MN: Llewellyn, 2006.

———. "Lilith." *Llewellyn's Magical Almanac 2003*. St. Paul, MN: Llewellyn, 2002.

———. *Natural Witchery: Intuitive, Personal & Practical Magick*. Woodbury, MN: Llewellyn, 2007.

———. "The Rose." *Llewellyn's Herbal Almanac 2004*. St. Paul, MN: Llewellyn, 2003.

———. *7 Days of Magic*. St. Paul, MN: Llewellyn, 2004.

Dunkling, Leslie. *A Dictionary of Days.* New York: Facts on File Publication, 1988.

Ferguson, Diana. *The Magickal Year.* New York: Book of the Month Club (originally UK: Labyrinth Publishing), 1996.

Gallagher, Anne-Marie. *Inner Magic: A Guide to Witchcraft.* London, UK: Octopus Publishing Group, 2007.

———. *Magical Spells for Your Home.* London, UK: Barron's, 2002.

———. *The Spells Bible.* Cincinnati, OH: Walking Stick Press, 2003.

Gant, Christy. "Ancient Amber." *Circle Magazine,* Issue 92, Winter 2004.

Gillotte, Galen. *Sacred Stones of the Goddess.* St. Paul, MN: Llewellyn, 2003.

Greenaway, Leanna. *Simply Tarot.* New York: Sterling Publishing, 2005.

Gundarsson, Kveldulf. *Teutonic Magic.* St. Paul, MN: Llewellyn, 1994.

Hallam, Elizabeth. *Gods and Goddesses:A Treasury of Deities and Tales from World Mythology.* New York: Simon and Schuster, 1996.

Helfman, Elizabeth S. *Celebrating Nature: Rites and Ceremonies Around the World.* New York: Seabury Press, 1969.

Illes, Judika. *The Element Encyclopedia of 5000 Spells.* London, UK: Element Books, 2004.

Jordan, Michael. *The Encyclopedia of Gods.* London, UK: Kyle Cathie Limited, 1995.

Koltuv, Barabara Black. *The Book of Lilith.* Berwick, ME: Nicolas-Hays, Inc., 1986.

Krasskova, Galina. *Exploring the Northern Tradition.* Franklin Lakes, NJ: Career Press/New Page Books, 2005.

Laufer, Geraldine Adamich. *Tussie-Mussies: The Victorian Art of Expressing Yourself in the Language of Flowers*. New York: Workman Publishing Company, 1993.

Marina Medici. *Good Magic*. New York: Simon and Schuster, Fireside Publishing, 1988.

Mercatante, Anthony S. *The Magic Garden*. New York: Harper and Row Publishers, 1976.

Monaghan, Patricia. *The Book of Goddesses and Heroines*. St. Paul, MN: Llewellyn, 1981.

Moon, Akasha. *The Little Book of Pocket Spells*. Kansas City, MO: Andrew McMeel Publishing, 2003.

Myth and Mankind: Sagas of the Norsemen. Amsterdam: Time-Life Books (First English Printing), 1997.

Nahmad, Claire. *Garden Spells*. Philadelphia, PA: Running Press, 1994.

O'Rush, Claire. *The Enchanted Garden*. New York: Gramercy Books, 2000.

Osborn, Kevin, and Dana L. Burgess. *The Complete Idiot's Guide to Classical Mythology*. New York: Alpha Books, 1998.

Paterson, Jacqueline Memory. *Tree Wisdom*. London, UK: Thorsons, 1996.

Penczak, Christopher. *Instant Magick*. Woodbury, MN: Llewellyn, 2006.

———. *The Outer Temple of Witchcraft*. St. Paul, MN: Llewellyn, 2004.

———. *The Temple of High Witchcraft*. Woodbury, MN: Llewellyn, 2008.

Perl, Lila. *Blue Monday and Friday the Thirteenth: The Stories Behind the Days of the Week*. New York: Clarion Books, 1986.

RavenWolf, Silver. *Silver's Spells for Prosperity*. St. Paul, MN: Llewellyn, 1999.

Redford, Donald B., editor. *The Ancient Gods Speak: A Guide to Egyptian Religion*. New York: Oxford University Press, 2002.

Rossbach, Sarah, and Lin Yun. *Living Color: Master Lin Yun's Guide to Feng Shui and the Art of Color*. New York: Kodansha International, 1994.

Skolnick, Solomon M. *The Language of Flowers*. White Plains, NY: Peter Pauper Press, Inc., 1995.

Starhawk. *The Spiral Dance*. Tenth Anniversary Edition. San Francisco, CA: HarperSanFrancisco, 1989.

Telesco, Patricia. *Folkways*. St. Paul, MN: Llewellyn, 1995.

Valiente, Doreen. *Witchcraft for Tomorrow*. Blaine, WA: Phoenix Publishing, 1978.

Vitale, Alice Thoms. *Leaves: In Myth, Magic and Medicine*. New York: Stewart, Tabori and Chang, 1997.

Walker, Barbara G. *The Woman's Dictionary of Symbols and Sacred Objects*. Edison, NJ: Castle Books, 1998.

Wodanson, Edred. *Asatru: The Hidden Fortress*. Parksville, BC: Wodanesdag Press, 1995.

Websites

http://eclipse.gsfc.nasa.gov/phase/phase2001gmt.html—NASA website with information on full moon phases for the years 2001–2025 Eastern Standard Time (accessed January 2009, July 2009)

http://www.shamanscrystal.co.uk/index.php—Crystal and gemstone information (accessed November 2008, July 2009)

http://www.bernardine.com/gemstones/gemstones.htm—Gemstone information, facts, and lore (accessed December 2008, July 2009)

http://en.wikipedia.org/wiki/Week-day_names—Information on the Weekday Heptagram (accessed November 2008, July 2009)

Index

THE WORTH OF a book is to be measured
by what you can carry away from it.

James Bryce

Venus, deity, 185–186, 189,
  197, 199, 202–204, 216

Venus, planet, xix, 185, 196–200, 202–203,
  205–206, 210, 222, 225, 292–293

Violet, xiv, 165, 185, 196, 198,
  212, 217, 292–293

Votive candles, xxv, 14, 50, 55, 63, 92–93,
  132–133, 141–142, 160, 163, 175,
  203, 222, 244–246, 257, 275, 293

Wheat, 145, 179–182, 215, 295, 297

White rose, 37, 45, 47, 57, 69, 208

Window boxes, 269

Wintergreen, 37, 68

Witch's jar, 100–101, 106

Wodin, 107–108, 110

Zeus, 111, 145–146, 148–149, 152,
  159, 161, 171, 182, 229

Free Catalog

Get the latest information on
our body, mind, and spirit products!
To receive a **free** copy of Llewellyn's consumer
catalog, *New Worlds of Mind & Spirit,* simply call
1-877-NEW-WRLD or visit our website at
www.llewellyn.com and click on *New Worlds.*

LLEWELLYN ORDERING INFORMATION

Order Online:
Visit our website at www.llewellyn.com, select your books, and order them on our
secure server.

Order by Phone:
- Call toll-free within the U.S. at 1-877-NEW-WRLD
  (1-877-639-9753). Call toll-free within Canada at
  1-866-NEW-WRLD (1-866-639-9753)
- We accept VISA, MasterCard, and American Express

Order by Mail:
Send the full price of your order (MN residents add 6.875% sales tax) in
U.S. funds, plus postage & handling to:

Llewellyn Worldwide
2143 Wooddale Drive, Dept. 978-0-7387-1584-1
Woodbury, MN 55125-2989

Postage & Handling:

Standard (U.S., Mexico & Canada). If your order is:
$24.99 and under, add $4.00
$25.00 and over, FREE STANDARD SHIPPING

AK, HI, PR: $16.00 for one book plus $2.00 for
each additional book.

International Orders (airmail only):
$16.00 for one book plus $3.00 for each additional book.

Orders are processed within 2 business days.
Please allow for normal shipping time. Postage and handling rates subject to change.

Garden Witchery

Magick from the Ground Up
(Includes a Gardening Journal)

ELLEN DUGAN

How Does Your Magickal Garden Grow?

Garden Witchery is more than belladonna and wolfsbane. It's about making your own enchanted backyard with the trees, flowers, and plants found growing around you. It's about creating your own flower fascinations and spells, and it's full of common-sense information about cold hardiness zones, soil requirements, and a realistic listing of accessible magickal plants.

There may be other books on magickal gardening, but none have practical gardening advice, magickal correspondences, flower folklore, moon gardening, faerie magick, advanced Witchcraft, and humorous personal anecdotes all rolled into one volume.

978-0-7387-0318-3
272 pp., 7½ x 7½ $16.95

To Write to the Author

If you wish to contact the author or would like more information about this book, please write to the author in care of Llewellyn Worldwide and we will forward your request. Both the author and publisher appreciate hearing from you and learning of your enjoyment of this book and how it has helped you. Llewellyn Worldwide cannot guarantee that every letter written to the author can be answered, but all will be forwarded. Please write to:

Ellen Dugan
℅ Llewellyn Worldwide
2143 Wooddale Drive, Dept. 978-0-7387-1584-1
Woodbury, MN 55125-2989
Please enclose a self-addressed stamped envelope for reply,
or $1.00 to cover costs. If outside U.S.A., enclose
international postal reply coupon.

Many of Llewellyn's authors have websites with additional information and resources. For more information, please visit our website:

HTTP://WWW.LLEWELLYN.COM

A BOOK IS like a garden
carried in the pocket.

Chinese proverb